A LICENSE TO KILL

A LICENSE TO KILL

Israeli Operations against "Wanted" and Masked Palestinians

A Middle East Watch Report

Human Rights Watch
New York • Washington • Los Angeles • London

Library of Congress Card Catalog Number: 93-79007
ISBN: 1-56432-109-6

HUMAN RIGHTS WATCH

Human Rights Watch conducts regular, systematic investigations of human rights abuses in some sixty countries around the world. It addresses the human rights practices of governments of all political stripes, of all geopolitical alignments, and of all ethnic and religious persuasions. In internal wars it documents violations by both governments and rebel groups. Human Rights Watch defends freedom of thought and expression, due process of law and equal protection of the law; it documents and denounces murders, disappearances, torture, arbitrary imprisonment, exile, censorship and other abuses of internationally recognized human rights.

Human Rights Watch began in 1978 with the founding of Helsinki Watch by a group of publishers, lawyers and other activists and now maintains offices in New York, Washington, D.C., Los Angeles, London, Moscow, Belgrade, Zagreb and Hong Kong. Today, it includes Africa Watch, Americas Watch, Asia Watch, Helsinki Watch, Middle East Watch, the Fund for Free Expression and three collaborative projects, the Arms Project, Prison Project and Women's Rights Project. Human Rights Watch is an independent, nongovernmental organization, supported by contributions from private individuals and foundations. It accepts no government funds, directly or indirectly.

The executive committee includes Robert L. Bernstein, chair; Adrian W. DeWind, vice chair; Roland Algrant, Lisa Anderson, Peter D. Bell, Alice Brown, William Carmichael, Dorothy Cullman, Irene Diamond, Jonathan Fanton, Jack Greenberg, Alice H. Henkin, Stephen L. Kass, Marina Pinto Kaufman, Alexander MacGregor, Bruce Rabb, Orville Schell, Gary Sick, Malcolm Smith and Robert Wedgeworth.

The staff includes Kenneth Roth, acting executive director; Holly J. Burkhalter, Washington director; Gara LaMarche, associate director; Susan Osnos, press director; Ellen Lutz, California director; Jemera Rone, counsel; Stephanie Steele, operations director; Michal Longfelder, development director; Allyson Collins, research associate; Joanna Weschler, Prison Project director; Kenneth Anderson, Arms Project director; and Dorothy Q. Thomas, Women's Rights Project director.

The executive directors of the divisions of Human Rights Watch are Abdullahi An-Na'im, Africa Watch; Juan E. Méndez, Americas Watch; Sidney Jones, Asia Watch; Jeri Laber, Helsinki Watch; Andrew Whitley, Middle East Watch; and Gara LaMarche, the Fund for Free Expression.

Addresses for Human Rights Watch

485 Fifth Avenue
New York, NY 10017-6104
Tel: (212) 972-8400
Fax: (212) 972-0905
email: hrwatchnyu@igc.org

10951 West Pico Blvd., #203
Los Angeles, CA 90064
Tel: (310) 475-3070
Fax: (310) 475-5613
email: hrwatchla@igc.org

1522 K Street, N.W., #910
Washington, DC 20005
Tel: (202) 371-6592
Fax: (202) 371-0124
email: hrwatchdc@igc.org

90 Borough High Street
London, UK SE1 1LL
Tel: (071) 378-8008
Fax: (071) 378-8029
email: africawatch@gn.org

TABLE OF CONTENTS

ACKNOWLEDGMENTS

The principal researcher and writer of this report is James Ron, a consultant to Middle East Watch. Kenneth Roth, the acting executive director of Human Rights Watch and Eric Goldstein, research director of Middle East Watch, also conducted research and wrote sections of the report. Eric Goldstein and Human Rights Watch consultant Cynthia Brown edited the report.

Richard Dicker, a staff attorney at Human Rights Watch, provided legal research. David Rosenberg, a volunteer lawyer, and interns Elizabeth Wilcox and Elena Ippoliti, also conducted research and copy-editing. Middle East Watch Associate Suzanne Howard helped with production.

Middle East Watch would like to thank the Palestinian eyewitnesses whose testimony forms a substantial component of this report. We are also grateful to the Israeli soldiers who agreed to speak with us about special-force activities.

This report would not have been possible without the aid of several local human rights organizations, although responsibility for the findings rests solely with Middle East Watch.

The staff of al-Haq, the Ramallah-based human rights organization, was exceptionally generous in providing suggestions, introductions and cooperation in the field, and in sharing their data and knowledge.

B'Tselem, the Israeli Information Center for Human Rights in the Occupied Territories, provided valuable advice and information, as well as assistance in the field. Other groups shared their time and knowledge, including the Palestine Human Rights Information Center and the Khan Younis-based Palestinian Lawyers for Human Rights. We owe thanks also to Gaza journalist Taher Shriteh for his help in the field, and to the many Israeli journalists and experts who shared their knowledge and insights.

Finally, Middle East Watch is grateful to the Israeli authorities who took the time to meet with us and to reply to our frequent requests for information. These include, in the IDF, officials with the Judge Advocate General's office and the Information Branch of the Spokesman's Office; and at the Justice Ministry, the State Attorney and her staff, and the Department of Human Rights and International Relations.

GLOSSARY

Border Police (משמר הגבו ל): The Border Police are a paramilitary force attached to the Israeli Police. Border Police units regularly patrol the occupied territories, often in coordination with IDF soldiers. When in the occupied territories, Border Police units are under the direct authority of the regional IDF military commander.

Uniformed Border Policemen are clearly distinguishable from IDF soldiers by the darker green color of their uniforms and vehicles. Border Police vehicles also typically have flashing blue lights and red license plates. Military vehicles have black license plates and do not have blue lights.

Criminal investigations into possible Border Police abuses are carried out by the Israeli Police and are overseen by the State Attorney's office (see separate entry).

Brigade (חטיבה): The IDF has divided the occupied territories into different military regions. Each regional command is considered to be a "regional brigade," commanded by a regional brigadier and his staff. The brigade staff includes a skeleton administrative framework dealing with local intelligence, operations, communications, supply and maintenance. With the exception of this skeleton staff, the actual manpower for the regional brigade comes from regular and reserve IDF units who rotate in and out of the regional commands. Thus, all IDF units are under the command of both the regional brigadier as well as the unit commander.

Civil Administration (המינהל האזרחי): The Civil Administration is the agency of the military government in the West Bank and Gaza Strip that handles most bureaucratic and administrative interactions between the authorities and the Palestinian population. These include such matters as licensing new businesses and issuing permits needed to travel overseas or to work inside Israel. Civil Administration offices are located in most population centers, many of them in the same compound as regional IDF headquarters. Most Civil Administration employees are military personnel.

Cold Weapons (נָשֶׁק קָר): The Israeli authorities use the term "cold weapons" to refer to implements other than firearms and explosive or incendiary devices. These include chains, stones, empty bottles, knives, axes, and iron bars.

Criminal Investigation Division (CID) (מְשטרת צבאית חֹן חֹן קֹרֹת): The CID is a branch of the IDF's Military Police that investigates possible offenses by IDF soldiers. According to official policy, the CID conducts an investigation of all deaths in the occupied territories in which the IDF appears to have been involved. The CID works under the supervision of the IDF Judge Advocate General (JAG). It does not investigate suspected offenses by Border Policemen (see separate entry).

Upon completion, the CID's investigation is submitted to the JAG for possible prosecution (see entry for Judge Advocate General).

General Security Services (GSS, also known as Shabak or the Shin Bet) (שירות ביטחון כללי): The GSS, Israel's internal security agency, is a secretive body with wide-ranging powers that have not been defined in any published law. The GSS is directly and solely responsible to the Israeli Prime Minister, with no substantive oversight by the Knesset.

In the occupied territories, the GSS works in coordination with the IDF regional commanders. GSS agents generally work in plainclothes and carry sidearms.

The main task of GSS agents is to collect intelligence on resistance activities by Palestinians. This is accomplished in part through the interrogation of Palestinians in custody and by maintaining a network of Palestinian informants. This information is factored into decisions by the authorities on policies and measures that are taken on security grounds.

According to officials and accounts by Israeli journalists and soldiers, the GSS plays a key role in compiling and updating the list of "wanted" activists.

Initiated Operation (פעילות יזומה): "Initiated operation" is the term typically used by the IDF spokesman to refer to operations carried out by IDF or Border Police special forces in the occupied territories. The term "initiated" distinguishes these operations from routine patrols carried out by regular military units. However, some activities of regular military units are also termed "initiated operations" by the IDF spokesman, such as when these units operate undercover.

Israel Defense Forces (IDF): The IDF is the army of Israel. The IDF has occupied and administered the West Bank and Gaza Strip since Israel took control of these lands in the June 1967 war.

The IDF has divided Israel, the occupied West Bank and Gaza Strip, and its self-declared "security zone" in southern Lebanon into three sub-regions: (1) **The Northern Command**, which includes northern Israel and the "security zone", (2) **The Central Command**, which includes central Israel and the occupied West Bank, and (3) **The Southern Command**, which includes southern Israel and the occupied Gaza Strip.

Judge Advocate General (JAG): The JAG is the IDF's chief legal officer. The JAG's responsibilities include reviewing investigations by the IDF Criminal Investigation Division (see separate entry) into possible wrongdoing by soldiers, and deciding on the next step. The JAG, upon reviewing an investigation file, may decide to court-martial the soldiers, recommend or order disciplinary action against them, return the file for continued investigation, or close the file.

Masked Activists (רעולי פנים): Many young Palestinian activists cover their faces when involved in resistance activities to avoid being identified by soldiers or Palestinians who provide information to the Israeli authorities. The mask is fashioned from a checkered headdress (*keffiyeh*) or other cloth. Masked Palestinians carry out a vast range of non-violent and violent activities. These include spray-painting political graffiti, leading marches, enforcing political strikes, stoning vehicles and carrying out often-fatal attacks on Palestinians accused of collaborating with the Israeli authorities. Masked youths who participate in one of these activities, such as graffiti-writing, do not necessarily participate in others.

Mukhabarat: The Arabic term used by Palestinians to refer to Israeli intelligence operatives, in particular those of the General Security Services (see separate entry).

Open-Fire Regulations (הוראות פתיחה באש): These are the written rules issued by the IDF high command to soldiers in the occupied territories regarding the use of their firearms. Border Police operating in the occupied territories are issued regulations that are virtually identical. The regulations, which are analyzed in Chapter One of this report, forbid soldiers from firing at persons except in two situations: in life-threatening situations and as part of the procedures for apprehending certain categories of fleeing suspects. Soldiers are required to be familiar with and obey the regulations.

The Procedure for Apprehending a Suspect (נוהל מעצר חשוד):

-**The Full Procedure (הנוהל המלא):** This procedure, spelled out in the open-fire regulations, governs the process of stopping a suspect when a soldier has reasonable grounds for suspecting that he has committed or is on his way to committing "a dangerous crime." The full procedure consists of three stages:

1. A shouted warning, in Arabic, "Stop or I'll shoot you!";
2. A warning shot, fired in the air;
3. A shot toward the fleeing suspect's legs.

After firing a single shot toward the suspect's legs, the soldier must then check whether the suspect has halted. If not, he may repeat step three until the objective has been met. The procedure for apprehending a fleeing suspect does not permit soldiers to aim above the suspect's legs.

-**The Official Abbreviated Procedure (הנוהל המקוצר):** The abbreviated procedure authorizes soldiers, in specified situations, to skip all or part of the two initial warning stages of the full procedure.

SHABAK: See General Security Services.

Shin Bet: See General Security Services.

Special Forces: The term "special forces" as it is used in this report refers to the four Israeli military and Border Police units that operate in the

xvi

occupied territories against "wanted" and masked Palestinians. Special-force operations typically involve troops operating undercover, although they sometimes wear full or partial military uniforms.

State Attorney: The State Attorney is a senior official within the Justice Ministry whose responsibilities include reviewing investigations by the Israeli police into possible wrongdoing by Border Police and deciding on the next step. In this respect the State Attorney is the counterpart to the IDF Judge Advocate General. Upon reviewing an investigation file, the State Attorney may decide to file charges against Border Police, recommend disciplinary action against them, return the file for continued investigation, or close the file.

Targeted Palestinians: This report uses the term "targeted Palestinians" to refer to the two categories of Palestinians who constitute the main objects of the security-force operations described in this report: "wanted" activists and masked activists.

"Unjustified" Killing: The term "unjustified" killing is used in this report to refer to killings by Israeli security forces that have occurred outside of situations of imminent mortal danger; or, in situations of imminent mortal danger, when the use of lethal force was either not necessary to counter that danger or was rendered necessary by the security forces' use of inappropriate tactics (see, for example the al-Mathloum case in Chapter Two). This definition is based on the internationally recognized norms of necessity and proportionality. Compliance with the open-fire regulations does not necessarily make a killing "justifiable"; many fleeing suspects who were posing no imminent mortal threat have been killed unjustifiably by soldiers following the procedures for apprehending suspects (see Chapter One).

Uzi: The Uzi is an Israeli-made weapon commonly used by the special forces. It uses a 9mm round and can be fired on automatic or semi-automatic.

"Wanted" (מבוקש; in Arabic: *matloub* or *mutarad*): "Wanted" Palestinians are, for the purposes of this report, suspected "hard-core" activists whom the GSS has placed on a high-priority list of fugitives. Israel alleges that these suspects are armed and dangerous, and that most have carried out attacks on Israeli servicemen, settlers or fellow Arabs suspected of collaboration. The term is not used in this report to refer to Palestinians who are sought by the authorities for other types of offenses.

ABOUT THE SOLDIERS QUOTED IN THIS REPORT

This report contains excerpts from interviews that Middle East Watch conducted in 1992 with Israeli soldiers who have knowledge of the special forces and of "initiated operations" against "wanted" or masked Palestinians. Four requested that we not identify them by name; Israeli soldiers are prohibited from providing information without authorization about IDF operations. They are identified throughout this report by their rank and a first initial that we have assigned them. They are no longer on active duty but continue to perform reserve service.

First Sergeant A.

First Sgt. A., twenty-two, spent three years as a combat soldier in an elite, all-volunteer infantry unit. First Sgt. A. was drafted in the summer of 1989, served until the summer of 1992, and was honorably discharged. First Sgt. A. is now a university student in the humanities.

While not a member of one of the full-time special forces, First Sgt. A. participated in a number of special force-style "initiated operations" against "wanted" Palestinians in the occupied territories. He also participated in operations against guerrillas in Israel's self-declared south Lebanese "security zone."

First Sergeant B.

During 1990-1991, First Sgt. B., twenty-one, spent one year as an administrative non-commissioned officer in the "Shimshon" special force.

Although First Sgt. B. never participated in actual Shimshon combat operations, First Sgt. B. participated in Shimshon training regimens, pre-operation preparations, and post-operation debriefings. First Sgt. B.'s knowledge of the unit stems also from living with Shimshon soldiers in their relatively small base in the southern Gaza Strip. Honorably discharged in 1991, First Sgt. B. is currently a university student in the humanities.

xix

First Lieutenant C.

First Lt. C., twenty-five, served first as a combat soldier, then as a platoon commander, and finally as a deputy company commander in one of the IDF's elite infantry brigades. First Lt. C. served as a soldier and later as a commander in both Israel's self-declared "security zone" and in the occupied West Bank and Gaza Strip. First Lt. C. served his mandatory three-year army tour of duty between 1987 and 1990, volunteered for an additional year, and was honorably discharged in 1991.

First Lt. C. has since returned to the military several times as a reserve infantry officer. In May 1992, First Lt. C. performed reserve duty in the northern West Bank district of Jenin. Although never a member of a special force, First Lt. C. had much contact with special-force soldiers. He is currently a university student.

First Sergeant D.

First Sgt. D., twenty-two, served as a combat soldier in the IDF's "Hermesh" Brigade, a special quasi-infantry brigade created shortly after the beginning of the Palestinian uprising. The brigade's primary task is suppressing Palestinian resistance; as opposed to most regular IDF units, Hermesh operates exclusively in the territories.

First Sgt. D. spent a large portion of his three-year mandatory military service in the Rafah refugee camp in the southern Gaza Strip. First Sgt. D. was stationed there March - July 1989, November 1989 - May 1990, and January - October 1991.

Although First Sgt. D.'s unit was not a full-time special force, it filled a variety of auxiliary roles in the offensive against targeted Palestinians. First Sgt. D. participated in numerous raids on the houses of "wanted" activists and in clashes with masked activists. First Sgt. D. is now a university student in the sciences.

INTRODUCTION

Since 1988, a pattern of unjustified killings by Israeli undercover security forces has emerged in the occupied West Bank and Gaza Strip. This report examines the killings during 1992 and the first two months of 1993, offering seventeen cases we investigated involving the use of excessive force. The forces responsible for most of these killings are special units from the Israel Defense Forces (IDF) and the Border Police operating under IDF command. Many of these killings, for which the Israel military command openly acknowledges responsibility, constitute violations both of international law and of the law that Israel professes to apply in the occupied territories; yet there has been no credible official effort to deter the practice. Not only are the members of undercover units encouraged to think of the victims as legitimate targets for lethal force, but the use of force in violation of the regulations routinely goes unpunished, with cover-ups extending from the rank-and-file to the senior military establishment, and relying on the acquiescence of the government of Israel.

The victims are of two types: (1) "wanted" men — Palestinians named on a security-forces list of militants who are suspected of being armed, highly dangerous, and responsible for politically motivated violence; and (2) youths who mask their faces, whose identities are not known to the security forces when they encounter one another, who generally are unarmed or carry at most "cold weapons" such as axes and chains, and who are routinely shot while posing no imminent mortal danger to security agents.

More than 120 Palestinians have been killed during special-force operations since the start of the intifada, or Palestinian uprising, in December 1987. Of these, nearly half were killed since January 1992. (It is often difficult to identify the force responsible for a killing; these figures represent the more conservative tallies prepared by local human rights organizations. See the statistical tables on pages three and four.)

This report documents seventeen cases in which twenty Palestinians were killed. These cases are intended to demonstrate a pattern of unjustifiable lethal force by undercover and other forces pursuing targeted Palestinians; these cases are not necessarily the only abusive killings that occurred during this period. Other human rights

1

organizations have identified additional cases where lethal force was apparently unwarranted.

Israel commonly misrepresents the work of the undercover forces by suggesting that their sole mission is to pursue dangerous "wanted" men with "blood on their hands." Less than half of the Palestinians they have killed were "wanted" suspects (see tables on pages three and four); the rest were masked youths, stone-throwers, and others whose identities were not known to the soldiers who shot them, and who were neither armed nor posing any imminent mortal threat to the security agents or anyone else.

The special undercover units are known in Hebrew as מסתערבים, or Arab-pretenders, because they often disguise themselves as Palestinians in order to penetrate Palestinian settlements. Although soldiers carry out the missions, and officials often slip into a vocabulary of military combat to describe their work, Israel has repeatedly affirmed that the units are bound by rules of conduct applicable in law-enforcement situations. They are ordered, under penalty of prosecution for deviations, to apprehend suspects using the minimum force necessary. By Israel's own declarations, the undercover units do not operate under wartime rules — rules that permit shooting to kill "combatants" rather than capturing them. Indeed, the use of civilian disguises, while a legitimate law-enforcement tool, would, if practiced by combatants in order to engage in hostilities, violate international law by blurring the mandatory distinction between combatants and noncombatants during armed conflict.

Despite Israel's declarations that law-enforcement rules apply, the Israel military command gives license to the special units to behave as if they were engaged in a military conflict — albeit a low-intensity one — with "wanted" and masked Palestinian activists. The resulting tactics include shooting on sight, shooting to kill, and shooting fleeing suspects dead — tactics appropriate to war but, as the cases presented in this report show, often entirely unjustified in terms of the law-enforcement principle of minimum necessary force that the units are obliged to uphold.

STATISTICS: PALESTINIANS KILLED BY UNDERCOVER FORCES

The statistics compiled by human rights organizations on undercover killings vary somewhat, due to differences in categorizing of some cases. While the IDF and Border Police generally acknowledge responsibility for killings in which their forces have been involved, they do not always specify whether the soldiers involved belonged to special units. Nor can Palestinian eyewitnesses be found in every case who can describe the soldiers involved.

Three human rights organizations, al-Haq, B'Tselem and the Palestine Human Rights Information Center (PHRIC), kept tallies of killings in which witnesses said the soldiers were wearing plainclothes, a characterization that coincides closely but not entirely with that of special-force personnel. Special forces sometimes operate in uniform, while non-special-force soldiers sometimes go undercover.

On the basis of its preliminary monitoring of cases and IDF statements, B'Tselem believes that undercover forces were responsible for 110 of the 920 Palestinians killed by security forces from the start of the intifada until November 30, 1992. B'Tselem breaks the figure down into those who were officially "wanted" and the rest, and found that only forty-two of the 110 were "wanted":

Year	Total
1988	5 killed, of whom 1 "wanted"
1989	26 killed, of whom 5 "wanted"
1990	13 killed, of whom 6 "wanted"
1991	23 killed, of whom 7 "wanted"
1992 (through Nov.30)	43 killed, of whom 23 "wanted"
Total thr. Nov. 30, 1992	110 killed, of whom 42 "wanted"

(continued on p. 4)

STATISTICS: PALESTINIANS KILLED BY UNDERCOVER FORCES

Although they have not broken down their data between "wanted" and others, PHRIC and al-Haq have compiled up-to-date tallies. According to the June 1993 Fact Sheet of PHRIC, 126 Palestinians had been killed by undercover forces through the end of May 1993:

Year	Total	Gaza Strip	West Bank
1988	8	5	3
1989	26	9	17
1990	11	5	6
1991	29	9	20
1992	43	13	30
1993 (thru May 31)	9	3	6
Totals	126	44	82

Al-Haq's figures for undercover killings are higher:

Year	Total	Gaza Strip	West Bank
1988	12	5	7
1989	35	12	23
1990	19	7	12
1991	32	9	23
1992	47	13	34
1993 (thru mid-May)	15	9	6
Totals	160	55	105

This data is provided here merely to suggest the magnitude of the phenomenon rather than to provide definitive numbers. For the purposes of this report, we refer, conservatively, to at least 120 undercover killings during the intifada.

BACKGROUND

The pursuit of targeted activists emerged as a priority of the security forces during the second phase of the Palestinian uprising. In its first year the intifada was characterized by mass demonstrations erupting almost daily and in several locations simultaneously. As these demonstrations became smaller and more sporadic, authorities directed more attention to identifying and pursuing Palestinians they considered to be hard-core activists responsible for perpetuating the unrest and killing suspected members of Israel's extensive network of Palestinian collaborators.[1]

A new strategy was adopted once the priority shifted from suppressing demonstrations to confronting identified individuals and categories of individuals, such as masked activists. In order to be able to enter Palestinian population centers and locate the targeted activists, security forces turned to special plainclothes forces operating in small groups and often disguised as Palestinians. In addition to the units that were created solely for the occupied territories, small infantry units trained for sabotage, ambushes and reconnaissance behind enemy lines were sent to the West Bank and Gaza Strip to carry out special-force operations. These units frequently carry out shoot-to-kill ambushes against guerrillas in Israel's self-declared "security zone" in southern Lebanon. Their participation against targeted individuals in the occupied territories, as well as the combat-oriented training that special-force soldiers receive, contribute to the tendency of these units to confront targeted individuals in a manner more akin to a combat operation than an attempted arrest.

NEW TACTIC: MILITARY ASSAULTS ON SUSPECTED HIDEOUTS...

The combat tendencies in Israel's pursuit of "wanted" activists have continued unchanged during Prime Minister Yitzhak Rabin's first year in office, and in some respects have intensified. While continuing to grant undercover units license to kill, the Rabin government has initiated

---

[1] From the beginning of the intifada until May 31, 1993, 732 Palestinians have been killed in the occupied territories on suspicion of collaborating with the Israeli authorities, according to the Associated Press.

a new tactic against "wanted" activists: sealing off and emptying neighborhoods in which suspects are thought to be hiding, and if they fail to come out and surrender, attacking the suspected hideout from a distance, using rockets, launched grenades, machine guns, and other heavy ordnance.

These assaults have in most cases destroyed or damaged a number of homes of families who were not suspected of any wrongdoing. In a study of the fifteen such assaults between September 1992 and April 1993, B'Tselem reported that forty-nine houses were destroyed and fifty-three damaged, and hundreds of residents were left homeless. In only seven of the assaults, were "wanted" persons found to be hiding in the targeted houses.

This new method of confronting "wanted" activists was begun in earnest after undercover soldiers were killed in separate incidents in August 1992. Thus far, the military-style assaults have achieved their stated goal of reducing the incidence of injuries both to soldiers and others during confrontations with "wanted" activists. No soldier, "wanted" person, or bystander has been killed during the unleashing of massive firepower, although "wanted" persons have been killed in ensuing incidents. While the drop in casualties is a welcome development, Middle East Watch cannot condone the tactic, because it has been responsible for destroying or damaging tens of homes and rendering homeless hundreds of Palestinians who have been accused of no wrongdoing. Although the IDF has claimed that innocent residents are entitled to compensation for damaged property, local human rights organizations report that they have heard of no case in which compensation has been paid.

In view of the fact that these operations have led to the arrest of only a handful of "wanted" persons — and in several operations, homes were destroyed and no one was captured — many of these attacks appear to have involved the use of force that was disproportionate to the objective of the operation.[2]

---

[2] See B'Tselem, "House Demolitions during Operations against Wanted People," May 1993; see also the monthly reports of the Gaza Center for Rights and Law; and David Hoffman, "Israelis Shift Tactics against Palestinians," *The Washington Post*, February 16, 1993. The B'Tselem report contains a three-page response by the IDF.

...WHILE THE PINPOINTED MISSIONS CONTINUE

These assault-type raids on suspected hideouts have not replaced the pinpointed missions of undercover units. More than thirty Palestinians have been killed by undercover units since Rabin became prime minister in July 1992, many of them in unjustifiable circumstances. Four special-force units concentrate on the pursuit of targeted Palestinians, while a range of other forces adopt similar tactics when they join in that pursuit. The special forces adopt a host of disguises, traveling in cars with the license plates of local Palestinians and walking in the streets disguised as masked activists, day laborers, women, or beggars. Undercover troopers have on occasion even participated in funerals and demonstrations in order to make contact with suspected leaders. (See, for example, the al-Mathloum case in Chapter Two).

In Israeli-annexed East Jerusalem, where the Israeli police force and not the IDF is responsible for security, the police operates an undercover force called the Gideon unit. Its conduct has attracted relatively little attention because the number of fatal shootings in Jerusalem has been small compared to the rest of the West Bank and the Gaza Strip. However, the recent trial of a youth who was shot by Gideonites illustrates two of the central issues that this report raises with regard to undercover units operating in the West Bank and Gaza Strip: the use of excess force in violation of the official open-fire regulations, and false testimony by security-force members to cover up their use of excessive force. This case is described in Chapter Five.

The special forces are often not readily identifiable as agents of the state when they move to intercept "wanted" or masked suspects. Several other types of armed persons in civilian clothes can be found in the occupied territories, including Jewish settlers (some of whom engage in vigilante-style raids on Palestinian communities), Palestinian militants, common criminals, and collaborators with the Israeli authorities. According to the open-fire regulations, undercover soldiers must shout "Army!" when they reveal themselves and draw their weapons. Eyewitnesses have informed us, however, that the soldiers often fail to do so. The dilemma faced by Palestinians who encounter undercover units was dramatically sketched by *Haaretz* correspondent Danny Rubinstein in 1992:

What happens if an Arab is walking down the street and
is suddenly threatened by young men in plainclothes
brandishing guns? What is he to do? In a split second he
is supposed to guess whether they are soldiers, members
of a terror squad [of Palestinian militants] who have
decided to kill him, or simply thieves. In accordance with
this guess he is then supposed to decide whether to run
or stop and raise his hands. The wrong guess is liable to
cost him his life.[3]

Two killings presented in Chapter Two illustrate this dilemma.
According to the authorities, in unrelated incidents that occurred on a
single day in April 1992, soldiers fatally shot Palestinians who appeared
armed but whose weapons, the authorities later acknowledged, turned out
to be children's toy pistols. Even if one accepts the official versions — and
our studies of the two cases bring these versions into question — it
appears that the ambushing soldiers gave the victims not even a fraction
of a second to show they were in fact not armed and to surrender.

Extensive preparations go into undercover operations in order to
surprise "wanted" individuals. As described in Chapter Four, these
activities include gathering information from surveillance, informants,
and other means. The preparations increase the burden of responsibility
on the undercover forces to evaluate reasonably the suspects' responses
before opening fire.

Israeli security forces use their resort to excessive force as a
means to pressure "wanted" Palestinians to turn themselves in. Military
sources have boasted to the press of the number of fugitives who have
surrendered to the authorities. During 1992, 143 fugitives turned
themselves in, according to Maj. Gen. Danny Yatom, the outgoing
commander of the Central Command, which includes the West Bank.[4]
Gen. Yatom boasted, "There were cases of fugitives who volunteered to
be deported to Jordan, but we did not agree. We have to fight them to

---

[3] Danny Rubinstein, "Dangerous Disguises," *Haaretz*, July 20, 1992.

[4] Israel Radio in Hebrew, March 10, 1993, as reported in Foreign Broadcast
Information Service (hereinafter FBIS), March 12, 1993.

the end."[5] During a period when undercover killings were particularly high, then-Minister of Defense Moshe Arens stated, "Hardly a day goes by when 'wanted' men do not turn themselves in. They seem to think that what they read in the newspapers about hit squads is true."[6]

Israeli authorities also target the families of "wanted" Palestinians for intimidation. Agents of the General Security Services (GSS, also known in Hebrew as *Shabak* or *Shin Bet*), the secret police agency responsible for intelligence collection, have visited many families to warn that unless their "wanted" sons turn themselves in, they face death at the hands of the special forces. In one case investigated by Middle East Watch, the father of Abd al-Qader Masarweh, a "wanted" twenty-one-year-old from the West Bank, was visited by plainclothes GSS agents and soldiers. The GSS agents warned Masarweh that his son would die at the hands of the special forces unless he turned himself in. Some three weeks later, on April 9, 1992, Abd al-Qader Masarweh was, according to testimony gathered by Middle East Watch, unjustifiably killed. (See Chapter Three.)

A PATTERN OF ABUSE

While Middle East Watch does not dispute Israel's decision to use undercover agents as a law-enforcement tool, or the right of these official forces to use firearms to defend themselves or others, we find that these units routinely use excessive levels of force against Palestinian targets. In many cases, the victims posed little or no grave danger to others, were given no opportunity to surrender, and could in all probability have been captured alive; in at least one case, security-force agents executed their victim after he was in *de facto* custody, that is, when he was posing no threat and had no real possibility of escaping.

Encounters with "wanted" activists can be dangerous. In some instances soldiers shot the targeted individuals only after they had drawn a gun or opened fire. At least six special-force soldiers have been killed

---

[5] *Jerusalem Post*, March 11, 1993.

[6] *Hadashot*, May 15, 1992, as reported in FBIS, May 18, 1992.

by Palestinian gunfire while pursuing "wanted" Palestinians.[7] These facts, however, do not relieve soldiers from the responsibility of assessing each encounter in terms of the level of danger inherent in that particular situation.

Middle East Watch believes that Israel must abide by internationally recognized standards governing the treatment of civilians in situations of a military occupation, particularly the Fourth Geneva Convention, and its requirements of humane treatment and protection against violence. While Israel rejects the *de jure* applicability of that convention,[8] it nevertheless accepts the basic premise that the activities of its security forces are governed by the principles of law enforcement rather than of combat. By its own definition, Israel is "administering" the West Bank and Gaza Strip, not waging war against its inhabitants.

---

[7] The IDF states that thirty-four soldiers have been killed by Palestinians in the occupied territories from the beginning of the intifada until May 31, 1993, but does not specify how many were special-force personnel. We reached a figure of six special-force soldiers by monitoring press accounts of the killings.

[8] Although it has ratified the Convention, Israel maintains that the land it captured in 1967 is not "occupied" within the meaning of the Convention because it was not previously part of a sovereign state: it views the West Bank as having been previously administered by Jordan and the Gaza Strip by Egypt as a result of illegal occupations. To recognize the applicability of the Geneva Conventions, Israel contends, might appear to accord Jordan and Egypt the status of an ousted sovereign with reversionary rights.

Virtually the entire international community, including the United States, as well as the International Committee of the Red Cross, which is regarded as the guardian of the Geneva Conventions, maintains that the Fourth Geneva Convention does apply to Israeli rule in the occupied territories. Among the principal arguments in favor of applicability are the strong precedents for viewing the laws of war, including the laws on occupation, as embodying important humanitarian principles that should apply even in cases that differ in some respects from the situations contemplated in the Hague Regulations and the Geneva Conventions.

In addition, because the territories were seized in an armed conflict which has not been concluded by a comprehensive peace accord, the Fourth Geneva Convention applies under a provision of Article 2 governing "all cases of declared war or of any other armed conflict which may arise between two or more of the High Contracting Parties...."

There is some dispute as to whether, under the international law governing a situation of military occupation, armed militants engaged in repeated acts of violence against the occupying authorities can be considered illegal combatants and, as such, forfeit their immunity from direct attack as legitimate military targets. In practical terms, that debate is not relevant to daily conditions in the occupied territories, because the undercover units of the IDF and Border Police do not have a mandate from the Israeli government or military to engage "wanted" persons as military targets. And, as noted, their undercover techniques would not be appropriate in combat situations. To its credit, Israel officially requires its security forces to employ the more restrictive standards of law enforcement, and to treat "wanted" activists as suspected offenders to be arrested and prosecuted.

For the most part, the official, written rules of engagement given to soldiers serving in the occupied territories are consistent with these principles, and restrict the use of lethal force to situations when such force is necessary to confront a life-threatening situation. With a couple of exceptions, Middle East Watch's quarrel is not with the rules as they are written but with the way that they are interpreted and often violated with impunity. In the context of the pursuit of targeted Palestinians, our main quarrel with the written rules is the discretion they give to soldiers to open fire on fleeing suspects even when those suspects are posing no imminent danger to others. This has led to many killings that may have been justifiable under Israeli laws, but were unjustifiable in terms of international norms for law-enforcement officers.

The written regulations governing the use of lethal force by soldiers in the occupied territories are based on the rules issued to police inside Israel, which prohibit the use of firearms except to avert a life-threatening danger. Israeli government officials have repeatedly asserted that Israel holds all soldiers and Border Police serving in the occupied territories to law-enforcement guidelines at all times. A Foreign Ministry statement issued in January 1990 observes: "Force is prohibited as a form of punishment or to deliberately inflict injuries; similarly, the use of force is forbidden against a person who, after having been arrested, shows no resistance or makes no attempt to escape."[9] In the same vein, the Justice Ministry wrote to Middle East Watch in December 1992, "The goal of the

---

[9] Israel Consulate General in New York, "Israel's Measures in the Territories and Human Rights," January 1990.

undercover security forces is to locate terrorists, apprehend them and bring them to trial...." (See Appendix.) Or, as Deputy Judge Advocate General Col. David Yahav told Middle East Watch, "[The undercover units'] job is to apprehend...terrorists, to bring them to prison, to investigate them, and use legal procedures. The purpose is apprehending, and not any other purpose."[10]

Thus, there is an official Israeli consensus that Palestinians suspected of even violent politically motivated offenses in the occupied territories — that is, "wanted" persons — must be granted the full range of protections accorded to suspected offenders, the foremost being the right to life and the right to a fair trial. Clearly those protections are also guaranteed to all persons, whether masked or not, who are posing no imminent mortal danger to security forces or others. Security-force units must therefore make every reasonable effort to arrest "wanted" and masked Palestinians, even when they are suspected of bearing arms or of having carried out attacks on Israeli forces. The requirement to use lethal force only as a last resort also imposes a duty on the undercover units to plan operations so as to minimize the likelihood of their needing to use lethal force.

Shooting to Kill

Middle East Watch finds, however, that there is a shoot-to-kill policy in at least a subset of cases. For example:

• There are cases that suggest a well-planned ambush, in which security forces could have effected an arrest but made little or no attempt to do so. For example, in March 1992, soldiers hiding behind a large boulder ambushed a group of three Palestinian men walking outside a village near Nablus, killing one and wounding another. The men, who were hit from a distance of about twelve meters, turned out to be neither "wanted" nor armed, and had not endangered the soldiers. (See the Dihmes case in Chapter Two. See also the Majadbeh case in Chapter Three.)

---

[10] Middle East Watch interview with Deputy Judge Advocate General Col. David Yahav, October 28, 1992.

• There are numerous cases in which undercover agents opened fire without warning — frequently against suspects who were either entirely unarmed or else carried "cold weapons" (see Glossary) in a way that did not threaten the lives of soldiers armed with automatic weapons, or others. For example, in the West Bank village of Ya'bad, a squad of undercover soldiers jumped out of their automobiles and immediately fired on a group of five masked youths holding clubs and exhorting villagers to observe a political strike, killing one and seriously injuring two others. (See the Hamarshe case, as well as the al-Khatib and Jadallah/Thiyab cases in Chapter Two.)

• In a significant number of other cases, undercover agents used the authorization given them by their written rules of engagement to fire at the legs of fleeing suspects and ended up hitting unarmed Palestinians in the upper body. Many of the victims in these cases reportedly suffered multiple gunshot wounds, indicating an intent to kill.[11] For example, in April 1992, undercover soldiers in Sa'ir, near Hebron, chased Mahmoud Shalaldeh, a suspected stone-thrower, out of a car in which he was riding and shot him dead as he tried to flee up a hill at the side of the road. (See also the Jabbar case in Chapter Two and the Taktak case in Chapter Three.)

A number of cases in which the "wrong" person was killed, suggest that undercover agents pursuing "wanted" activists are quick to open fire before carefully identifying their targets. Two examples:

• In January 1993, a soldier shot and killed sixty-four-year-old Muhammad Quweitah as he ran away from a soldier during a hunt for "wanted" persons in the Deir al-Balah refugee camp in the Gaza Strip. The dead man was neither "wanted" nor accused of any wrongdoing. (See Chapter Two.)

• On April 29, 1992, soldiers in the northern West Bank village of al-Yamoun hit seventeen-year-old Khalil Khamayseh with several bullets at close range. Documents obtained by Middle East Watch indicate that the dead youth was not "wanted" by Israeli intelligence. According to

---

[11] The testimony concerning multiple wounds comes from Palestinians who viewed the body. To our regret, Israeli authorities declined our requests to view autopsy reports in the cases we investigated.

the principal civilian eyewitness, Khamayseh was shot as he sat unarmed with his hands raised. The IDF claimed he had brandished a toy pistol at the soldiers, although it is hard to fathom why someone who was neither "wanted" nor armed would have done so and thus guaranteed his own execution. Evidence suggests that the soldiers were searching for someone else, a "wanted" activist who frequented the house where Khamayseh was killed. (See Chapter Two.)

Evidence of Premeditated Assassinations

Further, despite vehement denials by the IDF, Middle East Watch believes that in at least some cases, senior members of the security forces have targeted individual Palestinians for assassination. It is of course impossible to prove that a particular killing was premeditated without receiving a truthful account from soldiers or officers involved in the operation. The basis for our belief that such killings do occur is evidence presented in Chapter Four, including our interviews with soldiers and three cases that have possible earmarks of premeditation. An interview with a former sergeant in an elite infantry unit was particularly persuasive: he told us of a briefing he attended, during the winter of 1991-92, in which the commander of his unit characterized the objective of an upcoming operation as the assassination of a "wanted" Palestinian. According to this source:

> The unit commander said we were going to lay an ambush and that the objective was to "stick" (לחקן ע) the person....To "stick" means to kill. There is no doubt about that. That is the term we use in Lebanon all the time. It means to shoot to kill. That is what everyone in the briefing room understood....(See Chapter Four.)

Other soldiers denied that there were direct orders to kill specific individuals, but portrayed an aggressive hit-squad-like atmosphere within the units, nurtured and tolerated by their commanders. One former first sergeant told us of a 1991 briefing he attended, given by Gen. Matan Vilna'i (at that time in charge of the Southern Command, including the Gaza Strip), at which the general spoke about thirteen "wanted" Palestinians known to the undercover soldiers by name and photograph.

According to the first sergeant, "[Gen. Vilna'i] said, I believe that if these thirteen were to die the intifada would be over. At the least, we would have quiet for six months." Each time one of the thirteen was killed, said the sergeant, regional commanders sent his unit a bottle of champagne: "We received at least five bottles of champagne during the time that I was a sergeant." (See Chapter Four.)

Asked about this incident, Col. David Yahav, the IDF's Deputy Judge Advocate General, categorically denied that Gen. Vilna'i ever had made such remarks. But similar statements have been made for the record by other Israeli officers, who described the objective of operations as to "eliminate" "wanted" Palestinians. For example, on February 9, 1993, IDF Radio broadcast an interview with a company commander of the Givati infantry brigade who said, quite in contradiction of publicly stated official policy, that:

> My entire company is involved at this point in the hunt, in the pursuit after the terrorists walking around here. [My soldiers are not here] to deal with public disturbances and stuff like that, they move around like any force in Lebanon would now move. They are forces whose aim is to clash, to come into contact, to charge and to eliminate the terrorists; this is the only thing they [the company] are doing, and this is the sole thing they are preoccupied with....(See Chapter Four.)

Executions in *De Facto* Custody

Undercover forces have in some cases committed executions when the victim was effectively in custody, neither threatening his captors nor attempting to escape. Whether premeditated or not, such killings are never justifiable. In one case, on June 4, 1992, plainclothes soldiers repeatedly shot in the head and chest Sa'd Khalil abd al-Karim Miqdad, who was masked but not "wanted," as he lay wounded in the main street of Khan Younis refugee camp in the Gaza Strip. (See Chapter Two.)

Shooting on Sight

In contrast to executions in *de facto* custody, some killings occurred when the victims were not in custody but were nevertheless given no opportunity to surrender. Although the written rules of engagement require soldiers, whenever possible, to shout a warning and fire into the air before firing at a suspect, shooting on sight may be justified in circumstances when an agent comes upon a person wielding a gun in a threatening manner. But abbreviating or eliminating the warning steps is not justified in situations like the killing of 'Issam al-Khatib, an unarmed, masked youth who was manning a roadblock and was gunned down by plainclothesmen who jumped out of their car and opened fire immediately. (See Chapter Two.) A former first lieutenant told us why he ordered his soldiers to shorten the official procedure:

> By the time you shouted the warning in Arabic and fired in the air, the masked people are gone. If your aim is to stop them from escaping, it is absolutely counterproductive to go through the full, three-stage procedure for apprehending a suspect. It is simply too cumbersome.

> What I and others would do is order one soldier to yell, "Stop or I'll shoot!" I would order a second soldier to fire in the air, if we even bothered with that. Then I would take the best shot in the patrol and tell him to shoot toward the suspect to stop him from escaping.

> If we encountered a suspect — usually a masked person — all three would do what they were supposed to do at the same time. That way no one could say that he didn't hear a warning shout or didn't see a shot fired into the air. (See Chapter Four.)

Shooting at Fleeing Suspects

Israel's official open-fire regulations give personnel the authority to shoot at the legs of a fleeing suspect in order to prevent his escape, even if he does not pose an imminent threat. (See Chapter One.) This provision is more permissive than the international norms for law-enforcement agents and can, under field conditions, easily lead to death, as Israeli authorities readily acknowledge. This happens all too often when undercover soldiers are involved. (See, for example, the Shalaldeh and Hamarshe cases in Chapter Two.) When the supreme value is placed on preventing the escape of suspects, undercover soldiers know that they risk little scrutiny if a bullet "aimed at the legs" ends up hitting the suspect's back, a far easier target to hit.

According to the former first lieutenant cited above:

> What everyone does is fire to stop the person, and then later, if necessary, say that they had fired at the legs and missed. No one can give you a hard time for not being a good shot. (See Chapter Four.)

Field conditions during a chase or clash ensure that aiming at the legs is highly inaccurate. The requirement to aim at the legs is also virtually impossible to enforce. For example, in spite of the "Shimshon" trial in 1991-1992 (see Chapters Four and Five), in which the commander of an undercover unit was convicted for having ordered his soldiers to shoot at the torso of masked suspects who flee, this practice has continued, as indicated by the cases presented in Chapters Two and Three in which suspects were killed at close range by bullets supposedly aimed at their legs to prevent their escape.

FAILURE TO PREVENT AND TO PUNISH

The unjustified killing of targeted Palestinians is effectively condoned by the military establishment, which does not ensure that wrongdoing is uncovered by the IDF Criminal Investigation Division (CID) and then prosecuted by the office of the Judge Advocate General, according to evidence presented in this report. The same conclusions apply to the way that the Justice Ministry handles wrongful killings by the Border Police.

The office of the State Attorney, a senior official in the Ministry of Justice, oversees police investigations of killings by Border Police personnel. Whether the case involves IDF soldiers or Border Police, the authorities' options are the same: (1) close the file on grounds that personnel adhered to the rules or that there is insufficient basis for prosecution; (2) return the file to the investigators for additional information; (3) indict the responsible soldier or policeman in court — a criminal court for police, a military court for IDF soldiers; or (4) recommend internal disciplinary action. According to the IDF, the decision to indict a soldier is based on the ordinary standard of criminal law, i.e., a finding of "probable cause" to believe an offense has been committed.[12] Neither the Judge Advocate General nor the State Attorney needs to prove guilt beyond a reasonable doubt before bringing charges.

The established procedures do not provide accountability for wrongdoing by security force agents. Chapter Five discusses the irregularities that undermine the official probe that is required each time a Palestinian is killed by security forces. The cover-up begins when rank-and-file soldiers coordinate cover stories or lie to investigators who arrive at their unit soon after the incident. It continues when the investigators make little effort to collect evidence and cross-check and probe the soldiers' testimonies. The IDF spokesman's office, meanwhile, often issues statements to the press immediately after killings that are formulaic and distort the facts. The cover-up continues when the Judge Advocate General's office and the Ministry of Justice do not exercise their wide-ranging powers to ensure that investigations are pursued in good faith.

We are aware of only one court-martial resulting from the seventeen cases presented in this report in which we believe there is credible evidence of wrongdoing. And even rarer than prosecutions are punishments commensurate with acts of willful killing. In the court-martial mentioned above, the soldier was convicted of causing death through negligence because he had shot a twelve-year-old suspected stone-thrower in violation of the procedure not to carry out on children the procedure for apprehending a suspect who flees. He received a twelve-month sentence, of which six months were suspended; three of the remaining six months were to be served performing army work, and only three months behind bars. In the only other prosecution of a special-force soldier involving the death of a Palestinian, an officer who ordered his

---

[12] Middle East Watch interview with Col. David Yahav, June 8, 1989. At that time, Col. Yahav was head of the IDF's international law section.

men to fire at the torso of fleeing suspects, rather than at their legs as required by the official rules, was given a suspended one-month sentence and a one-rank demotion.

THE METHODOLOGY OF THIS REPORT

This report is based primarily on Middle East Watch's on-site investigations of killings of targeted Palestinians that occurred between March 1992 and February 1993.

Site Examinations and Testimony

In each case, Middle East Watch researchers visited the site of the incident and interviewed Palestinian witnesses to the shootings. The witnesses are quoted by name except when they requested anonymity. We made efforts to interview witnesses separately from one another and cross-examined them in order to separate what they saw and heard themselves from what they heard from others; and to probe their motivations, recollection of the incident, and truthfulness. Some of their claims could also be checked by visits to the scene of the killing itself. In some cases, we decided to dismiss testimony as unreliable. Several investigations were abandoned after we concluded that there was insufficient or no evidence of wrongdoing by the soldiers involved.

Official Information and Limits on Access

In October 1992, researchers met with Col. David Yahav, the IDF's Deputy Judge Advocate General, and members of his staff, with State Attorney Dorit Beinish and with Tamar Gaulan, director of the Human Rights and International Relations Department of the Ministry of Justice. These officials answered questions posed by Middle East Watch both during our meetings and in writing afterward. Their oral responses are cited throughout the report, and their written responses are reprinted in full as an Appendix to the report.

Israeli authorities refused Middle East Watch's request to interview the soldiers and Border Policemen who had participated in the incidents described in Chapters Two and Three. The authorities also turned down our request for access to another key body of evidence: the files of the official investigations, including autopsy reports. The IDF's spokesman wrote us, in May 1993, that "[W]e are unable to disclose them because of medical confidentiality. An autopsy report will be given only to a relative of the deceased if specifically requested." (See Appendix.) Autopsy reports specify the number, location, and direction of bullet wounds in the victims' bodies, and can in many cases help to corroborate or discredit civilian eyewitness testimony. This report sometimes quotes Palestinians who viewed the body and described the number and types of bullet wounds they saw. We would have preferred to complement these statements with the findings of the official autopsies.

The official account of cases involving Border Police was provided by the Justice Ministry. The official version of events in cases involving IDF personnel was provided to us by the office of the IDF Judge Advocate General.

Soldiers' Corroboration

Although the IDF refused to make soldiers in undercover units available for interviews, Middle East Watch was able to locate and interview IDF soldiers with some connection to the units involved in pursuing targeted Palestinians. Four soldiers gave us their names but asked not to be named in the report; it is an offense to disclose information obtained while serving as a soldier. None of the soldiers quoted was to our knowledge involved in the cases documented in Chapters Two and Three. We also quote the testimony of soldiers and officers from two trials involving killings by special forces.

Data from Human Rights Groups

This report also draws on the research conducted by other human rights groups into undercover killings, notably al-Haq, B'Tselem/Israeli Information Center for Human Rights in the Occupied Territories, the Palestine Human Rights Information Center (PHRIC), and the Gaza Centre for Rights and Law. Media coverage of the issue, particularly in the Israeli press, has also been helpful.

TARGETED PERSONS

The "Wanted"

The first category of persons targeted by the authorities consists of suspected militants whose identities are known to the authorities. The majority of these are believed by the authorities to possess guns. The IDF has stated, "As fugitives have used firearms against civilians and soldiers, they are considered highly dangerous and it is assumed that they would not hesitate to open fire if engaged."[12]

These men are frequently referred to as "wanted" (מבוקש in Hebrew; *matloub* or *mutarad* in Arabic). The agency with principal responsibility for drawing up the list of "wanted" persons is the GSS. According to the IDF:

> Wanted fugitives are designated as such only after a lengthy process. They must first be identified by the GSS, on the basis of concrete intelligence, as having committed dangerous crimes. They must then have been summoned to an investigation and failed to appear, their homes must be searched without their having been found and their families asked to bring them to an investigation, to which they do not arrive.[13]

It is not possible to substantiate the IDF's claim regarding the care with which the "wanted" list is compiled. The GSS is a powerful and secretive agency. It reports directly to the Office of the Prime Minister. The Knesset, Israel's parliament, has never defined the GSS's duties and jurisdiction, and exercises no substantive oversight over the organization.

The updated list of "wanted" persons in the territories, which includes photographs when available, is regularly circulated among troops. According to soldiers, the list has varied between 150 and a few hundred persons at any one time. An IDF statement of April 7, 1993 gave

---

[12] B'Tselem, *Activity of the Undercover Units in the Occupied Territories* (IDF response), 1992, p. 113.

[13] *Ibid.*, pp. 112-113.

the figure of about 200 "armed fugitives."[14] A "West Bank military source" cited by *Haaretz* in March 1993 stated that there were about ten armed groups in the West Bank and about seven in the Gaza Strip.[15]

The official "wanted" list contains only a fraction of all Palestinians who are sought by the authorities for security offenses. Authorities have not revealed the criteria used to compile the list, but claim that it contains "hard-core," usually armed, activists who are being sought for killing or seriously injuring soldiers, Israeli civilians, or Palestinians accused of collaborating with the authorities. Many of the activists have evaded arrest for months or longer by hiding in the homes of others or in the hills outside villages.

Masked Activists

The second category of targeted Palestinians is drawn from the thousands of men in their teens and early twenties who cover their faces to avoid identification by soldiers and Palestinian collaborators when they carry out politically motivated activities, both violent and nonviolent, that are illegal under Israeli law. Their mask usually consists of a hood or the traditional checkered Arab headdress (*keffiyeh*). Unlike activists on the "wanted" list, the identities of masked Palestinians are not known to the security forces when they confront one another.

The authorities' justification for targeting masked persons is provided in the written open-fire regulations:

> Local residents operating under the cover of disguises or special masks (that are not routinely used by the local residents) [are] causing harm to collaborators, imposing terror on the local population, and acting as chief inciters at violent demonstrations and riots. This activity, which is performed during the day and at night, constitutes a grave offense, and justifies their immediate arrest,

---

[14] IDF spokesman, "Response to B'Tselem Report Regarding the Demolition of Houses during Operations to Capture Fugitives," April 7, 1993.

[15] *Haaretz*, March 22, 1993, as reported in FBIS, March 23, 1993.

including the use of fire in the procedure for arresting a
suspect. (See Chapter One.)

In effect, the authorities treat masks as a strong initial indication
that the wearer is involved in serious violent activity. In a wide variety of
circumstances spelled out in the open-fire regulations, soldiers are
permitted to open fire at masked persons who attempt to evade arrest.
Special-force agents have been responsible for a number of unjustified
killings of masked persons who were posing no danger to others at the
time they were gunned down.

While some masked activists are involved in violent activity,
including the torture and execution of suspected collaborators, the
activities of masked Palestinians vary significantly. Some are guilty of
nothing more than spray-painting political slogans on public walls or
participating in marches. Other actions commonly carried out by masked
activists are announcing and enforcing commercial strikes, barricading
and closing streets, and stoning Israeli vehicles. Participation in one of
these actions is no proof that the masked person has committed any of
the others.

In fact, the large majority of masked activists do not carry
firearms. In some cases, they carry what Israeli authorities call "cold
weapons": sticks, iron bars, knives, chains, or hatchets. Middle East Watch
and other human rights groups have documented numerous killings by
security forces in which the victim was a member of a group of four or
five masked persons, one or two of whom were carrying cold weapons
while the others were carrying flags, megaphones, or spray-paint.

OFFICIAL JUSTIFICATIONS OF SPECIAL-FORCE OPERATIONS AND MIDDLE EAST WATCH'S RESPONSE

In response to previous critical scrutiny of the use of lethal force
by special-force operatives in the occupied territories, the IDF has offered
various justifications for the force employed and the deaths that have
resulted. Some of these were offered to Middle East Watch in the course
of our exchanges with Israeli officials. Others have been stated publicly
by IDF spokespersons. Unfortunately, many of these responses have had
the effect of obfuscating the issues at the heart of the criticisms made by
Middle East Watch and others.

In an effort to focus public discussion on the matters that we believe are genuinely at issue, we examine here the Israeli government's previous responses to findings of abuse similar to those presented in this report. The government's response is in italics; Middle East Watch's analysis follows.

Undercover units are an appropriate way to neutralize the threat posed by violent Palestinians. Police forces worldwide conduct undercover operations. Although the international laws of war prohibit *combatants* from disguising themselves as civilians in order to engage in hostilities, this prohibition does not forbid the use of such disguises in *police* operations. Because we agree with the Israeli government that Israeli security forces operating in the occupied territories should be evaluated under standards applicable to police rather than combat operations, we do not contest the use of undercover operatives per se. However, the legitimate power to conduct undercover operations does not imply a power to use lethal force, in violation of Israeli and international law, beyond that strictly necessary to meet an imminent threat to life. As this report shows, these laws have been violated repeatedly with impunity.

The special forces confront "armed, hard-core terrorists, who do not adhere to any code of law [and] have engaged in terror attacks."[16] *"It is assumed that [the 'wanted' Palestinian] would not hesitate to open fire if engaged."*[17] Middle East Watch is aware that many of the "wanted" Palestinians are armed and suspected of having committed violent crimes, including the murder of Israelis and of Palestinians deemed to have collaborated with Israeli authorities. The information available to the special forces is clearly relevant in assessing the degree of danger faced by a particular unit as it seeks to capture the "wanted" individual. Yet, contrary to the actions of Israeli security forces documented in this report, the identification of an individual as "dangerous" does not automatically justify the use of lethal force against the individual when other methods can be used to apprehend him. Nor does a generalized presumption of danger justify the use of lethal force against a particular class of individuals, such as masked youths, about whom no *individualized* information is known regarding their potential danger.

---

[16] IDF response in B'Tselem, *Activity of the Undercover Units*, p. 110.

[17] *Ibid.*, p. 113.

The special forces' restraint in using lethal force is demonstrated by the fact that some members of these units have been killed in action. Special forces encounter real risks in seeking to apprehend armed suspects, and Israel's security forces have the right to use lethal force to counter such risks in appropriate circumstances. However, these risks should not translate into the pre-approved characterization of all encounters as life-threatening and therefore warranting the use of deadly force, as appears to have occurred.

In addition, the risks encountered by security personnel may be due partly to the tactics chosen by special-force units. In some of the cases described in this report, undercover units engaged in high-risk tactics that placed them in potentially dangerous situations, leading to the use of lethal force that might otherwise have been avoided.

It is inappropriate to hold soldiers to the standards of police who encounter common criminals, because the armed Palestinians encountered by soldiers are "terrorists." When asked whether the rules of engagement should be the same as those a police force would use when confronting an armed bank robber, Deputy Judge Advocate General Col. David Yahav insisted that there were differences without specifying what those differences were. He responded:

> We expect [our soldiers] to act according to [police rules] — with a certain interpretation. The situations are different. We are dealing with terrorists whose interest is killing people. Soldiers have to confront armed killers.[18]

If Israeli authorities mean that the danger posed to security personnel or others may vary according to the motives of a suspect, they are of course correct. But if they suggest that the legal standards themselves should vary, they are wrong. To label someone a "terrorist" does not change the legal standards on police practices that govern efforts to apprehend him. Lethal force still may be used only as a last resort to prevent an imminent threat to life.

The Israeli government has not agreed to be bound by the international standards on police practices that Middle East Watch has used to assess the special forces. Israel has ratified the Fourth Geneva Convention, which virtually

---

[18] Middle East Watch interview in Tel Aviv, October 28, 1992.

the entire international community except the government of Israel recognizes as applying *de jure*. Israel does not recognize its *de jure* application, but its government has agreed to apply *de facto* what it considers to be its humanitarian provisions. While the Fourth Geneva Convention requires humane treatment and protection from violence, it provides only the broadest guidelines for assessing the conduct of soldiers toward various forms of violent resistance.

The most directly pertinent sources of codified law are the U.N. standards governing the behavior of law-enforcement agents. These are the legal standards that Middle East Watch has used to evaluate the conduct of Israeli special forces (see Chapter One). Although they have not been codified in a formal treaty, these standards have been ratified by General Assembly bodies and thus can be used to interpret less specific treaty provisions.

To their credit, Israeli officials have repeatedly stated that they require all security forces operating in the occupied territories, including special-force agents, to conduct themselves according to the restrictive law-enforcement rules of engagement. Both State Attorney Beinish and Deputy Judge Advocate General Col. Yahav told Middle East Watch that these rules, which are largely codified in Israeli criminal law, are consistent with international standards. The IDF has even stated, "[T]here is no contradiction between the Open-Fire Regulations given to IDF soldiers in Judea, Samaria and the Gaza District and regulations laid down by International Law....In fact [the regulations] do not allow IDF soldiers to use their weapons even in situations which International Law recognizes as warranting such use."[19]

Middle East Watch's findings cannot be trusted because most Palestinian witnesses lie. Deputy Judge Advocate General Col. Yahav told Middle East Watch in an interview on October 28, 1992, "I know there are [Palestinian] claims, affidavits that refer to our soldiers' terrible behavior, but in most cases, after investigation, we realize it was taken out of imagination."

---

[19] IDF response in B'Tselem, *Activity of the Undercover Units*, p. 122. Deputy Judge Advocate General Col. Yahav told Middle East Watch on October 28, 1992 that Israel required its soldiers to follow the open-fire regulations vis-à-vis "armed terrorists" even though international law viewed them as "illegal combatants" who could be shot on the spot.

Middle East Watch is aware that Palestinian witnesses may have motives to lie. But Israeli security personnel also may have motives to lie, including the soldiers who participated in an incident in which excessive force was used, their superiors, and those involved in the investigative process. By denying Middle East Watch access to the personnel involved in the incidents described in this report, as well as to the investigators' files and the autopsy reports, Israeli authorities have declined to furnish any hard evidence to support the official version of events.

To ensure the reliability and honesty of the testimony it collected from Palestinians, Middle East Watch took a variety of steps. We sought out individuals who were eyewitnesses to a particular shooting. Each was interviewed separately whenever possible, and testimony was probed on details that witnesses were unlikely to have thought to coordinate in advance. Middle East Watch investigators visited the site of each shooting, and asked witnesses to reenact the events they had described, again with the goal of checking their accounts and clarifying details. We discarded some Palestinian testimony as unreliable, and abandoned some cases for lack of credible evidence. We believe that the accounts included in this report are reliable, because of their consistency with each other, their credibility under our cross-examination, and their consistency with testimony taken unofficially from former Israeli soldiers.

In some cases the Israeli government did offer its own version of the events leading to a given shooting, but these were usually offered in summary form. Nonetheless, we have incorporated the government's claims in our descriptions of the shootings, and draw the conclusion that Israeli forces have acted illegally only when reliable Palestinian testimony demonstrates the government's justification for the shooting to be inadequate.

The Israeli government cannot be said to condone the unlawful use of force because so many soldiers have been prosecuted or court-martialed. The Israeli government periodically publishes statistics about the number of soldiers facing courts-martial or disciplinary proceedings (see Appendix). However, these statistics lump together a variety of lesser infractions, and do not give many details on the sentences meted out. On the basis of our evidence of misconduct, we conclude that it is more the exception than the rule that special-force soldiers who wrongfully kill Palestinians are punished. As noted above, we are aware of only one court-martial resulting from the seventeen cases presented in this report in which we believe there was unjustified killing by soldiers. Even in that single case,

the light punishment sent the wrong signal: a partially suspended
sentence and only three months behind bars for shooting a twelve-year-
old boy in the back.

*The undercover units are a more humane response to violent activity in
the occupied territories because they target only suspected participants in that
violence while leaving most Palestinian residents alone.* Middle East Watch
endorses the goal of a more discriminate response to violent activity, one
that spares those who refrain from participation in that violence. Indeed,
fundamental principles of due process and criminal responsibility compel
such discrimination in the application of criminal laws. However, a
discriminate response to violence is no excuse for the use of excessive
force against the targeted individuals.

*The undercover units have been a success because a substantial number
of "wanted" Palestinians have been captured or convinced to turn themselves in.*
The IDF told Middle East Watch that in the first eight months of 1992,
the IDF apprehended 491 "terrorists" while killing twenty-six; another
135 surrendered. Whether or not these figures are accurate, it is clear
that many suspects are captured unharmed and brought to trial for their
alleged offenses. Others are shot down only after they themselves draw
a weapon and thereby give soldiers cause to open fire.

But the fact that undercover units effect many arrests, or that
they sometimes face mortal danger, cannot excuse their resort to murder
in other cases. Furthermore, the above statistics on "terrorists" obscure
the fact that a large portion of IDF special-force operations are directed
not against "wanted" persons but against masked activists and sometimes
against stone-throwers, who are neither "wanted" nor carrying firearms
when killed. The IDF misleads when it portrays the undercover units as
exclusively involved in a battle against known and hardened "terrorists."

CONCLUSIONS AND RECOMMENDATIONS

• The undercover units operate according to a distinct, officially
denied set of rules regarding when they may open fire at "wanted" and
at masked Palestinian activists. These rules effectively give the undercover
forces a license to shoot to kill "wanted" and masked suspects in many
situations where the use of lethal force is unjustified. In so doing, the
unofficial rules violate Israel's official regulations for opening fire. They
also violate international norms that prohibit the use of lethal force

except, when used in response to a grave and imminent danger, they can be justified in terms of the principles of necessity and proportionality. Thus, while claiming to hold soldiers to the relatively exacting standards of law-enforcement agents with regard to the use of firearms, the Israeli military — with the tolerance of political and judicial authorities — in fact allows undercover units to employ methods that are closer to those of a combat operation.

• Despite official claims that undercover units concentrate their efforts on the pursuit of "hard-core," "wanted" activists who have blood on their hands, these units are also commonly used to ambush masked activists when they are engaged in non-life-threatening activities such as manning a roadblock or ordering shopkeepers to observe strikes. In these types of operations as well, the undercover units have a license to kill, even though these activists, whose identities are not usually even known to the soldiers conducting the ambush, are generally not the "hard-core" militants that are the supposed targets of the undercover units.

• Israel's unusual regulation directing soldiers to shoot at the legs of certain types of fleeing suspects, while seemingly humane, is in fact an invitation to use excessive force. Rather than instructing soldiers to use lethal force only when facing an imminent mortal threat, the IDF permits soldiers to aim at the legs, as if this practice employs something less than lethal force, in situations that are not necessarily life-threatening. As this report argues, a shoot-at-the-legs policy involves unacceptably high risks to the lives of the suspects. As a practical matter, it is impossible to prevent this from becoming a shoot-to-kill policy. It has led to a large number of unjustifiable killings with only rare adverse consequences for the soldiers.

In asserting that the undercover units have a license to kill, we are not saying they gun down every targeted activist they encounter. Indeed, many suspects are captured unharmed and brought to trial for their alleged offenses. Others are shot down only after they themselves draw a weapon and thereby give soldiers cause to open fire.

But the fact that undercover units effect many arrests, or that they sometimes face mortal danger, cannot excuse their resort to murder in other cases. The unjustified killings for which they are responsible are not aberrations, but rather constitute a pattern that could only continue with the complicity of the Israeli government.

In response to allegations of excessive force by its undercover units, the IDF has asked that its "credibility should be judged by the instructions given to soldiers, the way in which they are carried out, its supervisory mechanisms and the methods used to deal with irregularities."[20] This report addresses each of these criteria in turn.

Recommendations to the Government of Israel

Middle East Watch calls on the Israeli government to require, without ambiguity, that all of its security forces adhere to strict rules of engagement based on the norms of necessity and proportionality: that is, undercover security agents should use lethal force only when it is both proportional to the danger faced and necessary to prevent an imminent threat to life. Therefore,

(1) The government of Israeli should revise the official open-fire regulations where they are more lenient than the principles of necessity and proportionality permit, giving special attention to the rules governing the apprehension of fleeing suspects, including masked suspects. Shooting live ammunition at a suspect's legs is too dangerous to be considered anything less than lethal force. The rules should be revised to forbid opening fire except when the fleeing suspect is posing an imminent danger to life. No oral or unofficial instructions given to soldiers should be more permissive than the official regulations with regard to opening fire.

And

(2) The government of Israel should demonstrate the will to bring to justice soldiers and police, including elite special-force personnel, who violate the official rules. Inasmuch as IDF and Border Police investigations have, with rare exceptions, lacked the necessary impartiality and thoroughness, investigations of suspected misconduct

---

[20] IDF response in B'Tselem, *Activity of the Undercover Units*, p. 110.

should be transferred to an independent body capable of carrying out professional and impartial inquiries.

Recommendations to the U.S. Government

The U.S. government is aware that Israeli undercover units are responsible for grave abuses. The State Department's *Country Reports on Human Rights Practices in 1992* notes:

> Eyewitness accounts report that approximately two-thirds [of those killed by undercover forces] were unarmed at the time of death, although Israeli authorities say that half of those killed by the squads were armed....[N]umerous reports suggest that the units frequently killed suspects under circumstances in which it may have been possible to apprehend them without killing. In a number of cases, these squads also killed or wounded bystanders or individuals mistakenly identified as wanted persons.

Middle East Watch calls on the U.S. government to use its considerable influence with the Israeli government to encourage it to end the pattern of unjustified, state-sanctioned killings described in this report. Pressure should be applied through all appropriate means, including public criticism of abuses and of the failure to punish them appropriately; and linking the level of bilateral aid to Israel's human rights practices in the occupied territories.

Human Rights Watch, of which Middle East Watch is a component, has consistently urged successive administrations in Washington to comply with legislation that links U.S. aid levels to the recipient governments' protection of basic human rights, and to use other appropriate means to promote respect for human rights, such as actively monitoring rights conditions in the field and publicly criticizing governments that commit abuses.[21]

---

[21] See, for example, the Introduction and the sections on U.S. policy in each country chapter of the *Human Rights Watch World Report 1993*.

Israel receives annually between $3 and $4 billion in assistance from Washington, making it by far the largest recipient of U.S. bilateral aid, and making the U.S. Israel's largest provider of aid. Despite the opportunity that this assistance provides Washington to influence Israel's human rights practices, no U.S. administration has, to our knowledge, publicly suggested that the aid should in some fashion be conditioned on curtailing Israeli violations of the human rights of Palestinians living in the lands Israel has occupied since 1967.[22]

Such linkage is warranted by U.S. law. Section 502B of the Foreign Assistance Act states that "no security assistance may be provided to any country the government of which engages in a consistent pattern of gross violations of internationally recognized human rights" unless the President specifically requests an exception to this provision. The legislation states:

> The term "gross violations of internationally recognized human rights" includes torture or cruel, inhuman, or degrading treatment or punishment, prolonged detention without charges and trial, causing the disappearance of persons by the abduction and clandestine detention of those persons, and other flagrant denial of the right to life, liberty, or the security of person.

Section 116 of the Foreign Assistance Act imposes much the same condition on most forms of economic assistance that 502B imposes on security assistance.

That the conduct described in this report constitutes a "consistent pattern" should admit no doubt, since it is the product of a clear policy not to enforce vigorously either Israeli or international standards governing police practices. As for the term "flagrant denial of the right to life," it is not further defined in U.S. law, so there is no direction given as to whether it encompasses only summary and extrajudicial executions; or also the use of lethal force that is disproportionate under the circumstances. Either way, the intent is clear that the United States should

---

[22] However, the Bush administration held up approval for $10 billion in loan guarantees in 1991-1992 until the U.S. obtained Israeli promises to curb Jewish settlements in the occupied lands.

not become complicit in a pattern of unjustified killing through the continued unconditional provision of extensive assistance.

CHAPTER ONE
APPLICABLE LEGAL STANDARDS

This report analyzes the actions of soldiers both in terms of international legal norms and the IDF's open-fire regulations. As stated in the introduction, Middle East Watch believes that the norms of proportionality and necessity are applicable to the use of lethal force by Israeli soldiers operating in the occupied territories.

This chapter analyzes relevant portions of the official written regulations. Chapters Two and Three contain case studies of IDF conduct in the field. Then Chapter Four analyzes the relationship between the official written regulations and the norms followed in the field by undercover soldiers, drawing upon the case studies, soldiers' testimony and other material.

ISRAEL'S OBLIGATIONS UNDER INTERNATIONAL LAW

Middle East Watch believes that Israel must abide by internationally recognized standards governing situations of occupation, particularly the Fourth Geneva Convention and its requirements of humane treatment and protection against violence. While Israel rejects the *de jure* applicability of that convention, it nevertheless accepts the basic premise that the activities of its security forces are governed by the principles of law enforcement rather than of combat. Deputy Judge Advocate General (JAG) Col. David Yahav recently told *The New York Times*, "Our open-fire regulations follow the same legal principles that govern the police in Israel and in Western countries where there is no war."[1]

In an affidavit submitted to the Israeli Supreme Court acting as the High Court of Justice, then-Deputy Chief of Staff Gen. Ehud Barak (now chief of staff) stated that the rules of engagement governing the use of force by Israeli troops in the occupied territories were based on the view that "opening fire shall be justified according to the general

---

[1] Joel Greenberg, "Israelis Debate Army's Rights Record in Uprising," *The New York Times*, May 24, 1993.

principles of the Penal Law."[2] The Israeli government maintains that the pertinent Israeli law is compatible with international standards governing the use of force by law-enforcement officials, an assessment that, with certain exceptions, Middle East Watch shares.

The written regulations governing the use of lethal force by soldiers in the occupied territories are based on the rules issued to police inside Israel.[3] These regulations for soldiers prohibit the use of firearms with the exception of two situations: to avert a life-threatening danger to a person or, as a last resort, to shoot at the legs of Palestinians suspected of committing, or being about to commit, grave offenses who have ignored warnings to halt.

The legal and moral principle underlying these rules of engagement is that Israeli security personnel may not use lethal force except when they are forced to do so to protect their own lives or the lives of others. This principle applies also to opening fire at fleeing suspects, which is permitted when the person is suspected of what the rules call "a crime in which there is real danger to the life or the body of a person." However, in the occupied territories, the "real danger" need not be imminent before soldiers are permitted to fire at a suspect (see below).

Implicit in the acceptance of this principle is Israel's recognition of its obligations toward the West Bank and Gazan population to

---

[2] The affidavit was submitted in connection with *Yoav Hass* v. *Minister of Defense et al.*, HCJ 873/89, a legal challenge to the rules of engagement which the Court rejected on procedural grounds. Human rights attorney Avigdor Feldman prepared the petition. See also the letter from Deputy JAG Col. David Yahav to Middle East Watch, in the Appendix to this report.

[3] Section 22 of the Israeli Penal Law (as amended in 1992) permits an individual, civilian or law-enforcement officer, to escape criminal responsibility for the use of force in self-defense "if he acted in the way that he did against *an assailant to ward off an unlawful assault*, which placed his own or another's life...in danger of harm." (Emphasis added.) In other words, Israeli law provides that mere evidence that a person is "dangerous" is insufficient to justify the use of lethal force on the grounds of self-defense or defense of others, but force may be used only to ward off a concrete assault by that person. Moreover, to qualify for this defense, a person must act "reasonabl[y] in order to prevent [the] harm," and must not have "brought about the said assault by his improper behavior, while foreseeing the possible developments."

"maintain public order and normal everyday life." In other words, Israel is not in a state of war with the residents of these lands, even if it has put its army in charge of governing them. Rather, Israel, while attending to its own legitimate security concerns, is also obliged to attend to the welfare of the Palestinian population.

This general obligation derives from Article 43 of the Hague Regulations, which has the status of customary international law. Israel recognizes this obligation even while characterizing its role as "administering" rather than "occupying" the West Bank and Gaza Strip and rejecting the *de jure* applicability of the Fourth Geneva Convention.[4]

The Hague Regulations require in Article 46 that the "lives of persons...must be respected."[5] This requirement is fleshed out in the Fourth Geneva Convention, which we regard as legally binding on Israel with regard to its treatment of the population under occupation. The Convention requires that "protected persons...shall at all times be humanely treated, and shall be protected especially against all acts of violence" (Art. 27). Article 43 prohibits all "measures of such a character as to cause the physical suffering or extermination of protected persons...." These include "measures of brutality whether applied by civilian or military agents." The requirement of humane treatment is, virtually by definition, one of the "humanitarian" provisions of the Convention that the Israeli government has pledged to uphold *de facto*.

In addition, the Fourth Geneva Convention establishes a mechanism to enforce the duty of humane treatment by requiring that an occupying power investigate and punish those responsible for serious violations of this duty. Article 146 of the Convention requires the occupying power to investigate and prosecute "grave breaches" of the Convention. It obliges an occupying power to "search for persons alleged

---

[4] See, for example, Israel National Section of International Commission of Jurists, *The Rule of Law in the Areas Administered by Israel* (Tel Aviv: 1981), p. 1.

[5] Although Israeli conduct in the occupied territories must be judged under standards of international humanitarian law, or the laws of war, the same protection of the right to life can be found in international human rights law. Israel ratified the International Covenant on Civil and Political Rights in 1991. Article 6 of the Covenant secures the right not to be arbitrarily deprived of one's life. Under Article 4 of the Covenant, the right to life must be respected even in times of public emergency threatening the life of the nation.

to have committed, or to have ordered to be committed, such grave breaches, and...[to] bring such persons, regardless of their nationality, before its own courts."[6]

Article 147 provides that "willful killing" and "willfully causing great suffering or serious injury to body or health [of protected persons]" constitute "grave breaches" of the Convention. A "willful" killing can be defined as one which is both intentional and unnecessary or disproportionate under the circumstances. We believe that several of the killings documented in this report fit this definition.

While the Fourth Geneva Convention requires humane treatment and protection from violence, it provides only the broadest guidelines for assessing the conduct of soldiers toward forms of violent resistance that range from stone-throwing to the use of firearms. Given that the Israeli government accepts that its conduct is to be measured by standards for law enforcement, the most directly pertinent sources of codified law are the international standards governing the behavior of law-enforcement agents. The leading instrument in this regard is the United Nations Code of Conduct for Law Enforcement Officials, adopted by the General Assembly in 1979, and the Basic Principles on the Use of Force and Firearms by Law Enforcement Officials, adopted in 1990 by the Eighth U.N. Congress on the Prevention of Crime and the Treatment of Offenders.

Although they claim to hold soldiers to law-enforcement standards even when they are confronting armed Palestinians, Israeli officials frequently slip into the language of combat when discussing such encounters. Such references notwithstanding, Israeli officials have, to

---

[6] The same requirement can be found under international human rights law. Article 6 of the International Covenant on Civil and Political Rights, which Israel has ratified, prohibits the arbitrary deprivation of life. The Human Rights Committee, the authoritative body for interpreting the Covenant, issued the following pronouncement in its general comment 6:

> State parties should take measures not only to prevent and punish deprivation of life by criminal acts, but also to prevent arbitrary killing by their own security forces. The deprivation of life by the authorities of the State is a matter of utmost gravity. Therefore, the law must strictly control and limit the circumstances in which a person may be deprived of his life by such authorities.

their credit, clearly and repeatedly asserted that all soldiers operating in the occupied territories are obligated at all times to restrict their use of live ammunition to situations of mortal danger when lesser means have failed. This law-enforcement principle is said to apply to encounters with "armed terrorists" no less than to encounters with stone-throwing schoolchildren.

Indeed, as noted, the Israeli government's use of undercover units is evidence in itself that the security forces are operating in the framework of law enforcement. If they were to claim that their conflict with armed activists amounted to an armed conflict, then their disguising of soldiers in civilian dress in order to commit hostile acts — by blurring the distinction between combatants and noncombatants — would constitute impermissible "treachery" under the laws of and customs of war.

Both international and Israeli law on the use of force by law-enforcement officials are premised on the principles of necessity and proportionality. Force may be used only as strictly necessary to prevent specified threats of harm, and only insofar as the force used is proportionate to the harm to be avoided. These principles are set out in Article 3 of the U.N. Code of Conduct for Law Enforcement Officials, and in its official Commentary. Article 3 provides: "Law enforcement officials may use force only when strictly necessary to the extent required for the performance of their duty." The Commentary to the Code elaborates: "The use of firearms is considered an extreme measure....In general, firearms should not be used except when a suspected offender offers armed resistance or otherwise jeopardizes the lives of others and less extreme measures are not sufficient to restrain or apprehend the suspected offender." Article 9 of the Basic Principles states:

> Law enforcement officials shall not use firearms against persons except in self-defense or defense of others against the imminent threat of death or serious injury, to prevent the perpetration of a particularly serious crime involving grave threat to life, to arrest a person presenting such a danger and resisting their authority, or to prevent his or her escape, and only when less extreme means are insufficient to achieve these objectives. In any event, intentional lethal use of firearms may only be made when strictly unavoidable in order to protect life.

This obligation underlies Israel's official posture regarding the applicable rules on the use of force toward residents of the West Bank and the Gaza Strip. Throughout the intifada, which has included frequent acts of violent resistance by Palestinians, Israel has repeatedly affirmed that the behavior of its security forces is governed by the standards of necessity and proportionality — the standards appropriate to law-enforcement agents rather than to a combat army. For example, the Foreign Ministry said in January 1990:

> [S]pecial efforts have been undertaken to make clear to Israeli security personnel that, however great the provocation, their behavior must conform to strict regulations and standards, and that restraint must be exercised.
>
> According to regulations, force may be used to stop violent activity and to overcome resistance to arrest. Force is prohibited as a form of punishment or to deliberately inflict injuries; similarly, the use of force is forbidden against a person who, after having been arrested, shows no resistance or makes no attempt to escape.[7]

These principles, Israel insists, underlie all of its operations in the occupied territories, including its encounters with Palestinians who are armed and/or "wanted," and considered dangerous. The Justice Ministry wrote to Middle East Watch in a letter of December 21, 1992:

> The goal of the undercover security forces is to locate terrorists, apprehend them and bring them to trial....The members of the undercover units are subject to the same instructions as the rest of the security forces regarding the opening of fire. No license to kill has been given to the undercover units of the Israeli Police, the General Security Service (GSS), the Border Police, and the IDF, even as regards dangerous fugitives. The use of live

---

[7] Israel Consulate General in New York, "Israel's Measures in the Territories and Human Rights," January 1990.

ammunition is only permitted whether by undercover or regular security forces, in the following two situations: danger to life [and]...the arrest of a suspect...suspected of criminal offenses that endanger peoples' lives. (See Appendix.)

Deputy JAG Col. Yahav told Middle East Watch on October 28, 1992:

[The undercover units'] job is to apprehend...terrorists, to bring them to prison, to investigate them, and use legal procedures. The purpose is apprehending, and not any other purpose.

In contrast to killings during combat, all killings by special-force soldiers are, officials say, the subject of criminal investigations. "In cases where it is determined that enlisted personnel or officers have deviated from these orders, legal proceedings are taken against them, despite the fact that they are operating in difficult and dangerous situations against armed Palestinians who have murdered Jewish and Arab victims."[8]

Thus, according to both international consensus and Israel's own statements, the military authorities are obliged to ensure that Palestinians suspected of offenses are provided with the full range of basic rights, the most important of which is the right to life and the right to a fair trial. Soldiers must make every reasonable effort to arrest "wanted" and masked Palestinians, regardless of whether they are suspected of bearing arms or carrying out attacks on Israeli forces.

The requirement of using lethal force only when "strictly unavoidable" also imposes upon law enforcement officials a duty to plan operations in a manner that minimizes the likelihood that lethal force will be required, such as by laying siege to a suspect's hideout rather than storming it (to minimize the risk to arresting officials and thus the need for them to employ lethal force) or by surrounding a suspect to close off

---

[8] IDF response in B'Tselem, *Activity of the Undercover Units*, p. 110.

avenues of escape (to avoid the need to use force to apprehend him).[9]
This requirement can also be derived from the requirement under
Section 22 of the Israeli Penal Law that a shooting cannot be justified on
the grounds of self-defense or defense of others if a person "brought
about the said assault by his improper behavior, while foreseeing the
possible developments."

Middle East Watch believes that Israeli procedures for shooting
at the legs of fleeing suspects conflict with international standards by
authorizing fire at an excessively broad range of suspects. As this report
demonstrates, shooting at the legs of a fleeing suspect regularly has the
effect of shooting to kill, particularly as the distance between the firing
soldier and the fleeing suspect increases. The written rules of engagement
governing the use of live ammunition by Israeli soldiers contain no
limitation on the distance from which soldiers can shoot at the legs of a
fleeing suspect. Moreover, the pistols and shortened weapons preferred
by undercover soldiers because of the greater ease of concealment are
relatively inaccurate weapons. Finally, the distinction between the shoot-
at-the-legs requirement and shooting to kill is virtually impossible to
enforce because of the ease with which soldiers can aim above the legs
and then claim to have shot at the legs and accidentally hit vital parts of
the body. This problem is one of the reasons that neither the U.S. Federal
Bureau of Investigation (FBI) nor any U.S. urban police department of
which we are aware allows its agents to fire at the legs of a fleeing
suspect; the danger must be sufficiently grave and imminent for them to
use lethal force or they must not use it at all.

THE OFFICIAL OPEN-FIRE REGULATIONS
FOR SOLDIERS IN THE OCCUPIED TERRITORIES

Middle East Watch believes that the IDF rules of engagement,
which are binding on all IDF soldiers and Border Police operating in the
territories, are, with a couple of important exceptions, solidly grounded

---

[9] An example of the application of this requirement can be found in the U.S.
Federal Bureau of Investigation (FBI) Standards, which provide: "Emphasis must
be placed on planning arrests so that maximum pressure is placed on the
individual being sought and they have no opportunity to either resist or flee."
See *Legal Handbook for FBI Agents*, June 1992.

in international norms, particularly with regard to the use of force to counter mortal danger. For such situations, the regulations stress that the danger be imminent and life-threatening, and that the soldier has tried lesser means before firing on the suspect; the regulations then order the soldier to fire only at the person presenting the danger, and to stop firing as soon as the danger is removed. These instructions comport with the principles of necessity and proportionality. The problem with the IDF procedures on life-threatening situations lies not with the underlying principles so much as with the expansive notions of imminent mortal danger that soldiers have been permitted to adopt in the field.

In our view, it is with the IDF regulations on firing at fleeing suspects that the gravest violation of international norms is to be found. These regulations include those pertaining to firing on masked persons.

The regulation that enables soldiers to fire at the legs of fleeing suspects has been the Israeli legal framework in which hundreds of Palestinians have been shot dead without any finding of wrongdoing against the soldiers. Several cases are described in this report. Many of the victims were not suspected of life-threatening offenses and were posing no mortal danger when they were killed. Middle East Watch believes that this regulation, which on the surface may sound humane because it requires soldiers to fire at the legs, in fact violates the principles of proportionality and necessity by permitting soldiers to use lethal force in a wide variety of situations where there is no imminent threat to life. As the IDF readily admits, whenever shots are fired toward the legs under field conditions, there is a risk that the bullet will go astray and inflict a mortal wound. The order to aim at the legs is also virtually unenforceable, because a soldier can aim at the torso of a fleeing suspect and claim with little risk of being refuted that he aimed at the legs.

These themes are developed at length in Chapter Four, which describes how the open-fire orders translate into actual practice among the special forces. The purpose of this chapter is to lay out the written open-fire orders that are relevant to this study. We omit mention of several areas within the regulations, such as the sections that relate to opening fire "to stop suspicious vehicles" or to the use of plastic bullets against "rioters."

Israeli authorities have never made public the full open-fire regulations that apply to soldiers operating in the occupied West Bank and Gaza Strip, claiming that if the rules were publicly known,

Palestinians would "exploit" that knowledge.[10] Police departments worldwide charge that criminals exploit their knowledge of the rules that constrain police conduct. However, bearing in mind the police-style rules of engagement that Israel claims to uphold in the occupied territories, it is noteworthy that the two U.S. police departments we checked, those of New York and Los Angeles, informed us that all open-fire regulations issued to their personnel were a matter of public record.

Middle East Watch believes the open-fire regulations should be in the public domain in view of the great number and unabated pace of casualties that Israeli soldiers have inflicted in questionable circumstances in the occupied territories. There is a compelling public interest in holding soldiers accountable for deviations from their rules, which requires that the rules be publicly known.

This chapter notes two aspects of the rules of engagement that have been characterized by a lack of clarity during the intifada; in one of these areas — the rules on firing at masked persons — IDF officials conceded that soldiers' confusion about the rules had led them to open fire more liberally than had been intended. The need for clarity, we believe, is ill-served by treating the rules as inappropriate for public scrutiny.

The Israeli government published a detailed account of the rules of engagement in a document distributed by the Israeli consulate in New York in 1990.[11] The regulations are contained in a periodically updated *Pocket Booklet for the Soldier Serving in Judea and Samaria and the Gaza Strip* (פנקס כיס לחייל המשרת באיו"ש ואזח"ע). All IDF soldiers serving in the territories are supposed to carry the *Pocket Booklet* with them. This chapter quotes translated excerpts of the January 1991 version. We note, however, that there have been modifications to that version which have not been disclosed in detail, including an abbreviated procedure for apprehending suspects and an expanded definition of "life-threatening" situations to include all encounters with suspects carrying firearms; both of these amendments provide us cause for concern, as explained below.

---

[10] Middle East Watch interview with Lt. Col. Arik Gordin of the IDF spokesman's office, March 4, 1990.

[11] Israel Consulate General in New York, "Israel's Measures in the Territories and Human Rights," January 1990.

According to the *Pocket Booklet*, IDF soldiers are permitted to fire live ammunition at suspects in the occupied territories in two basic situations: when soldiers or others are placed in life-threatening danger and in order to prevent the escape of a "dangerous" suspect who has disobeyed orders to halt.

Opening Fire in Situations of Mortal Danger

The rules divide life-threatening situations into two basic scenarios: when a person is at risk of injury by a lethal weapon; and when a group of "rioters" endangers his life through the use of physical force or "cold weapons" (see Glossary). In our view, this section of the rules adheres to the principles of necessity and proportionality and is reasonable. Virtually all situations in which a soldier is at immediate risk of being hit by gunfire or a molotov cocktail can be regarded as life-threatening and would justify opening fire at the attacker.

The picture grows more complicated when the suspect is sighted carrying a firearm but is not holding it in a threatening manner. For example, a soldier with binoculars may spot a person walking in the distance with a pistol tucked in his belt, away from other people and unaware of the soldier. Is this scenario life-threatening? Israel's recent decision to expand the definition of life-threatening to include the mere carrying of a firearm is a violation of the principle of necessity. Permission to shoot on sight anyone carrying a gun conflicts with both Israeli law and international standards. Section 22 of Israeli Penal Law, cited above, permits police and others to use force "against an assailant to ward off an unlawful assault" that places his own or another's life in danger of harm. In other words, the assault that is being prevented must have some concreteness.

The same idea is found in the requirement that the danger be imminent in the Basic Principles on the Use of Force and Firearms by Law Enforcement Officials.

In the year during which the killings in this report occurred (March 1992-February 1993), there was much public ambiguity over the rules applicable to persons sighted with firearms. On March 30, 1993, the Israeli cabinet appeared to end the confusion by approving regulations authorizing soldiers to shoot armed Palestinians on sight, regardless of whether they were preparing to fire their weapons when sighted.[12] Deputy Defense Minister Mordechai Gur told Israel Radio he had "no doubt that the new rules, all of them built on the international law and the Israeli law, will enable the soldiers to act in a more efficient way."[13]

It is not entirely clear when this rule had been conveyed to soldiers. In February 1992, the Israeli press reported that the IDF had modified its definition of a "mortal danger" to include any visual contact between armed Palestinians and IDF personnel, meaning, apparently, that any Palestinian *carrying* a firearm could be shot dead on sight. The Nablus district commander said on Israeli television in March 1992:

> Anyone carrying a weapon is in fact a potential attacker, and from our point of view he is a danger. In light of that, as long as he has a weapon, we'll hit him.[14]

Maj. Gen. Danny Yatom, the commander of Israel's central military region (which includes the occupied West Bank), said in a May 1992 news conference:

> When somebody carries in a clear way a weapon or holds a pistol in his hand, he poses danger to life, and he will be shot without warning. Even if the terrorist does not open fire, we will be the first to open fire in order to defend the lives of our soldiers. I don't think we have to wait until terrorists open fire first at our people.[15]

---

[12] Israel Radio in Hebrew, March 30, 1993, as reported in FBIS, March 31, 1993.

[13] Israel Radio in English, March 31, 1993, as reported in FBIS, March 31, 1993.

[14] Clyde Haberman, "Killings of Palestinian Suspects Raise Questions about Israeli Army Agents," *The New York Times*, April 12, 1992.

[15] "Israel Asserts Armed Palestinians Will Be Killed Without Warning," *The New York Times*, May 7, 1992.

Hadashot reported that IDF officers had requested alterations in the definition of a life-threatening situation long before February 1992 but that the IDF legal department had withheld approval for fear that the new regulation would be abused in the field.[16]

Despite the above-cited clear statement of policy by Gen. Yatom, the new rules were not publicly disclosed, and they remained the subject of contradictory statements. At roughly the same time as Gen. Yatom made his remarks, the IDF wrote: "B'Tselem's claim, that in the framework of the changes in the opening of fire instructions it has been permitted to fire at armed men without warning, even when they could otherwise have been apprehended without threatening soldiers' lives, is baseless."[17] The Deputy IDF Chief of Staff, Amnon Shahak, was quoted on Israel Radio as saying:

> [T]he rules of engagement have not been changed; we have merely clarified them. We have not instituted a more liberal approach toward opening fire and any attempt to portray things as such is misleading the public.[18]

On October 28, 1992, Gen. Yatom's comments were apparently contradicted again, in an interview that Deputy JAG Col. Yahav gave to Middle East Watch. Col. Yahav said, "Generally, you can't shoot an armed person on sight." He refused to discuss exceptions. Five months later, the cabinet announced a shoot-on-sight policy toward armed Palestinians in the occupied territories, an amendment that seemed to have already been implemented in the field.

Later in this chapter, we discuss another aspect of the rules of engagement that was also highly ambiguous in the months following its inception: the orders for confronting masked persons. Whether deliberate or negligent, the lack of clear rules tends to subvert the sense of

---

[16] Alex Fishman, "The Safety Catch is Off and the Finger is on the Trigger," *Hadashot*, May 1, 1992.

[17] IDF spokesman in B'Tselem, *Activity of the Undercover Units*, p. 121.

[18] Israel Radio in Hebrew, May 2, 1992, as reported in FBIS, May 4, 1992.

accountability that the IDF should instill in its personnel if it wishes to prevent abuses.

Opening Fire as Part of the Procedure for Arresting a Suspect

The regulations provide for a three-stage procedure for opening fire on a suspect: Stage 1, calling a warning in Arabic; Stage 2, firing a single warning shot upward, ascertaining that this does not endanger persons or property; and Stage 3, firing "in order to hit the legs only" and "always...on the single shot setting, with utmost caution...." It is stipulated that "no fire is to be directed toward the upper part of the suspect's body" and that fire "is not to be opened, except against a specific attacker who has been identified as endangering human life."

This procedure is to apply except in the event that IDF personnel are attacked by gunfire or sabotage. In a sub-section headlined "THROWING ROCKS: ATTENTION!", the regulations emphasize: "Do not fire at a person throwing rocks, except as a part of the procedure for the arrest of a suspect, and only when the rock-throwing constitutes real and immediate danger." "Real danger" is defined as "the throwing of rocks toward a moving vehicle with intent to hit it, or rock-throwing in other circumstances that endangers human life...." The regulations on rock-throwers continue, "Do not open fire unless the arrest procedure is performed close to the rock-throwing. If the suspect has not been arrested immediately and close to the incident, weapons are no longer to be used as part of the arrest procedure."

The regulations state that personnel may "not open fire except as a last means to arrest a suspect, when all other means have failed." There is an additional note to "[a]void firing at *children* under the age of fourteen and at *women*."

We have quoted these portions of the regulations because the cases described in this report offer evidence of their violation. That is, persons have been shot by undercover units when they have presented no imminent danger (e.g. rock-throwers not posing a threat to security forces' or others' lives); they have been shot without the three-stage procedure being followed, and absent the exhaustion of all other means to apprehend them.

In part, the doctrine of using lethal force to apprehend a fleeing suspect is grounded in principles of self-defense. The U.N. Basic

Principles on the Use of Force and Firearms by Law Enforcement
Officials require that firearms cannot be used to arrest a fleeing suspect
except when such person presents a danger involving an "imminent
threat of death or serious injury" or a "grave threat to life."[19] The
requirement that the threat posed by a fleeing person be immediate and
not remote is explicit in the requirement of an "imminent" threat and
implicit in the reference to a "grave" threat.

But the use of lethal force to apprehend a fleeing suspect is also
grounded in a desire to maintain the integrity of the law-enforcement
process. If a suspect can simply run away from a law-enforcement official,
the rule of law might be undermined. Historically, some nations have
permitted the use of lethal force to apprehend a fleeing suspect
(particularly a felon) even if he poses no immediate threat to life.
Although international standards remain imprecise in this respect, there
is clear movement toward a requirement that lethal force (as opposed to
lesser forms of coercion) can be employed against a fleeing suspect only
if an immediate threat to life is posed. In other words, there is growing
appreciation in the international community that the public's interest in
avoiding summarily taking the life of a fleeing suspect outweighs its
interest in apprehending criminal suspects, unless the fleeing suspect
threatens immediate death or serious physical harm to others. This
conclusion is only reinforced by the fact that the rule of law is hardly
served by killing a suspect before he can be brought to trial, whereas a
suspect who escapes can be caught and tried another day. Accordingly, we
believe that the ambiguity in the law governing the use of lethal force to
apprehend a fleeing suspect should be interpreted in favor of a

---

[19] The pertinent provisions read as follows:

> Law enforcement officials shall not use firearms against persons
> except in self-defense or defense of others against the imminent
> threat of death or serious injury, to prevent the perpetration of
> a particularly serious crime involving grave threat to life, to
> arrest a person presenting such a danger and resisting their
> authority, or to prevent his or her escape, and only when less
> extreme means are insufficient to achieve these objectives. In
> any event, intentional lethal use of firearms may only be made
> when strictly unavoidable in order to protect life. (Annex, Basic
> Principles on the Use of Force and Firearms by Law
> Enforcement Officials, p.114.)

requirement of immediate serious harm to others before lethal force can be used against him.[20]

---

[20] The leading U.S. Supreme Court case governing the use of lethal force to apprehend a fleeing suspect contains similar ambiguity on the issue of how immediate a threat to life posed by the fleeing suspect must be. In *Tennessee* v. *Garner*, 471 U.S. 1 (1985), the Court seemed to suggest that an immediate threat was required before lethal force could be used, when it stated: "Where the suspect poses no immediate threat to the [arresting] officer and no threat to others, the harm resulting from failing to apprehend him does not justify the use of deadly force to do so." *Ibid.* at 11.

However, the Court also suggested that this standard would be satisfied not only "if the suspect threatens the officer with a weapon" — a clear example of an immediate threat — but also if "there is probable cause to believe that he has committed a crime involving the infliction or threatened infliction of serious physical harm," so long as a warning, if feasible, has been given. *Ibid.* at 11-12. This language suggests that past commission of a violent crime is alone enough to create an immediate threat — an expansive understanding of the immediacy requirement. Yet the Court at the same time required the arresting officer, before concluding that a fleeing suspect posed an immediate threat to life, to have "probable cause" to believe that he had posed such a threat in the past. This more-likely-than-not standard requires far more certainty than, for example, a requirement of reasonable suspicion. It is also an objective standard, which rests not on the subjective belief of the arresting officer but on the way in which a reasonable person would have responded to the situation faced by the arresting officer.

The National Law Enforcement Policy Center of the International Association of Chiefs of Police, in commenting on the Association's Model Policy, provides an effective statement of the reasons for restricting the use of lethal force in apprehending fleeing suspects to situations of an immediate threat to life:

> [P]olice officers may use deadly force to prevent the escape of a fleeing felon whom the officer has probable cause to believe will pose a significant threat to human life should the felon escape. In this case, the more demanding test of probable cause must be employed before deadly force can be used. In such a case, a threat of further violence and/or death must impose clear and immediate justification to use deadly force.
>
> For example, the use of force would be justified in instances where an officer was attempting to stop the escape of a felon whom the officer had positively identified as one who had just

A landmark ruling by the Israeli Supreme Court in *First Sgt. David Ankonina* v. *Chief Military Prosecutor*, C.A. 57/53 P.D. 7 1126 (1989) affirmed that lethal force may be used against a fleeing suspect only when it is proportionate to the danger being prevented. The Court's reference to Section 22 of the Penal Law, with its limitation of the justification of self-defense to the warding off of an assault, suggests that the imminence and not only the magnitude of the danger posed by a fleeing suspect are factors in determining when it is permissible to open fire. The Court stated:

committed a violent crime or homicide, and who is fleeing the scene with a weapon. The potential escape of other felons, however, may not pose the same degree of imminent risk to the public or the officer, and the use of deadly force to prevent their escape would be eminently more difficult to justify under this policy.

Of the two circumstances in which deadly force may be used, that involving the fleeing felon is unquestionably the most difficult to regulate through policy. Because there can be a greater risk of error in these circumstances, some agencies may prefer to disallow the use of deadly force entirely in the case of fleeing felons. Those who prefer this approach point to the problem associated with positive identification of suspects, the fact that many serious felonies may not involve actual violence or death and that, even in the case of repetitive violent offenders, one cannot accurately predict the offenders' future behavior. Given these and related problems, this approach assumes that if an error is to be made it is best that it be made through restraint rather than face the risk of the unwarranted taking of a human life. (IACP National Law Enforcement Policy Center, "Use of Force: Concepts and Issues Paper," February 1, 1989, pp. 3-4.)

A similar policy has been adopted in the United States by the Commission on Accreditation for Law Enforcement Agencies, which permits the use of deadly force against a fleeing felon only when a police officer "reasonably believes that the action is in defense of human life, including the officer's own life, or in defense of any person in immediate danger of serious physical injury." (Commission on Accreditation for Law Enforcement Agencies, November 1990, pp. 1-2.)

Public interest in the apprehension and arrest of offenders is formed, *inter alia*, by the desire to defend the members of the public, the offender's potential victims.

The official or the citizen works toward the protection of human life and the physical well-being of the offender's victim or of those liable to become his victims if the offender is not arrested. However, this aspect of the public interest has two facets: just as it serves as a motive for the apprehension of the offender to prevent harm being done to another person, so it provides normative guidance regarding the degree of force to be employed against the offender. In both instances the underlying goal is the desire to avoid as much as possible the taking of life. This goal becomes a limitation on the use of force, so that human life should not be taken nor bodily harm inflicted when this does not stand in reasonable proportion to the degree of danger one wishes to prevent, even when what is involved is the offender's apprehension. In order to realize the said interest, a higher threshold must be set for grounding the justification for the use of lethal force in executing the law, than one which stems exclusively from the formal classification of the offenses according to the maximum punishment accruing to them.

It is therefore proper that we base our tests on a theoretical foundation comparable to the rules of reasonable proportionality which, for example, form the basis for the provisions regarding responsibility for an offense relating to the use of force by a public official in the course of personal self-defense, as stated in Sec. 22 of the Penal Law....As is stated there, a reasonable correlation must exist between the degree of the danger and the degree of the force employed.

In conclusion, the logical inter-relationship between the means employed and the offense one seeks to prevent, dictates the setting of narrow boundaries for the public official who is required, or who wishes, to exercise his authority in order to arrest an offender or prevent his escape.[21]

The U.N. Basic Principles require that even when a fleeing suspect poses an immediate threat, lethal force may be used "only when strictly unavoidable in order to protect life." The meaning of this requirement is clarified in Principle 10, which provides:

> In the circumstances provided for under Principle 9, law enforcement officials shall identify themselves as such and give a clear warning of their intent to use firearms, with sufficient time for the warning to be observed, unless to do so would unduly place the law enforcement officials at risk or would create a risk of death or serious harm to other persons, or would be clearly inappropriate or pointless in the circumstances of the incident.

The Basic Principles do not stipulate that the warnings given in advance of using lethal force involve a warning shot. Indeed, in some countries, warning shots are prohibited because of the danger that they pose to others.[22] Yet international standards are clear that whenever possible, some warning must be given and the fleeing suspect must be given ample opportunity to heed the warning before lethal force is employed.[23]

---

[21] Cited in B'Tselem, *Activity of the Undercover Units*, pp. 28-29.

[22] See, e.g., the standards governing the use of firearms by the FBI which provide: "No warning shots are to be fired by Agents in an effort to stop a fleeing person or for any other purpose." *FBI Legal Handbook for Special Agents*.

[23] See, e.g., the Model Policy of the International Association of Chiefs of Police of February 1989 ("Before using a firearm, police officers shall identify themselves and state their intent to shoot, where feasible."); FBI Standards ("Whenever feasible, verbal warnings should be given before deadly force is applied."), *ibid*.

Israeli law contains a similar requirement. In the above-
mentioned *Ankonina* case, Israeli Supreme Court Chief Justice Meir
Shamgar stated:

> [F]orce should not be used unless it is the last resort in
> the specific circumstances....[L]ethal action is not to be
> taken unless it is essential to take it, because more
> moderate means have proved fruitless and the result
> could not be prevented in any other way....
>
> The necessity should be immediate, involving the need to
> take action on the spot, and the action should be the least
> drastic possible which still serves the purpose.

Justice Shamgar then set forth the steps that ordinarily must be
followed before using force to apprehend a suspect:

> The methods are, in the first place, a warning given by
> voice or by a sign; second, expressing the intention to
> take more decisive action, including a warning given by
> voice or by a sign; third, expressing the intention to take
> more decisive action, including the use of firearms, this
> by means of firing warning shots in the air; and finally
> — and only finally — aimed fire, but even then in a
> manner calculated to reduce the degree of bodily harm.
> Naturally, the order of the actions and other limitations
> do not apply if a grave immediate danger is posed to the
> official or to the person he is protecting, which justifies
> immediately taking every means required for self-defense
> or for the protection of others.[24]

Middle East Watch believes that Israeli procedures for shooting
at the legs of a fleeing suspect should be scrutinized in terms of the
principles outlined above governing the use of lethal force. We criticized
the shooting-at-the-legs policy in our 1990 report *The Israeli Army and the*

---

[24] Cited in B'Tselem, *Activity of the Undercover Units*, pp. 29-30.

Intifada.[25] By allowing soldiers to shoot at the legs the IDF is introducing lethal force into a variety of situations where the suspect is posing no imminent threat to life. In practice, the shooting-at-the-legs rule has been virtually impossible to enforce. Once a soldier finds himself in a situation in which the regulations permit him to fire at a suspect's legs, he enjoys near-total impunity concerning where the bullet lands. He can aim at the relatively more substantial and stationary targets of the head or abdomen, and then claim that he had aimed at the legs, with little or no evidence likely to contradict him unless the victim was only a few feet away. Or, he can earnestly aim at the legs but hit the suspect's back or head due to a variety of factors for which he cannot be faulted, as the IDF readily concedes:

> [T]he use of firearms for the purposes of arrest always includes the danger of a fatal outcome or harm, to the other person, even if used carefully. And that is due to the possibility of unpredictable accidents which can always occur. (See IDF comment on the killing of Mahmoud Shalaldeh, in Chapter Two and the Appendix.)

The Chief Military Prosecutor elaborated on this point in a 1990 interview:

> The intention is not to kill the suspect, but to catch him. However, if you shoot from fifty meters at the legs, there's a five percent chance you won't hit the legs. Hitting someone who is running is a very difficult task. He jumps, falls, climbs a wall. The bullet ricochets, there are slopes in the ground.[26]

The 1991 *Pocket Booklet* contains no limits on the distance from which soldiers may fire on fleeing suspects. However, Col. Yahav told Middle East Watch in October 1992 that such limits had been imposed.

---

[25] See also al-Haq, "The Illegal Use of Lethal Force against 'Fleeing Suspects,'" May 1, 1991.

[26] Middle East Watch interview with Col. Menachem Finkelstein, March 4, 1990.

He refused, however, to specify the range, saying it was classified. In this regard, it is worth noting the relative inaccuracy of the pistols and shortened weapons that are preferred by undercover soldiers because of the greater ease of concealment. For these and other reasons, neither the FBI nor any U.S. urban police department of which we are aware permits firing at the legs of a fleeing suspect; the danger must be sufficiently grave and imminent for them to use lethal force or they must not use it at all.[27]

The principles of necessity and proportionality are violated in several respects by the conditions stipulated in the booklet for opening fire at a fleeing suspect. The conditions are permissive with regard to the required level of danger, but even more so with regard to the imminence of the danger. The *Pocket Booklet* authorizes soldiers to shoot a fleeing Palestinian if there is a reasonable suspicion that he has committed or is on his way to committing "a dangerous crime." Thus, if the suspect allegedly committed a "dangerous" crime in the past, it is simply accepted that he poses some future danger; there is no requirement that he be posing any sort of imminent danger before firing on him if he refuses to halt.

The problem is best illustrated by comparing the *Pocket Booklet*'s appropriately worded language on stone-throwing to the language on other "dangerous crimes." The procedure may be executed against stone-throwers only when "real [mortal] danger exists and the arrest is performed immediately during the incident." There is no comparable requirement with regard to other offenses that the danger be immediate.

---

[27] This is true of New York, Los Angeles, and Houston, among other cities. The Houston Police Department's policy on deadly force states:

> Rule 1: Police officers shall not discharge their firearms except to protect themselves or another person from imminent death or serious bodily injury....

> Rule 4: Police officers shall not discharge their firearms to subdue an escaping suspect who presents no imminent threat of death or serious bodily injury. [Reprinted in *Deadly Force: What We Know, A Practitioner's Desk Reference on Police-Involved Shootings* (Washington, D.C.: Police Executive Research Forum, 1992), p. 598.]

Perhaps the most ominous aspect of the definition of "dangerous crimes" meriting the procedure is the inclusion of *"membership* in a hostile organization *or activity* therein in a manner likely to endanger a person's life or physical integrity." (Emphasis added) The booklet does not specify what information would enable the soldier to develop a "reasonable" suspicion that a Palestinian is a "member" of a particular hostile organization. Is information from the GSS required, or is it sufficient, for example, to spot a person writing pro-Hamas graffiti, or participating in a march or funeral procession where pro-Fatah banners are being waved and slogans are being chanted?

Another disturbing aspect of the treatment of "membership" is that the rules seem to treat it as a "dangerous crime" by itself. This would be consistent with Israel's long-standing insistence that a member of a "hostile organization" is a party to its violent activities even if he himself is not directly involved in those activities.[28]

---

[28] For example, in a letter to Amnesty International dated May 30, 1988, Attorney General Joseph Harish challenged the premise that it is possible for individuals to be members of the Palestine Liberation Organization without necessarily espousing or becoming involved in violence:

> Membership in the PLO requires unqualified adoption of and allegiance to its credo of terror....A member of that terrorist organization may be called upon to carry out acts of violence at any time, irrespective of his previous activities or personal beliefs....[T]he contention that within the PLO it is possible to distinguish between activities which are decidedly political and terrorist activities was recently addressed by Israel's Supreme Court in the case of *Faisal Abd'l al-Khadr Hussaini* v. *The State of Israel* [A.A.D. 1/87]. The Court stated, *inter alia*:

> The State of Israel finds itself in the midst of a protracted struggle with an octopus called the terrorist organizations. That struggle is not a war in the ordinary sense. There is no head-on clash of the fighting forces of the two sides. It is a war waged against the State in every possible way: by ... terrorist activities against the Israel Defence Forces and the civilian population, as well as by demonstrations, disturbances of the peace, business strikes, the blocking of roads, the throwing of stones and incendiary bottles in Judea and Samaria and the Gaza Region, the whipping-up of popular feelings, the sowing of

It is possible that the ambiguously worded regulation concerning membership is meant to be read as "membership in a hostile organization...in a manner likely to endanger a person's life or physical integrity." Deputy JAG Col. Yahav told Middle East Watch in October 1992 that in order to fire at a fleeing suspect who refuses to halt, "It's not enough that it's a felony by law. It has to be connected to a threat to the life of people." If this requirement excludes certain types of members of banned organizations, that is not made clear. While specific *activities* can be reasonably seen as life-threatening, the booklet does not explain when *membership* becomes life-threatening.[29]

The booklet does not specify, once the soldier reaches the third stage of the procedure and has fired at the legs of the suspect, what conditions must be met before he fires again at the legs of the suspect. The rules specify that the weapon "shall always be used on the single shot setting, with the utmost caution...." But how much time must a soldier pause each time before firing again, in order to ascertain whether he has wounded the suspect? The booklet's silence on these matters seems to give soldiers leeway to fire shots in rapid succession.

---

discord between Arabs and Jews, incitement by newspapers and other means, and the like. All these activities and the various bodies engaged in them require organization, financing and coordination. *Inter alia*, they require a ramified intelligence network and the concentration of material that may serve them as a basis for planning and execution. It is therefore impossible to make a distinction between one sector of the system and other sectors and to argue that this sector does not engage in actual violence and should be considered separately from the other....

Thus, Israel's countermeasures must focus on each of the links that form the chain of terrorism and must damage or weaken it. (*Ibid.*, pp. 5-7.)

[29] Israel maintains a list of "hostile organizations" that includes all factions and support groups of the Palestine Liberation Organization, Islamic Jihad, and Hamas. It is an offense under the emergency laws that Israel applies in the occupied territories to belong to or provide services to the proscribed groups, and Palestinians are commonly sentenced to prison terms of two years or longer for these offenses.

Commenting on the killing of fleeing suspects in 1990, Middle East Watch pointed out:

> The fatalities are a predictable outcome of the IDF's policy on apprehending suspects. Even if the five percent margin of error cited by the chief military prosecutor is correct, it is unacceptably high when it may result in the killing of a suspect who is unarmed, running away, and posing no imminent threat to anyone. Continuing this policy of shooting at such fleeing suspects is a clear violation of the principles of necessity and proportionality and an important contribution to the number of unjustified killings.[30]

ABBREVIATING THE THREE-STEP PROCEDURE FOR APPREHENDING SUSPECTS

In some of the cases presented in this report, eyewitnesses stated that soldiers skipped all or part of the three-step procedure before opening fire at suspects. Official accounts reported that the soldiers had followed the procedures for apprehending suspects. The existence of classified orders requiring soldiers to abbreviate the procedure under certain circumstances makes it impossible for the public to judge whether the soldiers who bypassed the three-step procedure did so in compliance with their regulations. This sort of confidentiality in the open-fire regulations undermines accountability for abuses.

Deputy JAG Col. Yahav confirmed to Middle East Watch on October 28, 1992 that there are shortened procedures, but said he could not discuss them with us. We are aware of an IDF document that specifies two situations in which security personnel are obliged to shorten the three-step procedure for apprehending fleeing suspects. Titled "Sheet on Situations and Responses" (דף מקרים ותגובות), the document addresses various situations soldiers may face and specifies what actions they are required to take in these circumstances. In two of the situations mentioned in the document — "stone-throwing against vehicles" and "if an attacker flees and is not holding a weapon" — soldiers are ordered to use

---

[30] Middle East Watch, *The Israeli Army and the Intifada*, p. 44.

the shortened procedures. The document, which does not define the shortened procedure itself or the exact circumstances in which it may be used, is typically carried by soldiers together with the *Pocket Booklet*.

PURSUING MASKED ACTIVISTS

The problematic nature of the written open-fire regulations is most marked in its discussion of masked activists. According to the *Pocket Booklet*, soldiers are permitted to use fire to apprehend a masked person when certain specified "additional suspicious circumstances" exist. Those specified circumstances include many that involve no imminent danger to security agents or other persons. Rather, the examples given range from "hanging around in a group while carrying means (chain, knife, axe) or other dangerous activity" to "a background of violent and dangerous activity in the neighborhood/village at a close date preceding [the encounter]" such that "a reasonable suspicion" exists that the masked persons "participated...or are about to participate" in a warned-of violent activity.

The *Pocket Booklet* explains that masked persons merit special consideration in the regulations because "there is much grave activity by local residents operating under the cover of disguises or special masks," including reprisals against collaborators, terrorizing the local population, and "acting as chief inciters at violent demonstrations and riots." This activity "justifies the immediate arrest [of these masked persons], including the use of fire in the procedure for arresting a suspect." The conditions attached to the opening of fire toward a masked person are virtually identical to those specified in Stage 3 of the general orders for apprehending fleeing suspects.

In order for the use of fire against a masked person to be justifiable under the regulations, "there is a need for circumstances in which the commission of a dangerous crime is suspected or in which the suspect is thought to be on his way to commit a dangerous crime....[That is,] there must be a reasonable suspicion that the suspect committed, is committing, or is about to commit a dangerous crime (such as a violent attack on troops or local residents, damage to property in a manner likely to endanger human life, carrying an axe, knife, or other weapons, etc.) or if the wearer of the mask is suspected to be on his way to committing a dangerous crime as delineated above."

The orders for apprehending masked persons lacked clarity when first issued in 1989 and were consequently interpreted in the field more liberally than was intended, the chief military prosecutor acknowledged to Middle East Watch.[31] Soldiers told us that during that period they were instructed to open fire at any masked Palestinian they encountered; some testified to IDF investigators and to military courts that they believed they were supposed to shoot to kill masked activists. (See Chapter Four.)

In an attempt to clarify the rules that seemed to raise more questions than it answered, Brig. Gen. Zvi Poleg, commander of the IDF troops in the Gaza Strip, explained in September 1989:

> there are two types of masked men....There are masked men who lead local disturbances by children, etc. The order is not aimed at that population....Fire is opened only against masked men who deal with violent activity against locals and impose terror.[32]

Gen. Poleg did not, at least in this interview, explain how soldiers were to distinguish between the two types of masked men. Carrying a weapon is no litmus test, since soldiers are permitted to use live ammunition to apprehend masked persons in "suspicious" circumstances whether or not they are armed.

In October 1989, Yesh Gvul, a solidarity organization for Israeli selective conscientious objectors, filed a petition to Israel's Supreme Court, sitting as the High Court of Justice, challenging aspects of the open-fire orders, including the permissive rules on shooting masked suspects.[33] The court rejected the petition one year later on the grounds that the petitioners had no direct stake in the issue.

Nevertheless, the instructions found in the current *Booklet* represent a refinement of the vaguer earlier rules on confronting masked activists. Following the passages quoted above on the apprehension of

---

[31] *Ibid.*, pp. 37-39; see also Chapter Four, below.

[32] Tel Aviv Educational Television in Hebrew, September 13, 1989, as reported in FBIS, September 14, 1989.

[33] *Yoav Hass* v. *Minister of Defense et al.*, HCJ 873/89.

masked suspects, the *Booklet* contains a section titled "Firing for the Arrest of a Suspect — Persons Wearing Masks — Emphasis for the Briefing of Troops," which refers to a Supreme Court ruling and stresses that a masked person is not to be shot if "walking alone in daylight in a quiet civilian neighborhood" and appearing not to carry any weapons, or engaged in nothing more violent than "drawing a slogan on a wall." Rather, there must be a "reasonable suspicion" that the suspect "committed, is committing, or is about to commit, a dangerous crime (such as a violent attack on troops or local residents, damage to property in a manner likely to endanger human life, carrying an axe, knife, or other weapon, etc.)...[or that the] person wearing the mask is suspected to be on his way to commit a dangerous crime as delineated above."

These refinements of the rules concerning masked persons represent an effort to address the ambiguity of the orders to date, and to limit the circumstances in which lethal force is officially permitted against masked suspects. Despite these refinements, undercover forces continue in many instances to shoot dead masked activists where they are posing no imminent danger. Evidence of this practice is presented in several cases in Chapter Two and in the testimony of soldiers in Chapter Four.

CHAPTER TWO
CASE STUDIES, PART ONE
KILLINGS OF PALESTINIANS
WHO WERE NEITHER ARMED NOR "WANTED"

This chapter analyzes thirteen special-force-style operations involving the deaths of fourteen Palestinians who were not carrying firearms and who, to the best of our knowledge, were not officially "wanted." In our view, each of these killings was in some measure unjustified, and together they demonstrate that special-force soldiers have a license to kill that extends beyond the pursuit of armed and "wanted" fugitives. The license emanates from (1) unofficial rules of engagement that apply to special-force-style missions and (2) the difficult-to-enforce command in the official rules to aim at the legs when firing at fleeing suspects.

In most of the cases, we conclude that the killings cannot be plausibly justified with reference to the level of danger faced by the soldiers. In a few cases, such as those of Rami Zakariya al-Mathloum (Case Five) and Muhammad Isma'il abd as-Salaam al-Ja'afreh (Case Thirteen), we lack the evidence to assert that the soldiers did not face a serious danger when they opened fire, but we show that the operation that led to the death was itself abusive.

These killings, which occurred between April 1992 and February 1993, are of various types. Seven of the victims were wearing masks or hoods, including two who were killed in a single incident. Three were not masked but were allegedly throwing stones. The other four victims appear to have been none of the above, but were killed after unwittingly falling into an ambush for "wanted" persons. Officials justified the latter four by explaining that the victims were shot, in three cases, after waving a stick or a toy pistol in a menacing manner, and in the fourth case, after ignoring orders to halt. Official statements on each incident are summarized in the case section below and are reprinted in full in the Appendix.

The official investigations into these killings have been completed in only three of the thirteen cases, according to the last information provided to us by officials as we went to press. According to the final or the interim findings provided by officials, soldiers invoked self-defense in eight of the killings and in the other five claimed to be following the

63

procedures for apprehending a fleeing suspect. Only one of the thirteen cases has so far led to a court-martial, the Amjad Jabbar case.

Note: Witnesses were sometimes inconsistent when asked the ages of those killed. The ages provided below are to the best of our knowledge correct and certainly very close to the actual age.

KILLING OF MASKED ACTIVISTS

Case 1: Basel Umar Jadallah and Ahed Muhammad Thiyab

Ages: both 15
Date of incident: February 10, 1993
Place: Nuseirat refugee camp, Gaza Strip
Remarks: One of the two was carrying a makeshift iron sword, the other a hatchet.

Summary of Incident

Basel Umar Jadallah and Ahed Muhammad Thiyab were stopping traffic and sticking political posters on the walls of Nuseirat refugee camp. One of them was carrying a makeshift sword fashioned from an iron bar, while the other was carrying a hatchet. Plainclothes soldiers in an unmarked car pulled up next to the youths, emerged from their vehicle, and shot both of them dead. One was shot without warning with his back facing the soldiers, while the other was killed attempting to flee. A third youth who had been with them escaped.

Description of Incident

On February 13, 1993, we traveled to Nuseirat refugee camp and questioned three eyewitnesses to the killings. Interviewed separately, they gave virtually identical versions of the event.

According to the three witnesses, at approximately 2:30 p.m. on February 10, 1993, three persons wearing green hoods, shirts, and pants were blocking traffic and glueing political posters to the wall along a narrow road in the middle of Nuseirat refugee camp. While one of the hooded persons stood in the middle of the street stopping traffic, the other two applied glue to the posters and then pasted them onto the wall. After affixing a number of posters to one storefront, they moved down the street and began applying glue to a second batch of posters.

The hooded youth stopping traffic moved to a spot several meters in front of a grocery store, where witness #1, a recently married twenty-five-year-old man, is employed. Witness #1, who declined to give us his name, was standing at the entrance of the store and watching the activity outside. About fifteen meters to his left, two other hooded youths were busy with glue and posters.

A second eyewitness, sixteen-year-old Ashraf Sharif, stood to the left of witness #1, close to the two youths with the posters. Sharif was not hooded. A third witness, a man of about thirty-five who also declined to give his name, stood some twenty meters to witness #1's right.

Several cars were lined up to the right of witness #1, waiting for the hooded youths to allow them through. A blue Peugeot moved up close to the hooded youth in charge of the traffic, and the driver told the youth he was in a hurry and asked to be allowed to pass. The youth waved the car on.

Then a second vehicle, a white Volkswagen van loaded with what appeared to be wooden crates, stopped only meters from the hooded youth. The youth raised his hand, motioning the driver to stop. There were three or four persons dressed in civilian clothing inside the vehicle, witness #1 said. Witness #1 heard the hooded youth first tell the driver of the van to wait and then saw him turn around, as if to check the road behind him. When he turned, witness #1 said, the hooded youth's back was to the van. The other two hooded youths, Sharif said, were preoccupied with their glue and posters and paid no attention to the van. Witness #1 recalled:

> The driver and the passenger next to him got out of the van. They started shooting, and I saw the hooded person fall down, right in front of me. He was only two meters away from the soldiers. Then I ran back into my shop and hid behind the counter.

All three witnesses agreed that the first hooded victim had his back to the van when the plainclothesmen emerged from the vehicle and opened fire without warning and at close range.

Sharif, who had been standing near the two youths with the glue, began to creep down the street, away from the plainclothesmen, with his back to the wall. He watched one masked youth run past him and escape. The second youth dropped the glue and dashed across the street toward an alley situated directly across from the spot where he had been preparing the posters. Then, Sharif said, he saw

> the hooded person get shot and fall down, right there, in
> the middle of the street. He fell into the puddle. He was
> still moving, kind of twitching. He fell down maybe ten
> meters in front of the white van.

According to the third witness, the soldiers continued to fire at the second youth after he fell into the puddle:

> When he [the second hooded victim] was in the water,
> they kept on shooting from where they were standing.
> The first one who was shot, the one stopping the traffic,
> was lying face down on the ground.

The plainclothesmen dragged the two victims, who were apparently unconscious, into their van. Throughout this time, the witnesses said, several additional soldiers who had exited from the van during the shooting took up positions in the street and fired into the air. Several moments later, the witnesses said, a military jeep arrived on the scene. The two vehicles then turned around and drove off together.

Note: it is not clear which of the two slain youths was Jadallah and which was Thiyab. Both were wearing hoods.

The Official Version[1]

On the day of the killings, the IDF spokesman said the youths were shot in self-defense. According to the IDF, the soldiers ran into the group of masked youths while on a mission "aimed at 'wanted' suspects" known to be operating in the area. The masked youths were wearing uniforms and carrying knives and hatchets, the army said. One of the masked youths threatened a soldier with a knife, forcing the soldiers to open fire in self-defense, killing one of the masked men on the spot and wounding another, who died later in the hospital. The spokesman added that the soldiers said they had heard a gunshot from among the Palestinians near them, but could not determine who had fired.[2]

Analysis of the Official Version

The official version is brought into doubt both by the testimony of Palestinian eyewitnesses and by the nature of the official statement itself. The statement alleges that one of the masked youths threatened a soldier with a knife, and that the soldiers came under gunfire from unknown assailants. Even if these assertions were accepted, they do not explain the killing of the second youth. The statement did not claim that any of the masked youths were carrying firearms or were responsible for the alleged shooting. By releasing the official autopsy findings, the IDF could support its claim that one of the youths was killed while threatening a soldier with a knife, rather than shot in the back, as the Palestinian witnesses assert.

---

[1] The following is a summary of official comments on the case that were gathered by B'Tselem, which monitored the IDF's statements after the killing.

[2] Radio Israel in English, February 10, 1993, as reported in FBIS, February 11, 1993.

Case 2: 'Issam al-Khatib

Age: 18
Date of incident: October 10, 1992, died: October 23, 1992
Place: Ar-Ram, West Bank
Remarks: Al-Khatib was among a group of youths manning a roadblock where cars had been stoned and/or turned back shortly before the incident. He was not armed.

Summary of Incident

A group of youths, including two or three who were masked, erected low stone roadblocks on the main road of Ar-Ram. An army jeep that approached the area was stoned. Soldiers got out, fired in the air, and retreated. After the jeep withdrew, the youths stood at the roadblocks, chanted slogans, and prevented cars from passing. A white Mercedes then drove quickly into the midst of the youths. Men in plainclothes jumped out and fired immediately at the youths, injuring at least two, including al-Khatib, who died from chest wounds thirteen days later.

The way that the undercover soldiers sped past several youths and stopped near al-Khatib suggested that they had targeted him in some fashion. He may have been selected because he was one of the few youths on the scene who was masked, and/or because he may have been directing the youths' obstruction of traffic. The undercover units may have acted on the basis of information relayed to them by soldiers who were parked in a jeep near the incident.

Description of Incident

On October 25 and 26, 1992, Middle East Watch researchers traveled to Ar-Ram to interview four persons who had witnessed different parts of the incident in which 'Issam al-Khatib was fatally wounded by special-force soldiers. Ar-Ram is a suburb of Jerusalem, just north of the area that was annexed after the 1967 war.

On October 10, 1992, between 4:30 and 5 p.m., a group of youths were scattered over a stretch of the main street of Ar-Ram. Stones littered the street, and there were a couple of roadblocks made from stones. The roadblocks were low enough that cars could drive over them. Two or three of the youths had their faces covered, either with checkered headdresses or with shirts pulled over their heads.

One of the masked youths was 'Issam al-Khatib. He was in his last year in high school. According to relatives, he was not wanted by the authorities, but he was politically active and had been twice imprisoned, once for three and-a-half months and once for ten days.

Earlier in the day there had been a demonstration at the same location in solidarity with Palestinian security prisoners, who were staging a hunger strike. Residents of Ar-Ram assembled on the street and then traveled in buses to demonstrate in front of the office of the International Committee of the Red Cross in Jerusalem.

When the demonstrators returned to Ar-Ram in mid-afternoon, youths milled around on the main street. Some vehicles that approached were stoned, according to witnesses.

Khaled Omran Razem, forty-six, was in the live poultry shop he owns on the main street of Ar-Ram, some 100 meters west of where the killing occurred. He recalled:

> There had been an incident earlier in the afternoon, when a jeep drove up and was stoned by youths. A soldier got out and fired into the air, and then the jeep withdrew.
>
> The youths hung around afterward, stopping traffic and turning back most of the cars. Most of the cars were Arab; Israeli cars generally don't come this way.

Mohamed Sirhan Ramadhan Sulaimeh, a sixty-two-year-old retired grocer, lives in a house up an alley that intersects with the main road at precisely the point where the killing took place. At about 4:30 p.m., Sulaimeh was returning from Jerusalem. A driver had dropped him off on the main street some two hundred meters west of the incident.

Sulaimeh walked about thirty meters down the main street and passed an army jeep, in which a uniformed soldier was speaking in Hebrew on a walkie-talkie. In front of the jeep was a stone roadblock that the youths had made. Because of a jog in the road after the roadblock, the soldiers and the youths were not in view of one another.

After Sulaimeh passed the jeep the next stretch of the main road came into view. He described what he saw:

> There were about fifteen or twenty youths on the street, spread out. Three or four of them wore masks. Several were acting as lookouts. I saw one of the masked ones ordering a car, a civilian Arab car, to turn around. The youths were chanting slogans. I did not see any stones being thrown.
>
> As I walked toward them, a white Mercedes taxi drove very quickly from behind me. It rode over the roadblock, passed some of the youths, and then stopped in the middle of the road, in the midst of the youths.
>
> Four men jumped out from all four doors of the car, and all of them immediately began firing with M-16s and pistols, all over the place. They were shooting automatic fire.
>
> The soldiers wore civilian clothes, and had "phosphorus" bands on their heads.[3]

Sulaimeh said the soldiers did not shout any warning before opening fire.

One, and possibly two others were wounded in addition to Khatib. A youth in his early teens, identified by Sulaimeh as "Ibn Burqan," was shot in the upper leg; another youth reportedly suffered a light injury and escaped.

There was only one round of shooting. Immediately afterward, according to Sulaimeh, the uniformed soldiers in the jeep fired a flare into the sky. They stood by and watched as the undercover soldiers controlled the area around the shooting.

One of the undercover soldiers chased the injured "Ibn Burqan" as he tried to flee down a hill on the south side of the road. According to

---

[3] In a few cases, Palestinians described the undercover soldiers as wearing what they described as *"fosfoor"* (phosphorus) markings on their heads. The soldiers apparently don some distinctive markings shortly before they go into action in order to reduce the risk of their firing on one another.

Sulaimeh, "The soldier brought him back up the hill and threw him down on the asphalt street." The youth remained there until soldiers permitted an ambulance to transport him to a hospital. "Ibn Burqan" was treated and released; he declined to be interviewed by Middle East Watch.

Meanwhile, al-Khatib lay injured on his stomach. According to Sulaimeh:

> One of the undercover soldiers was leaning over him and seemed to be looking at his injuries. Another soldier came over and with his foot turned him over on his back. Khatib was moaning softly. Ambulances came from UNRWA [the United Nations Relief and Works Agency] and from Ramallah, but the soldiers did not allow them to take 'Issam [al-Khatib], and they were ordered to leave. By the time an ambulance took him away he had lost consciousness.

The events were witnessed from a nearby rooftop by a twenty-two-year-old man who asked that his name not be used in the report, explaining that he had not answered a recent summons from the Israeli authorities. (His name is on file at Middle East Watch.) According to the man:

> After the march in solidarity with the prisoners, the youths closed down the main street with stones. An army jeep came at 3:50 or 4 p.m. The youths threw stones at it, from a long way up the road. The soldiers fired in their direction two tear gas cannisters and three bullets in the air, and then drove back.

> After the jeep retreated, the youths were walking around normally. They turned back cars. They were not throwing any stones.

> Then a Mercedes drove up very quickly and stopped right in the middle of the youths. All of the doors opened at the same time, and five men got out. Four had pistols and one had an Uzi. They began firing in several

directions. After they fired, the soldiers put on caps with
yellow "phosphorus" bands.

'Issam [al-Khatib] was wounded in his leg and his chest,
and another youth who was wounded ran down the hill.
One of the men went after him and grabbed him by the
shoulder, brought him back and put him on the
pavement on his back. He asked him his name in broken
Arabic. The men were talking to each other. People
began to gather in the street. The men pointed their
guns at them and shouted at them in Arabic, cursing.
Jeeps started coming after a couple of minutes, until
there were about ten jeeps.

Two military doctors came in the jeeps. They put glucose
into the arms of both of the wounded ones. A Palestinian
doctor came, and they let him take care of 'Issam. At the
beginning 'Issam was moving his head, but then he lost
consciousness.

When an ambulance came from el-Bireh, the men
ordered the driver to leave. They would not let him take
'Issam. They allowed another ambulance to take him at
about 5:30 or 5:45.

The undercover soldiers let a Palestinian doctor who has an office
on the main street approach and examine al-Khatib. (The doctor declined
to be interviewed by Middle East Watch.) Ambulances evacuated "Ibn
Burqan" after ten minutes, and al-Khatib more than twenty minutes after
the shooting. Several witnesses said that both the undercover and the
uniformed soldiers on the scene refused to permit the first ambulance
that arrived on the scene to evacuate al-Khatib.

Nada Khazmo, an editor at the weekly political magazine *al-
Bayadir as-Siyasi*, lives in a house on the main road, less than twenty
meters from where the incident occurred. She recalled:

When I heard shots I ran from the kitchen to the
[second-floor] veranda. The shots sounded like ta-ta-ta-ta
[automatic fire]. I saw one youth on the ground, and a

white Mercedes. There were five men, all in civilian clothing wearing "phosphorus" bands on their heads. There were no other soldiers present.

People came out to see what was happening. The undercover soldiers yelled at them to go home. The youth [al-Khatib] was lying on his back, moaning.

Khazmo said she saw no weapon in al-Khatib's hands or at his side.

When the Palestinian doctor came, the soldiers let him treat the youth. When an ambulance arrived, they let the ambulance staff treat him, but they wouldn't let them evacuate him at first.

"Ibn Burqan" was treated and released from the hospital. Al-Khatib was taken to Ramallah Hospital, where he died from his wounds on October 23. According to one youth, when al-Khatib passed away local youths brought his body back home for burial. No autopsy was conducted.

Hospital records obtained by B'Tselem indicate that al-Khatib had eight bullet wounds: four in the abdomen, three in the legs, and one in the left arm.

The Official Version

One day after the shooting, the IDF stated that in the course of an initiated operation by an IDF force in the area of Ar-Ram, the force encountered at 5 p.m. masked persons stoning passing Israeli cars. The soldiers called on them to stop. When they refused to do so, the soldiers opened fire. As a result of the shootings two persons were wounded, one seriously and one moderately.

In May 1993, seven months after the incident, the IDF reported that it was still being investigated.

Analysis of the Official Version

The IDF's initial statement, while vague, suggests that the soldiers opened fire in order to apprehend fleeing masked youths who had been stoning cars. The written open-fire orders seemingly state that the procedure for firing at the legs of a fleeing suspect should not be executed against a stone-thrower except when he is suspected of "the throwing of rocks toward a person or a vehicle when real danger exists and the arrest is performed immediately during the incident." In this particular incident, the "arrest" was not performed "immediately during the incident." The undercover unit arrived in response to earlier stone-throwing.

The written regulations are arguably more permissive toward opening fire when the fleeing stone-throwers are masked, as they were in this incident, although the point is not clear. But according to witnesses, there was in this case no attempt to make an arrest or to hit the legs only; the soldiers sped up to the scene, opened fire without warning, and fatally injured one suspect with several bullets in the upper body.

Case 3: Abdullah Dibash Hamarshe

Age: 16
Date of incident: September 9, 1992
Place: Village of Ya'bad in Jenin district
Remarks: Hamarshe was among a group of youths who were holding wooden clubs; it is not clear whether he was holding one when shot.

Summary of Incident

Hamarshe was among a group of masked teenage youths who were walking on a street in Ya'bad, carrying sticks and megaphones, exhorting villagers to observe a political strike. Plainclothes Border Police drove up and jumped out of a car and began firing at the youths. Hamarshe was reportedly wounded in the leg and tried to flee, but was chased and fatally shot at close range. Two of the other masked youths were wounded in the legs, one with several bullets that were fired as he lay on the ground.

Description of Incident

On October 23, 1992 two Middle East Watch researchers visited Ya'bad and interviewed witnesses to the killing of Hamarshe.

At about 9 or 9:30 a.m. on September 9, five masked youths from Ya'bad were walking at the western edge of the village, on the main road that leads to the village of Zabda to the west. Among them were Abdullah Hamarshe, Samir Fahmi Zeid, Saleh Khalil Kabaha, Hisham Ahmed Kabaha, and a fifth young man.

A man in his twenties, whose house overlooks the site where the incident began, said that the youths were calling out orders to shopkeepers to remain shut that day in observance of the strike. (The ninth of each month is observed as a strike day in commemoration of the start of the intifada.) The witness declined to give his name to Middle East Watch.

Samir Fahmi Zeid, one of the five youths, told Middle East Watch that they were carrying clubs. Hamarshe was talking into a megaphone about the strike.

Saleh Jamil Amarleh, a thirty-six-year-old butcher from Ya'bad, was driving east in his Volkswagen van from Zabda with his wife, two of his children, and five other passengers. After entering Ya'bad on the main road, he noticed a white Peugeot 404 mini-van parked on the right side of the road in front of him. Later he saw that there was also a white Volkswagen minibus with blue (Palestinian) license plates, stopped on the road some fifty meters west of (behind) the Peugeot, but he did not notice it at first. Amarleh also noticed a group of masked youths walking west together on the street, at the point where a school stands on the north side of the road. He did not count the masked youths at the time, he said, but later learned there were five. The youths were walking between the Peugeot and the white minibus.

When Amarleh had driven past the youths and the parked Peugeot, he heard two gunshots and turned his head. He saw the youths running toward his van. There were more gunshots, and Amarleh kept driving ahead, but bullets struck his vehicle and the engine died. He told the passengers to drop to the floor. Before he finished saying this, the cabin window was shattered, and Amarleh was struck in the back and head with flying objects, apparently either bullet fragments or pieces of glass from the cabin window. He showed us three small scars on his back which he attributed to this incident, and said some of the other passengers were wounded by flying glass. He also showed us bullet holes in the back of his van. (According to al-Haq, Hamarshe had tried to escape by jumping onto the back of Amarleh's van.[4])

After Amarleh was wounded he got out of his car and looked back. He saw two youths lying on the main road in front of the school and men in plainclothes standing over them. Amarleh did not count the plainclothesmen, but said there were at least ten on the scene. Amarleh said he saw one soldier hold up one of the youths, Samir Fahmi Zeid, and fire at his legs. A second youth, Saleh Khalil Kabaha, also had been wounded in the legs by gunshots. A third youth, who turned out to be Abdullah Hamarshe, ran past Amarleh's vehicle, pursued by two soldiers. Hamarshe was limping. One of the soldiers caught up with him as he descended a hill into the village, and fired at him at close range, fatally injuring him. A physician from the village whom the soldiers allowed to examine Hamarshe said he was dead when the soldiers evacuated him.

The witness mentioned above, who lives nearby, went to his window after hearing gunfire. He said he saw two youths lying on the street, bleeding. Each was guarded by an armed soldier. Eventually, he said, the youths were evacuated in a government ambulance to a Nablus hospital. Afterward, Ya'bad was placed under curfew for the rest of the day.

Samir Fahmi Zeid, one of the youths, told Middle East Watch that the men in the Volkswagen were the first to open fire. They hit Saleh Khalil Kabaha. Then the men in the Peugeot got out with short Uzis. Zeid said that the soldiers shouted no warnings to the youths before opening fire. One of them hit Zeid in the lower right ankle. He limped two meters and then fell down. Then, he said, a soldier from the Peugeot put his foot on Zeid's chest and fired seven more bullets into his lower legs, three in the right leg and four in the left. When he was interviewed by Middle East Watch six weeks after the incident, both of Zeid's legs were in full casts and appeared swollen. He could not walk.

---

[4] Al-Haq, "Willful Killings: A Sustained Israeli Policy in the Occupied Palestinian Territories," November 21, 1992, p. 16.

Zeid recounted that two of the youths ran up an alley. One escaped and one, Hisham Ahmed Kabaha, was caught and arrested. Six weeks after the incident, Zeid told Middle East Watch that Kabaha was still in prison.

The soldiers permitted a Palestinian doctor to care for Zeid. Twenty minutes after the shooting, a government ambulance arrived and took Zeid to the military compound in 'Arrabeh, where he received preliminary care. He was briefly taken to Afula hospital in Israel and then to Rafidiya hospital in Nablus, where he spent fourteen days. He said that during that time, two policemen and one soldier came and questioned him in Arabic about the incident and then had him sign a statement in Hebrew.

Saleh Khalil Kabaha, another of the youths, declined to recount the incident to Middle East Watch. When we saw him six weeks after the shooting, he was walking with a cane. He said he had been hit in the left leg by five bullets and spent twenty-seven days in the hospital.

According to Zeid, none of the five youths was "wanted" or had been previously arrested. Since the shooting, he added, none of the youths was arrested. The one who was seized at the scene, Kabaha, was charged with being masked and possessing axes and clubs, al-Haq reported.[5]

The Official Version

According to the initial official statements on the incident, Border Policemen "were confronted" by six youths with knives and axes. The police ordered them to stop, and when they did not obey, the police opened fire. In May 1993, the Justice Ministry summarized its interim findings pending a legal decision by the regional prosecutor. The Ministry stated:

> Hamarshe was one of a group of young, masked men carrying various weapons (such as knives, axes, metal bars, chains and swords) who confronted a Border Police unit. When the Border Policemen called for them to stop they attempted to escape. After calling them again

---

[5] *Ibid.*, p. 17.

to stop, and shooting in the air to warn them to surrender, Hamarshe continued to escape. According to testimony that was taken, a Border Policeman then fired at Hamarshe's legs. Hamarshe, however, was fatally wounded by the bullet.

Analysis of the Official Version

The interim official version of this event is consistent with Palestinian testimony about the general circumstances of the incident, but diverges on significant details. It is, by all accounts, another case of a masked youth who, while carrying cold weapons but posing no imminent danger, is shot dead while fleeing.

The Justice Ministry makes no claim that the youths attacked or endangered the policemen. Witnesses said the masked youths were ambushed by the undercover agents who, contrary to official claims, opened fire immediately without warning. The official version does not explain how a bullet aimed for Hamarshe's legs ended up causing his death, even though the policeman reportedly fired from close range.

Also disturbing is the police's apparently gratuitous firing of several bullets into the legs of Samir Fahmi Zeid. Given that Zeid's activities were considered sufficiently dangerous to merit being shot several times, it is noteworthy that he was, by his account, neither detained nor charged in connection with the incident. This suggests that the undercovers agents were intent on delivering summary punishment rather than making lawful arrests.

Case 4: Nuri Sharif abd al-Qader al-Aqqad

Age: 16
Date of incident: July 27, 1992
Place: Khan Younis refugee camp, southern Gaza Strip
Remarks: Al-Aqqad was initially holding an axe, but reportedly dropped it while attempting to flee.

Summary of Incident

Al-Aqqad was pursued by the undercover troopers into a private dwelling after being surprised while spray-painting slogans on a wall in Khan Younis refugee camp. He was gunned down after being trapped in the small room into which he had fled. Although he may have been holding an axe before fleeing into the bedroom, he was, witnesses said, unarmed at the time of his death.

Description of Incident

On July 28, 1992, the morning after al-Aqqad's death, a Middle East Watch researcher traveled to Khan Younis and interviewed two witnesses to the killing as well as several others who saw the beginning of the incident on the street.

The witnesses said that at approximately 7:30 p.m. on July 27, al-Aqqad, whose face was covered by a mask, was spray-painting graffiti on the wall of the Qutaiba mosque in Khan Younis refugee camp. A second youth, sixteen-year-old Shukri al-Aqqad, masked and carrying a hatchet, stood guard across the street from the mosque. One witness stated that Nuri al-Aqqad had an axe in his belt.

Several moments later, a civilian car pulled up at the intersection near the mosque. H. L.,[6] a twenty-nine-year-old male resident of Khan Younis who was standing in front of the mosque, said he saw

> a Peugeot 404 come from south to north on the main road and suddenly brake to a halt when it was in view of the masked persons. Three men got out of the Peugeot. Two were wearing army pants and civilian t-shirts. One was wearing jeans. Another was wearing a beige shirt. One had a green shirt. One had a yellow shirt.
>
> Two of them opened fire at the masked persons immediately. They did not warn them first. After they had opened fire, one of them yelled at the youths in Arabic to stop.

---

[6] Mr. H. L. requested that his name not be used in this report. His name, address, and identity card number are on file with Middle East Watch.

The masked youth painting on the wall, Nuri al-Aqqad, appeared to have
been wounded in the leg, H.L. said. The wounded youth ran from the
soldiers, disappearing around the corner of the mosque. The second
masked youth, Shukri al-Aqqad, appeared unhurt, H.L. said, and fled in
the opposite direction. Soldiers caught up with him after a short chase.
One of them stood above Shukri al-Aqqad and fired a number of shots
into the ground near his body, according to sixty-two-year-old Ms. R.,[7]
who said she was watching from a nearby doorway:

> The masked youth fell down right over there, next to the
> metal pole. His axe fell down in the street. A man in
> civilian clothes carrying a gun shot all around him, in the
> dirt. I don't know why he fired. He did not wound him.
> The youth pleaded with him, "Don't kill me."

> Then the soldier pulled the masked youth up, twisted his
> arm behind his back, and began to walk away with him.

Meanwhile, the other youth, Nuri al-Aqqad, fled some twenty
meters down the road from the mosque and into a nearby home. A
second car, a Peugeot 504, pulled up in front of the Qutaiba mosque. It
contained four armed men in blue jeans and t-shirts. Three got out and
pursued Nuri al-Aqqad into the house he had entered. The fourth
remained with the car.

Ms. J., who requested that her name not be published in this
report, was in the kitchen when Nuri al-Aqqad dashed into her home, a
cramped shack typical of many dwellings in Gaza's refugee camps. Her
kitchen is a one-meter-by-two-meter alcove, adjoining the bedroom,
immediately to the left of the doorway. The kitchen alcove has no door
of its own; it is separated from the bedroom by a curtain. The bedroom,
approximately three meters square, contains a queen-size bed to the right
of the door, and a wooden armoire set against the opposite wall from the
doorway.

Ms. J. said that al-Aqqad ran into her bedroom and tried to hide
next to the armoire, facing the entrance:

---

[7] Ms. R. requested that her name not be used in this report. Her name is on
file with Middle East Watch.

My husband was with me in the kitchen. We heard shots.
A few seconds later, a masked person came running
through the bedroom doorway. He rushed over to the far
wall, by the armoire opposite the door. He was wearing
green-looking clothes.

He tried to hide behind the armoire, but it was too heavy
for him to move. He only managed to shift it a little, not
enough to hide. He remained there, facing the doorway.

Ms. J. said that the masked person had nothing in his hands.

Ms. Y.M.,[8] who was in the bedroom, said that she ducked into
the kitchen when al-Aqqad burst in. Seconds later, she said, an armed
man in jeans and a white shirt appeared at the door, stepped into the
room, and fired at the masked person from a range of less than two
meters:

The soldier came in right behind the masked youth and
started shooting. If I had been a little slower, he would
have shot me as well, because I was right in front of the
doorway.

Ms. J., standing only meters away, described what happened next:

The soldier was holding a gun in his hand. It looked like
a big pistol. He stepped into the room and stood at the
edge of the bed, right across from where we were
standing in the kitchen. He shot at the masked person,
many shots. I don't know how many. A second soldier
appeared immediately after. I don't know if he fired as
well.

Both women said that al-Aqqad was holding nothing in his hands when
shot.

---

[8] Ms. Y.M. requested her name not be used in this report. Her full name is
on file with Middle East Watch. She is too young to have an identity card
number.

One of the two armed men then went over to the masked youth while the other pointed his weapon at the persons in the kitchen and told them in Arabic to shut up. Then they led Ms. J.'s husband, who was in the kitchen with his wife, outside, where a Border Police jeep had arrived.

Ms. J. left the alcove, ran through the bedroom, and followed the soldiers outside to the jeep. She said she saw an axe lying on the floor:

> When I came out of the room I saw an axe in the hallway. There were lots of soldiers there, some of them in uniform, others in regular clothes. One of the soldiers picked up the axe and held it in his hand.

The soldiers released Mr. J. several moments later, and drove away with al-Aqqad's body in their jeep. Ms. J. said she believed he was already dead when he was carried from her home.

When visiting the scene of the killing on the day after the incident, the Middle East Watch researcher photographed a chest-high cluster of seven bullet holes in the wall near the armoire. However, his film was later confiscated by IDF soldiers when he was investigating a special-force killing in Jenin.

The Official Version

According to *Haaretz* of July 28, 1992, officials said that a Border Police force encountered two masked persons armed with axes in Khan Younis camp and began pursuing them. In the course of the chase, one of the masked persons suddenly turned on the policemen and raised his axe, yelling *"Allahu Akbar!"* (God is great!) One of the Border Police, who felt that his life was in danger, shot and killed the masked person. The other masked activist was arrested.

In May 1993, the Justice Ministry informed us that the investigation into this case was not yet complete.

Analysis of the Official Version

The initial IDF account of this killing is at variance with the eyewitness testimonies we gathered, which suggest that al-Aqqad was killed while unarmed and posing no threat to his pursuers. Yet even if he was still clutching his axe when shot, as officials claim, the decision by the Border Policeman to chase a suspect he saw holding an axe into an unfamiliar dwelling, rather than pausing and giving him a chance to surrender, virtually guaranteed that he would enter the house with his guns blazing. Indeed, the seven bullet holes in the wall are evidence that the Border Policeman used massive force against al-Aqqad.

This kind of pursuit, with its predictably deadly outcome, cannot be justified by the "offenses" that triggered it: wearing masks, holding cold weapons, and writing graffiti. Indeed, in our view, it is an excessive use of force even to fire at the legs of such suspects, when they are posing no imminent threat to others. That the soldiers did so in this case without first shouting the required warnings, as witnesses claim, compounds the abuse.

Case 5: Rami Zakariya al-Mathloum

Age: 20
Date of incident: July 12, 1992
Place: Sabra neighborhood, Gaza City, Gaza Strip
Remarks: Al-Mathloum was carrying a makeshift sword.

Summary of Incident

Six plainclothes special-force soldiers approached a group of between seven and nine masked persons who were leading a demonstration of more than 200 persons in Gaza City. Some of the participants said they believed that the arriving men were members of a rival political group. A fight quickly erupted, in which al-Mathloum joined in with his makeshift sword. The undercover soldiers — who had not, until that moment, either identified themselves as undercover agents or attempted to make an arrest — drew back and opened fire, shooting al-Mathloum in the head and wounding several others, two seriously.

This killing is noteworthy because of the way the special forces infiltrated a gathering in which they were vastly outnumbered and left themselves little choice but to shoot their way out of a threatening situation once they revealed themselves to be security forces.

Description of Incident

On July 28, 1992, a Middle East Watch researcher traveled to the Sabra neighborhood in Gaza City and separately interviewed three eyewitnesses to the killing, two of whom were among the group of masked persons leading the demonstration. One of the masked persons had been shot in the stomach and legs during the incident and was recovering from an operation. The three testimonies were consistent except on minor details.

According to the witnesses, at approximately 8:45 p.m. on July 12, 1992, more than 200 persons were assembled outside a mosque for a political demonstration. The square was illuminated by electric lights in the mosque.

The demonstration was led by a group of seven to nine masked persons. Two of the masked persons were standing well in front of the crowd. One carried what appeared to be either a metal bar or a wooden stick, while the other carried a makeshift sword or stick. The other masked organizers stood several meters behind the first two, carrying wooden sticks or metal bars. The rest of the demonstrators stood well behind the masked leaders.

The demonstration was organized by supporters of the Islamist movement Hamas. During the previous week there had been clashes between supporters of Hamas and Fatah, the PLO faction, in the Gaza Strip.[9] On July 10, two days before the demonstration, the two organizations announced an agreement to end the clashes.

Witness #1,[10] a forty-year-old high-school soccer coach, stood watching the demonstration from the roof of his three-story apartment block, where he lives with his wife and five children. His roof commands a view of the square where the demonstration took place and of the side streets running from the square to the surrounding neighborhood.

---

[9] See, for example, David Hoffman, "Rival Palestinian Factions Step Up Struggle in Gaza," *The Washington Post*, July 10, 1992; Clyde Haberman, "Violence in Gaza Pits Arab vs. Arab," *The New York Times*, July 12, 1992; and Patrice Claude, "Violents affrontements entre Palestiniens islamistes et partisans du processus de paix," *Le Monde*, July 10, 1992.

[10] Witness #1 asked that his name not be used in the report. His name is on file at Middle East Watch.

The soccer coach saw two white Peugeots drive slowly down a side street and park some 100 meters from the square. Six men, dressed as Palestinian laborers, emerged from the cars and walked toward the square, passing directly beneath the coach's building. Just before entering into the square, the men stopped and put on armbands and caps which had a faint yellowish glow.[11] The coach said he realized then that the men were undercover forces.

The six men then turned into the square and approached the leaders of the demonstration. Witness #2,[12] who said he was one of the masked persons leading the demonstration, said he saw the men approaching from across the square. He said:

> They looked normal: they were wearing regular pants and t-shirts, and I didn't see anything different about them. They were walking toward us, and I thought they were coming to join the demonstration, as many others were doing....They called out *"Allahu Akbar!"* [God is great!] to us as they approached.

The six men approached until they stood face-to-face with the two masked persons leading the demonstration. Then, the coach recalled, "One of the six men lunged ahead of the others and grabbed the masked person standing on the right. Both men fell to the ground."

Witness #2, masked and by his own account holding a stick, said he thought they were being attacked by members of Fatah:

> All of a sudden, they tried to grab three of us, so we raised our sticks....I thought they were from Fatah....If we had known they were special forces, we wouldn't have done that.

Witness #3, who did not give his name, said that the special-force soldiers grabbed a youth standing next to him in a bear hug. According

---

[11] He was apparently referring to the "phosphorus" markings that undercover soldiers sometimes put on shortly before going into action. See footnote earlier in this chapter.

[12] Witness #2 refused to give his name to Middle East Watch.

to the coach, a masked person carrying a makeshift sword (the witnesses participating in the demonstration said the implement was a stick), set upon the man who had grabbed their comrade, striking him several times with his weapon. At that point, the coach said:

> The other five men took a few steps back and pulled out guns. They were carrying short guns, like Uzis. They shot at the masked person with the sword from a distance of about five meters. Then all the masked people began to run, and all the people in the street as well.

The masked person who was shot turned out to be al-Mathloum. The coach said that once al-Mathloum fell to the ground, soldiers dragged him back to the side street in front of his house. The soldiers also kept holding the man they had first grabbed when the fighting began. The coach watched the soldiers jog back to their cars. Border Police jeeps then transported al-Mathloum and the arrested suspect from the area.

According to the United Nations Relief and Works Agency (UNRWA) spokesperson's office, in addition to al-Mathloum, six persons were wounded by military gunfire during the incident, one seriously.

The Official Version

On the day after the incident, Radio Israel reported that soldiers dressed as Arabs infiltrated a march of Hamas activists who were masked and carrying axes and clubs. According to the IDF spokesman, Hamas activists attacked an officer and soldiers opened fire. In the confusion, one of the Hamas activists was beaten to death by his comrades.[13] On July 14, the Israeli newspaper *Hadashot* quoted official military sources as saying that their men were not responsible for al-Mathloum's death. The army claimed that soldiers had found the body with beating wounds but no bullet holes.

In response to a query by the Israeli human rights group B'Tselem, however, Captain Avital Margalit of the IDF spokesman's office wrote on July 20, 1992:

---

[13] Radio Israel in English, July 13, 1992, as reported in FBIS, July 14, 1992.

[A]n investigation is now underway by both the Israeli Police as well as the IDF's Criminal Investigation Division into the circumstances of the above person's death. The investigation has only just begun. It is unclear whether the youth was killed by fire from our forces or by Palestinians.

The IDF statement that you refer to in your letter [i.e. B'Tselem's letter questioning the initial army claim that it was not responsible for the killing] was published immediately after the incident and was based on information taken from preliminary investigations.

The up-to-date facts we have given you in this letter are based upon the autopsy results. The autopsy discovered that there were bullet entry and exit wounds in the back of Mazloum's head. There were also signs of severe beating, so it is unclear what was the cause of Rami al-Mazloum's death.

The army provided new details in December, in response to a query from Middle East Watch. It acknowledged that soldiers shot al-Mathloum, but said that on the basis of the ongoing investigation, his killing was a justifiable act of self-defense:

The investigation to date suggests that the deceased was shot when he attacked an IDF soldier with a club. According to the investigation, an IDF force entered into a fight with a group of masked men armed with clubs and axes. During the clash the deceased was shot. Two soldiers were injured and needed medical attention. (See Appendix.)

In its latest communication with Middle East Watch before this report went to press, the IDF stated that the investigation had not been completed.

Analysis of the Official Version

In the scant details made available in the ten months since the incident, the official version in no way contradicts the testimony collected by Middle East Watch. The undercover force apparently set themselves the goal of identifying and confronting the leaders of a political demonstration. To do so, they sent a small group of undercover soldiers face-to-face with the masked leaders, who were holding cold weapons. A fight ensued — with the demonstrators apparently mistaking the still-unidentified men as members of a rival political faction. Had al-Mathloum known that the men who had confronted the demonstrators were undercover soldiers with automatic weapons, he may not have suicidally set upon one of them with his stick or homemade sword.

The undercover forces designed the operation in such a way that almost guaranteed that they would have to shoot their way out of a face-to-face encounter with a vastly greater number of young marchers, many of whom carried cold weapons. If eyewitness testimony is accurate that soldiers lunged at one of the marchers before identifying themselves, then this operation was tantamount to a shoot-to-kill operation based on entrapment. If they can ever be justified, such tactics are not justifiable when the targeted individuals are suspected only of offenses no more serious than wearing masks, carrying cold weapons, and leading demonstrations.

Case 6: Sa'd Khalil abd al-Karim Miqdad

Age: 18
Date of incident: June 4, 1992
Place: Khan Younis refugee camp, southern Gaza Strip
Remarks: Miqdad was carrying an axe when first confronted and shot; he was deliberately shot again when lying wounded and unarmed on the ground.

Summary of Incident

Miqdad was shot repeatedly at close range in the head and chest by two plainclothes soldiers while he lay wounded in the main street of

Khan Younis refugee camp. Miqdad was masked and had held an axe prior to being wounded. He was shot after he and a group of four other masked youths were ambushed by plainclothes soldiers while the youths were spray-painting nationalist graffiti.

Description of Incident

On July 19 and 20, 1992, a Middle East Watch researcher went to Khan Younis refugee camp and spoke with four eyewitnesses to Miqdad's killing. The witnesses, who viewed the incident from different angles, gave testimony that was consistent except for several minor discrepancies.

According to the eyewitnesses, at approximately 6:30 p.m. on June 4, 1992, a group of five masked youths began to spray-paint graffiti on the walls of a kiosk bordering the main street of the camp. Two youths painted slogans dictated to them by a third, while the other two, carrying axes, blocked traffic coming from both directions. A crowd of approximately forty children gathered to watch.

A Peugeot 404 with Gaza license plates and carrying six Arab-looking men drew up and stopped in the line of cars waiting for the masked youths to permit traffic to move again. After several minutes, the Peugeot swung around into the lane nearest the graffiti writers. The masked person responsible for stopping traffic from that direction approached the car and motioned for it to stop. He held an axe.

Ms. Amina Miqdad, a forty-year-old resident of Khan Younis camp who is related to the victim, was driving with relatives when her car was stopped by the youths. The masks prevented her from identifying any of the youths, she said. She was several meters away from the Peugeot when it was approached by the youth holding the axe and obstructing traffic. The youth, she said,

> took four or five steps toward the car, and was standing near the car's headlights. His right hand was raised. The axe was in his left hand, which was down by his side, like this [she showed how the hand holding the axe was at his side]. The blade was down, toward the ground. He did not seem alarmed by the Peugeot.

When the youth raised his right hand to motion them to stop, Amina Miqdad continued, the doors of the Peugeot swung open, and the men emerged and almost immediately began shooting toward the masked youths. (Another witness said the soldiers had first shot in the air.) According to Amina Miqdad, the youth who had motioned the car to stop "turned toward the graffiti writers, and yelled, 'The army, guys!' ('*Ej-jeish, ya shabab!*') With his back turned to the armed men, he threw the axe down on the ground, in front of him, in the opposite direction of the armed men."

The children and four of the five masked youths fled the scene through the alleys behind the kiosk. Two of the armed men, Amina Miqdad stated, ran forward and managed to shoot one of the masked youths in the leg, who then fell down on the concrete traffic island in the middle of the street.

Mou'in Rajab al-Batsh, a thirty-one-year-old father of two, witnessed the events from outside his grocery store bordering the same road. He was about twenty-five meters away, on the opposite side of the events from where Amina Miqdad's vehicle was stopped. He recalled:

> When the masked youth got to the traffic island he fell down. It looked like he had been hit in the leg, because he grabbed hold of his leg and then spun around. He lay on the ground face down, on his stomach.
>
> I saw him raise his hands over his head and then also lift up his neck so that he was looking up, straight ahead.
>
> One of the gunmen from the Peugeot ran toward him and stood near his head. The gunman was wearing a brown shirt and held a pistol in his right hand, and an Uzi in his left....Another soldier, with a grey shirt, stood in the middle of the street, about eight or nine meters away from the masked person.
>
> The one in the brown shirt fired two shots with his Uzi. The masked person's head jerked up, as if it had been hit. When the shots hit his head his body sort of raised up, so that his chest was exposed toward the one with the grey shirt.

Then, the one with the brown shirt fired a long burst
into the masked person's chest. The one with the grey
shirt stood there pointing his gun in my direction.

Muhammad Khamees Thabet Mustafa abu Taha, the eighteen-
year-old son of the owner of the kiosk whose wall was being painted by
the masked graffiti writers, said he was close enough to hear the wounded
masked person surrender to the soldier standing near his head before he
was shot:

When the masked person was wounded, a soldier came
up to him. The masked person raised his hands and head
and looked right at the soldier. Then he said to him, "I
surrender."

Muhammad abu Taha's father and the owner of the kiosk, fifty-
seven-year-old Khamees Tahabat Mustafa abu Taha, said:

While the youth was lying looking up, with his hands in
the air, the soldier wearing the dark shirt, standing near
the masked youth's head, shot him in the head.

Several seconds later, the younger abu Taha said, another soldier
approached the youth lying on the ground and fired an additional burst
into his upper body. In describing the same event, Amina Miqdad said:

The soldier with the plain shirt bent over and fired from
very close at the masked person. He fired over twenty
shots. He "cultivated" him. [Amina Miqdad made a
motion like a peasant using a scythe.]

The witnesses were not consistent on whether the victim was the
same masked youth who had approached the Peugeot at the beginning
of the incident. Two witnesses said that the youth who was shot had been
stopping traffic coming from the opposite direction, on the side nearest
to Mou'in al-Batsh. They said that the masked youth who had initially
motioned the Peugeot to wait managed to escape with the crowd fleeing
the area.

After the youth had been wounded on the ground, both Amina Miqdad and the younger abu Taha stated that the two soldiers held him by the legs and dragged him toward their Peugeot. They picked him up and put him inside. At that point a Border Police jeep arrived carrying uniformed soldiers. These soldiers took the body out of the Peugeot and carried it to their jeep. The jeep was parked in front of abu Taha's kiosk, allowing the younger abu Taha to get a clear view of the body as it lay in the back of the vehicle. "The masked person's head was hanging out of the back," he said. "Even with the hood it was clear that his head was all smashed up and full of bullet holes." Both the Peugeot and the Border Police jeep then drove away.

Middle East Watch representatives spoke with foreign relief workers who said they visited Miqdad's family shortly after the funeral. The family, the relief workers said, told them that his body had several bullet wounds in the head and multiple exit and entry wounds in his back and chest. The Israeli authorities did not respond to Middle East Watch's request for a copy of the official autopsy report or a summary of its findings.

The Official Version

According to *Haaretz* of June 5, 1992, the IDF stated that a force of Border Policemen on an "initiated operation" in Khan Younis saw four masked persons blocking traffic on the road. One of the masked persons charged the policemen with an axe in his raised hand. The policemen shot and seriously injured the masked person who was then evacuated to a nearby military base. The masked person was pronounced dead on arrival.[14]

In response to questions about the case that Middle East Watch submitted in writing in November 1992, the Justice Ministry and the IDF initially provided no information. When questions were again submitted in April 1993 the Justice Ministry replied that an investigation was under way.

---

[14] See also, "A Masked Person Charged with an Axe — And Was Shot Dead," *Hadashot*, June 5, 1992.

Analysis of the Official Version

The official version is contradicted by the four witnesses interviewed by Middle East Watch. Although they stated that Miqdad was masked and carrying an axe, he did not attempt to charge the soldiers, who, they said, jumped from their car and opened fire. They also asserted that the soldiers shot Miqdad again while lying wounded and disarmed on the ground. The official autopsy report might lend credence to one version or the other, but the authorities did not respond to our request for a copy.

KILLINGS OF PALESTINIANS WHEN OTHER PERSONS WERE TARGETED

Case 7: Muhammad Salah abu Quweitah

Age: 64
Date of incident: January 14, 1993
Place: Deir al-Balah refugee camp, Gaza Strip
Remarks: Abu Quweitah was not armed.

Summary of Incident

Muhammad abu Quweitah was shot in the back while running away from a plainclothes soldier during a large-scale operation to surround a suspected hideout of "wanted" persons. Officials have accused the sixty-four-year-old abu Quweitah of no wrongdoing other than ignoring calls to halt. During the operation in which abu Quweitah was killed, the homes of three families were demolished by the IDF's heavy fire, and no "wanted" persons were apprehended or killed. (See the Introduction for background on these kinds of operations against suspected hideouts of fugitives.)

Description of Incident

On February 8, 1993, a Middle East Watch researcher traveled to Deir al-Balah and interviewed witnesses to the search for "wanted" men that cost abu Quweitah his life. There are apparently no witnesses to the shooting other than the soldier(s) involved in the incident. However, we interviewed one man who fled from a special-force soldier into the alley in which abu Quweitah was killed moments later. We also spoke with witnesses to other aspects of the army's operation in Deir al-Balah that night.

Al-'Abd abu Libdeh, a thirty-eight-year-old laborer employed in Israel, lives with his wife and four children on an alley that is next to the site of abu Quweitah's killing. On the night of January 14, 1993, abu Libdeh saw a number of flares over Deir al-Balah from his window and decided to leave his house and investigate. He walked down the alley and when he reached a larger street he saw, at a distance of some twenty meters, a young man adjusting a white *keffiyeh* (traditional Arab headdress) on his head.

> I thought to go and ask this guy what was going on. I walked toward him and when I was about ten meters away, I called out a greeting.

> All of a sudden, this guy turned toward me and yelled "Stop, Army!" (*"Waqqif! Ej-jeish!"*) I turned around and began to run. I was so scared. I thought that if I stayed, he would beat me up.

Abu Libdeh turned into the side alley that led toward his home but sprinted past his doorway, heading for narrow side streets that lead into the camp. The special-force soldier gave chase and then opened fire:

> I heard shooting, maybe five bullets. It was so dark, you couldn't see anyone. I ran around a corner and rushed into someone's house to hide.

Abu Libdeh said that moments later he heard a second burst of shooting. He said he heard no warning before the shots rang out.

Ali al-Basrah, fifty-seven years old, who lives across from abu Libdeh with his two wives and fourteen children, returned home apparently only moments after the shooting. He heard no gunfire, but when he turned into his alley, he saw two uniformed soldiers standing over an inert body in front of his doorway.

> The body was lying in the sewage that runs through the middle of the alley. In addition to the soldiers, there was a young Palestinian man trying to pull the body up.

One of the soldiers ordered al-Basrah to help the other Palestinian with the body. Together, the two men pulled abu Quweitah from the street, and he was evacuated by the soldiers.

Abu Quweitah's wife, fifty-year-old Muyissar Ihmidar Ibrahim abu Quweitah, said that her husband had left their house as soon as he heard rumors of a raid. She said that the couple routinely split up when soldiers entered the camp; Ms. abu Quweitah usually stayed in their main home, while her husband hurried to a second shack they owned, fearing, she said, that soldiers would vandalize it.

Authorities returned abu Quweitah's body to his wife a few days after the killing. According to thirty-four-year-old Taysir Ziadeh, who is related to abu Quweitah and who saw the body, the victim's body had two entry and two exit wounds. One of the bullets entered the back of abu Quweitah's head and exited from his face. The second bullet first penetrated into his upper right shoulder and exited through the front of his right shoulder. Both wounds indicate that abu Quweitah was shot from behind.

On February 6, 1993, Ms. abu Quweitah was summoned by the Civil Administration. When she went to the local headquarters on February 8, an officer asked her what had happened on the night of the shooting and what her husband had been wearing that evening. He also asked her why he did not halt when he had been ordered to do so.

Middle East Watch also spoke with neighbors of abu Quweitah whose homes were destroyed or damaged by rocket fire during the course of the raid. Shortly after the killing of abu Quweitah, uniformed soldiers surrounded several nearby houses inhabited by twenty-two members of the Mazrou'a and abu Thrim families. According to fifty-seven-year-old Wasfi Nafah Mazrou'a, he was ordered by loudspeaker to leave his house together with his wife and eight children.

> They blindfolded everyone, women, children, everyone.
> They put us all together for over four hours near the
> beach, while we heard shooting and explosions.
> After[ward], we came back, and I saw that our house was
> completely destroyed.

The Official Version

According to a statement by the IDF spokesman of January 15, 1993:

> In the course of an initiated operation by security forces
> this evening in Deir al-Balah against armed wanted
> persons, the area where these persons were hiding was
> sealed off. In the course of the closure one person tried
> to flee the area. One of the soldiers, who saw the fleeing
> man, called on him to stop and carried out the full
> procedure for apprehending suspects. When he [the
> fleeing person] refused to obey, the soldier fired two
> bullets in his direction, killing him.

An IDF statement of April 7, 1993 maintained the same version of events: abu Quweitah "was hit by IDF fire and killed after he ran away from a building and did not heed the call of soldiers to stop." The statement did not indicate whether any disciplinary measures against the soldier were contemplated.[15]

Analysis of the Official Version

The IDF's statements assert that the full procedure for apprehending a suspect was carried out, an assertion that was disputed by the witnesses interviewed by Middle East Watch. But even if the soldier did carry out the full procedure, the IDF has not explained how the soldier arrived at a reasonable suspicion that the sixty-four-year-old,

---

[15] IDF response in B'Tselem, "House Demolitions during Operations against Wanted People," May 1993.

unarmed abu Quweitah had committed or was on his way to committing a serious crime. Such a "reasonable suspicion" is required of a soldier before he carries out the procedure for apprehending a suspect. If such a reasonable suspicion is absent, the soldier should be held accountable for a wrongful death.

When ordered to halt by an armed man in plainclothes, many Palestinians flee whether or not they have done anything wrong. While soldiers are entitled to be suspicious of anyone who thus disobeys their orders — perhaps more so when they are closing in on a suspected hideout of armed activists — the IDF open-fire regulations make clear that such suspicion is insufficient to warrant the use of lethal force against any person who flees. It is worth noting that, during the four-hour operation in Deir al-Balah that night, the IDF did not claim to have encountered any violent resistance or to have captured any fugitives.

Also, the IDF has not, to our knowledge, commented on how in this case a soldier supposedly firing at the legs of a fleeing suspect fatally injured him in the upper body, reportedly in the shoulder and head. Whether the upper-body wounds were intentional or not, this unjustified killing underscores the deadly consequences of permitting soldiers to fire at the legs of fleeing suspects in a variety of non-life-threatening circumstances.

Case 8: Jawad As'ad Rahal

Age: 28
Date of incident: April 29, 1992
Place: Village of 'Arrabeh, Jenin district, northern West Bank
Remarks: Rahal was not armed, but he was holding a toy pistol shortly before, and perhaps when, he was gunned down.

Summary of Incident

Border Policemen in plainclothes ambushed and shot Rahal as he was walking with two young nephews on a path outside his village. The troopers shot Rahal repeatedly, including after he had fallen, according to eyewitnesses. Rahal was not masked or armed and, to the best of our knowledge, not "wanted," although he was holding a toy pistol that belonged to his nephew. His nephew claimed that Rahal had handed him the toy pistol moments before the ambush.

Description of Incident

On August 20, 1992, a Middle East Watch researcher visited the West Bank village of 'Arrabeh and spoke with two eyewitnesses to the killing. The witnesses are the fourteen-year-old and ten-year-old nephews of the victim, who were walking with him when he was ambushed. A third, adult eyewitness was not present on the day of Middle East Watch's visit, but shortly after the incident gave al-Haq an affidavit, which is excerpted below.

In mid-afternoon, Rahal, a recently married carpenter, was walking along a dirt path leading from his family's fields north of 'Arrabeh toward his home in the village. Rahal was accompanied by two nephews, fourteen-year-old Amjad Hassan Ali 'Ardah, who was walking by his side, and ten-year-old Abd al-Jabbar Muhammad abd al-Rahman Mardawi, who was trailing some thirty meters behind, according to both boys. Rahal was carrying Amjad's toy pistol, according to Amjad.

Rahal and his nephews ran into Rahal's brother, thirty-seven-year-old Majed As'ad Rahal, who was heading in the opposite direction toward the family's fields. The two men stopped for a few moments to talk and then continued on their separate ways.

According to both boys, Jawad Rahal stopped near a large cactus to urinate. At this point, according to Amjad, he handed the toy gun to Amjad, who continued to walk southward along the path toward the village. Amjad said he was holding the toy pistol throughout the entire shooting incident. At that moment, Abd al-Jabbar, who was walking in the same direction some thirty meters behind his uncle, noticed

> two men with guns. One was wearing jeans and a black
> shirt. The other was wearing army pants and a blue-
> striped shirt. They were in the wheat field right next to
> the cactus tree. The wheat was high, so they were hidden
> until they stood up.

According to Abd al-Jabbar, the black-shirted gunman reached the path to Rahal's north and opened fire at Rahal from a distance of less than ten meters. Neither of the three witnesses mentioned hearing the gunmen cry a warning before opening fire, and in its account of the case, the Justice Ministry also mentioned no warning.

Amjad, who was some fifteen meters away from the shooting, turned at the sound of shots and found himself facing Jawad Rahal's back. The boy said that his uncle appeared to realize that he was being attacked by undercover special forces:

> When I heard the shooting, I turned around, and saw my uncle with his hands in the air, near the cactus. He was yelling [in Arabic], "I'm not wanted, stop shooting!"

Abd al-Jabbar, standing near Majed Rahal and facing Jawad Rahal's front side, said he thought his uncle had been wounded in the leg before calling out that he was not wanted. At that point, Abd al-Jabbar said, his uncle hopped backward several times on one leg and fell to the ground, lying on his back. According to all three of the eyewitnesses, the gunman wearing the black shirt continued to fire at Rahal after he had fallen. Amjad said of both plainclothesmen:

> They were firing at Jawad, who lay between them. They shot him on the ground. Then, the one turned toward me and shot in my direction. I ran away, toward the village.

At the sound of the shooting, Majed said he was thirty meters away from his brother and facing away. He told al-Haq:

> I heard gunshots and turned to see what had happened. I saw my brother Jawad with his hands in the air. Three persons were standing near him, dressed in civilian clothes. One aimed a small gun at my brother, and was shooting at him. My brother had fallen on the ground, but I saw the gunman continue to shoot the body of my brother.

Several moments later, a number of military vehicles and a civilian van arrived on the scene. The plainclothes troopers mounted the vehicles with Rahal's body and left the village.

Thirty-five-year-old Saleh Muhammad Mardawi, Jawad Rahal's brother-in-law, told Middle East Watch that when the army returned his body, he saw about fifteen bullet wounds in the front of Rahal's body, including in the chest, neck, head, and legs. Authorities did not comply with Middle East Watch's request for information about the autopsy.

The Official Version

The day after the shooting, *Haaretz* reported that according to military sources, Border Police engaged in an initiated operation in 'Arrabeh observed two suspects and ordered them to halt. The suspects refused to obey the order and one drew a pistol. In response, the article said, the Border Policemen opened fire. The military sources acknowledged that the gun was discovered to be a toy. They added that a knife was discovered on Rahal's body.

In a letter to Middle East Watch dated May 20, 1993, the Justice Ministry stated that the inquiry into Rahal's death was still under way. The letter reported that according to intelligence information, Rahal was believed to have a pistol in his possession at the time he was shot. However, after the shooting, a search of his body did not reveal any firearms.

Analysis of the Official Version

The initial official reports that Rahal was shot after he drew a pistol were later retracted. It is still conceivable that he was ambushed by undercover Border Policemen who mistook a toy pistol he had been carrying for a real gun. Even if they had this impression, it was they who were lying in ambush and in apparent control of the situation, and they could have offered Rahal a chance to surrender before opening fire. According to the Palestinian witnesses, the troopers emerged from the field and shot Rahal without warning. The claim made in the initial reports that he had pointed a gun at them seems unlikely, since pointing a toy gun would have served no purpose other than to guarantee his own death.

The continued assertion by authorities that Rahal was "wanted" also raises suspicion, since information provided by Rahal's relatives indicates that he was not "wanted." They told Middle East Watch that Rahal had been issued a permit to work in Israel shortly before his death. They added that two days before being killed, Rahal had visited the local Civil Administration compound to arrange a visitor's permit for his sister. It is highly improbable that a "wanted" person would have walked into a well-guarded government office to file an application on which his name would have been required.

Case 9: Khalil Nader Khamayseh

Age: 17
Date of incident: April 29, 1992
Place: Village of al-Yamoun, Jenin district, West Bank
Remarks: Khamayseh was not armed, but a toy pistol was found at the scene of the killing; the main Palestinian eyewitness told Middle East Watch that Khamayseh was not holding it when shot; the IDF said he had pointed it at the soldiers.

Summary of Incident

Khamayseh was shot repeatedly at close range while on the roof of a friend's home. The principal Palestinian eyewitness said a soldier, who was among a group of uniformed soldiers who approached the roof, shot him repeatedly even though he had raised his empty hands in the air. The IDF claimed that Khamayseh had pointed a gun at the soldiers. The IDF acknowledged that the gun turned out to have been a toy pistol that Khamayseh had not been "wanted."

Description of Incident

On September 5, 1992, Middle East Watch visited al-Yamoun and spoke with an eyewitness to the killing, Nasser Nayef Muhammad Kamanji, a thirty-five-year-old unemployed clothes salesman and father of three.

According to Kamanji, Khamayseh had come to his house on the afternoon of April 29 to discuss an insurance claim the two men were planning to pursue after they had both been in an automobile accident a month earlier.[16] At 5 p.m., Khamayseh and Kamanji went up to the roof of the house, which is situated on the edge of the village. The house is built into a slope that is lined with olive trees. The roof is visible from most areas above it on the slope. It is possible to walk down the slope and onto the roof.

The two men sat on a sofa located in the center of the roof. Ms. Kamanji brought them tea and went back into the house. According to Mr. Kamanji:

> As I raised my hand to sip the tea, something caught my eye among the olive trees on the hillside in front of us. I looked toward it and saw two soldiers, in uniform, looking out from behind an olive tree, about fifty meters away from us. I then saw about eight soldiers scrambling on their backsides over a stone terrace directly behind the tree. They were coming down single file, one by one, and I could see them all as they tried to hide behind the tree.
>
> I said to Khalil, "The army!" ("*Ej-jeish!*")

Kamanji said neither he nor Khamayseh was alarmed, since they were not "wanted" and had no reason to believe that the soldiers moving through the brush were after them. If either had been inclined to flee, Kamanji said, they would have tried to do so. Several moments later, Kamanji recalled:

> The soldiers fanned out from the tree and spread out in a line facing us. They were moving in a crouched position, jumping sideways, in little spurts. They were about twenty meters away from us, pointing their guns.

Both men remained in their seats, watching the soldiers with growing alarm. At that point, Kamanji continued:

---

[16] Kamanji showed Middle East Watch researchers photocopies of the police reports regarding his accident. They are signed and stamped by the Israeli police station in Nablus.

One of the soldiers ran forward, to a spot right on the
edge of the roof. He pointed his gun at us and then
another one ran forward and crouched next to him.
There were still another six or seven soldiers spread out
behind them, pointing their guns at us.

Kamanji said one of the soldiers shouted in Arabic, "Stop or I'll
shoot you!" Khamayseh said that he and Kamanji remained seated and
raised their hands in the air.

Then, Kamanji said, the soldier moved forward until he was
standing at the edge of the roof, less than ten meters away from where
the two men were sitting. He was panting from the effort of descending
the slope and looked exhausted. At that point, Kamanji said:

The soldier pointed his gun at Khalil and then simply
shot him, repeatedly. I was terrified; I thought he was
shooting at me as well.

After the shooting, the soldiers all came up onto the roof.
One of them threw Khalil down on the ground. Blood
was pouring out of his stomach.

Kamanji was forced to his knees and handcuffed with thick plastic
bindings. He watched the soldiers search Khamayseh's body and pull his
identity card from his pocket. They then looked at the scattered police
and insurance forms the two men had been reviewing. Kamanji, who
speaks fluent Hebrew, said of the soldiers:

They found his I.D. card and his work permit.[17] They
also saw his medical reports from the hospital and the
report from the Nablus police station about the accident.
Khalil had brought all that paperwork over to discuss

---

[17] The permit allows the bearer to work inside Israel, and would have
indicated to the soldiers that Khamayseh was probably not "wanted." The Israeli
authorities rarely, if ever, issue permits to Palestinians convicted for or suspected
of security offenses. A photocopy of Khamayseh's permit is on file at Middle East
Watch.

with me. I heard one of them say, "This is the wrong
person."

Kamanji said one of the soldiers turned over the sofa where the
two men had been sitting, picked up the toy pistol, looked at it and then
threw it on the ground. Kamanji told Middle East Watch that the pistol
was lying under the sofa where Khamayseh was sitting, and may have
been visible to the soldier who pulled the trigger. Kamanji said that
Khamayseh had made no attempt to reach for the pistol when he was
confronted by the soldiers.
    A large military force then arrived, in jeeps, a civilian van, and
a helicopter. Kamanji was blindfolded and arrested. He was detained for
thirty-seven days, during which time he said he was interrogated by the
GSS and accused of harboring "wanted" persons in his home. He was then
released without charge.
    Khamayseh's brother Ali, who also speaks Hebrew, told Middle
East Watch that shortly after the killing he went to the nearby Civil
Administration compound, where an officer told him that his brother had
been on the "wanted" list for five years. Then, Ali Khamayseh recalled:

> The officer said to me in Hebrew, "Your brother was
> holding a pistol when he died. He tried to draw the pistol
> from his belt and because of that, the soldiers acted to
> defend themselves."

Ali Khamayseh said he was surprised to hear his brother had been
"wanted," since he possessed a permit to work in Israel. Ali Khamayseh
showed Middle East Watch travel and work permits that had been
recently issued to Khalil by the Civil Administration. No "wanted"
Palestinian would have been able to apply for these permits in his own
name without being arrested.
    Ali Khamayseh said he informed the Civil Administration officer
that if his brother had been "wanted" for five years, this would mean that
he had been a fugitive from the age of twelve. Ali said he also told the
officer that during that time the army had never attempted to arrest his
brother at home. In contrast to many "wanted" individuals, Khalil always
spent the night at his family's home, Ali said.
    Ali Khamayseh said he counted the wounds in his brother's body
when authorities returned it to the family for burial. He said there were

nine bullet entry wounds in the front of the body: one in the face, two in the right side of the rib cage, three in the left side of the rib cage, and three in the left leg. The IDF did not grant Middle East Watch's request to review the official autopsy report. However, Deputy JAG Col. Yahav said in an October 28, 1992 interview with us that the autopsy noted four bullet wounds, one of which was caused by a bullet exiting the body.

The Official Version

On the day after the killing, *Haaretz* quoted military sources as reporting that Khamayseh was killed after soldiers on an initiated operation in the village of al-Yamoun encountered two residents, one of whom drew a pistol and aimed it at them in a threatening manner, forcing the soldiers to fire in self-defense.

This is the one case presented in this report that Middle East Watch was able to discuss orally with the IDF JAG's office. In an interview on October 28, 1992, Deputy JAG Col. Yahav provided the following version of events:

> There were two young men on the roof, one of them looking through binoculars, with a gun in his hand. The soldiers were running down the hill in order to engage him. They warned him, in Arabic, to stop or they would shoot. He turned with the gun in his hand and a soldier felt threatened [and opened fire]. Apparently it was a toy gun.
>
> The soldiers were there for a reason. We had information that on this roof, there were armed terrorists from the Black Panthers.[18] This was the reason. As for Khamayseh, I do not know whether he was "wanted." For us [in investigating the killing], it's not important. We "freeze" the situation. We don't check all of the secret information. The soldier believed he was in a state of

---

[18] The Black Panthers is an armed group operating in the West Bank that is affiliated with the PLO's Fatah faction.

danger to his life, based on the fact that he saw the suspect with a gun pointed toward him.

Deputy JAG Col. Yahav added that the soldiers removed from the scene a toy gun and a large knife.

In response to questions posed by Middle East Watch, Col. Yahav wrote in December 1992:

> [A]fter checking of the investigative material, the Military Advocate General decided to close the inquiry file without taking any steps against any of the soldiers. It was found that the soldiers fired since they were convinced that their lives were in danger....The inquiry file was closed after it became apparent that the reason for the incident was a mistake on the part of the officer, who was concerned with the danger to his life. This was a completely honest mistake....(See Appendix.)

In his letter of December, Col. Yahav summarized the same version of events he had given to Middle East Watch orally in October. The soldiers told CID investigators they spotted Khamayseh standing on the roof of Kamanji's house "armed with a weapon and binoculars, which he was using to scan the area." Convinced they were dealing with an "illegally armed terrorist," the soldiers ran toward the roof and ordered him to halt. They charged him from a distance of fifteen meters. When he turned toward them while holding the pistol, a soldier "who saw that the deceased was aiming the pistol at him" shot him dead from a distance of ten meters. The soldiers later discovered the weapon was a toy.

Analysis of the Official Version

The official assertion that Khamayseh was killed while pointing a toy pistol at approaching soldiers, while not impossible, runs counter to common sense. The openness of the area surrounding the house supports Kamanji's statement that he and Khamayseh spotted the soldiers well before they drew close to the house. If the two Palestinian men did in fact see a group of armed and uniformed soldiers approaching, it is unlikely that Khamayseh would have continued to hold a toy pistol in a menacing manner, knowing he might be shot for doing so. But if he was holding a pistol, it is unlikely that the soldiers, closing in on a suspect holding a gun whom they believed to be a Black Panther, would have risked their lives by shouting a warning to him before opening fire. Both the IDF and Kamanji told us that a warning was indeed shouted, but Kamanji said that Khamayseh was unarmed when it was shouted, and that the soldier opened fire immediately afterward.

Another point that heightens suspicion of the IDF version of events is the account provided by Khamayseh's brother, according to which authorities told him after the killing that his brother had been wanted for five years. It is possible that the soldiers involved in the incident mistook Khamayseh for Bassem Sbeihat, a "wanted" activist who frequented the house where Khamayseh was killed, according to the house's owner. If the soldier who pulled the trigger held this mistaken impression, it may have contributed to his decision to open fire when he did. (Sbeihat was killed by special forces in a nearby village in August 1992.)

Case 10: Ra'ed Abd ar-Rahman Dihmes

Age: 19
Date of incident: March 18, 1992
Place: Village of Kufr Qadoum, Nablus district, West Bank
Remarks: Dihmes was not armed.

Summary of Incident

At dusk, three young Palestinian men were walking in a valley outside of the village of Kufr Qadoum. None of the youths was armed or masked. Suddenly a voice called out, "Halt! Army!" (*"Waqqif! Ej-jeish!"*) Immediately thereafter, gunmen lying in ambush opened fire, mortally wounding Dihmes and seriously injuring a second man. The IDF claimed that soldiers hunting for "wanted" men opened fire when confronted by the youths after one of them waved a stick in a threatening fashion. Middle East Watch's interviews with the two survivors and a visit to the scene of the incident strongly indicates that the shooting was not justified and may have been a shoot-to-kill ambush.

Description of Incident

On October 22, 1992, three Middle East Watch researchers visited the scene of the killing, one mile outside the village of Kufr Qadoum, and interviewed separately the two surviving civilian witnesses, Muhammad 'Abbas and Muntasir Barham. Barham, a carpenter, says he has been unable to work since the shooting. His face has been disfigured by two bullets which struck him in the jaw.

According to the two youths, on the evening of March 18, 1992 they and Dihmes were returning home to Kufr Qadoum from the nearby village of Hajjeh, along a path that leads through fields. Barham said he was walking with a stick for support because he had stepped on a nail some time earlier. Barham and 'Abbas said that none of the three was wearing a mask or head covering.

About half-way between the two villages, the path descends from Hajjeh into a valley. The valley is a dry riverbed strewn with boulders. The two youths said that during the intifada, local activists had dumped along the valley's dirt road the bodies of several Palestinians whom the activists had slain on suspicion of collaborating with the Israeli authorities.

The men reached the intersection of the path from Hajjeh and the valley road at about 6:40 p.m., at dusk. The youths turned left on the valley road to head toward Kufr Qadoum. When they had taken a few steps along the valley path, several bright lights were suddenly focused on them from a distance of some twelve meters to their right. The light beams, the witnesses said, originated next to large boulders situated on the bank of the riverbed.

The boulders in question are well-placed for staging an ambush, since they provide persons hiding behind them good cover and an excellent view of the valley and the path descending into it.

'Abbas said that a second after the lights blinded him he heard a voice shouting at them, "Halt! The army!" 'Abbas recalled, "As I raised my hands in the air the shooting began."

Immediately after the shooting began, 'Abbas said that Dihmes leaped forward and tried to push 'Abbas behind him. 'Abbas dropped to the ground to protect himself. He saw Dihmes fall to the ground.

Barham said he was hit by four bullets, the first hitting his leg and the others hitting his face and stomach. The shooting was over within seconds, he said:

> It all happened together. I didn't have a chance to be afraid. The lights, the shooting, the wounds all happened at the same moment. I did not even have time to raise my hands.

'Abbas said that as he lay on the ground, three gunmen emerged from behind the boulder and walked toward them. "They were wearing dark clothes and hoods over their heads with openings for their faces," he said.

While one of the armed men shined a light in his eyes, another approached and began to search them, 'Abbas said. A third crouched nearby, guarding the scene. After searching Dihmes's body, the gunman spoke into a walkie-talkie and then fired a flare into the air.

Moments later, 'Abbas said, tens of uniformed soldiers arrived on the scene. They were joined by a man in a white shirt and dark pants who, 'Abbas said, appeared to be a doctor, since he began attending to Barham and Dihmes.

The soldiers searched for the youths' identity cards, finding only Barham's, since 'Abbas and Dihmes did not have theirs with them. The soldiers said nothing to 'Abbas other than ordering him not to move. He sat still, with his hands raised.

Some fifteen minutes later, 'Abbas said, a helicopter landed in the ravine. The soldiers loaded Barham onto the helicopter, which then departed. Barham said he lost consciousness in the helicopter and awoke to find himself in Tel Hashomer Hospital inside Israel.

The soldiers loaded Dihmes's body into one of the two jeeps that had arrived. 'Abbas said they placed a sack over his own head, removed his shoes, tied his hands and legs with tight plastic bindings, and placed him into the jeep.

'Abbas said that after several minutes' drive, the jeep reached a nearby army roadblock in the village of Imattain. The soldiers took him out of the jeep and removed the sack from his head. 'Abbas then saw

"Captain Ron,"[19] a GSS officer responsible for Kufr Qadoum. "Captain Ron" ordered 'Abbas to explain what he was doing in the valley and who had sent him there. He refused to believe 'Abbas's denial that the three men had been engaged in resistance activity. According to 'Abbas, "Captain Ron" told the soldiers nearby, in Arabic, "I want to shoot him like his friend. Take him to the mountains and kill him like you did to the other."

Instead, the soldiers drove 'Abbas to Tulkarm prison, where he spent eight days in detention. During that time, he said, he was questioned once about the shooting by a uniformed police officer, and once about Dihmes's family. He was not otherwise interrogated and not threatened or physically mistreated. A few weeks after 'Abbas was released, the head of the local Civil Administration office in Qalqilya, "Captain Gideon," summoned 'Abbas to his headquarters and took a statement from him about the killing. His statement was accurately recorded in Arabic, 'Abbas said, and he was not questioned again by officials about the incident.

Barham said he spent fifteen days in Tel Hashomer Hospital, during which time he was questioned by a uniformed soldier about the incident. The soldier questioned him in Arabic and took notes in Hebrew. Barham was not imprisoned, and after his release from the hospital he was not questioned again, he said. He said that Tel Hashomer did not ask for payment for his hospital stay. After his release, he required further treatment at al-Maqassid Hospital in East Jerusalem.

Barham said he had never been arrested or detained by Israeli authorities. He said he carries an orange I.D., which indicates a clean security record and entitles him to apply to the authorities to enter Israel and annexed East Jerusalem.

Barham and 'Abbas said they did not believe that Dihmes was "wanted" by the authorities at the time he was killed. They said he had been "wanted" a long time ago in Qalqilya. About four years ago, he settled in Kufr Qadoum, where he helped his uncle in construction work. During these years, authorities had stopped him and checked his I.D. a number of times without detaining him.

A friend of Dihmes, Abd ar-Rahman Ishtawi, attended Dihmes's burial. He said that there were numerous bullet holes in the right side of

---

[19] GSS agents commonly assume false first names by which they are known to Palestinians in the area where they operate.

Dihmes's body. The IDF did not respond to Middle East Watch's request for the findings of the autopsy of Dihmes.

The Official Version

The day after the incident, *Haaretz* quoted "official military sources" saying:

> [A]n IDF force encountered three masked men. One of them brandished a knife and a large stick at the soldiers. The latter shot at him and killed him. His friend was critically injured.

In response to specific questions from Middle East Watch, Deputy JAG Col. Yahav wrote in December 1992 that the case was still being investigated, and provided the following preliminary account:

> [T]he soldiers, whose aim was to arrest murderous and armed terrorists, fired at the legs of the deceased and his friends. During the operation the soldiers saw the deceased waving an object which seemed to be a rifle. The soldiers, who feared for their lives, shot and killed him. (See Appendix.)

In May 1993, the IDF informed us that the legal deposition had not yet been given and therefore it could provide no further details of the investigation.

Analysis of the Official Version

The IDF initially claimed that the three youths were masked and that Dihmes brandished a knife and stick at the soldiers. Deputy JAG Col. Yahav's later account states that the soldiers were on a mission to confront "armed terrorists" and shot Dihmes when he appeared to threaten them. He states that Dihmes had "an object which seemed to be a rifle," and suggests that the soldiers first fired at the legs and, only when sensing mortal danger, shot to kill. He does not repeat the earlier claim that the youths were masked, and does not explain why soldiers opened fire in the first place.

It is difficult to imagine why a man, especially one who was not "wanted," would wave a stick in a threatening manner at soldiers who were pointing their guns at him some twelve meters away. Moreover, both of the survivors interviewed by Middle East Watch said that Barham, not Dihmes, was holding the stick.

Both men stated that Dihmes and Barham were shot in one, continuous burst of fire. The survivors made no mention of two separate volleys, as suggested by Col. Yahav.

If the soldiers indeed intended to arrest rather than kill the persons they were hoping to confront, it is unclear why they opened fire so quickly. The circumstances of this encounter favored the soldiers more than nearly all of the other cases presented in this chapter. They had set up their position well in advance, hiding behind large boulders in a valley far from residential areas, where they could monitor all approaches. The fact that, in spite of this favorable situation, the soldiers opened fire so quickly at Palestinians some twelve meters away who turned out to be unarmed strongly suggests the soldiers may have intended to kill suspects whom they had reason to believe would be using the path between Kufr Qadoum and Hajjeh.

KILLINGS OF STONE-THROWERS WHO WERE NOT MASKED

Case 11: Amjad abd ar-Razeq Thalji Jabbar

Age: 12
Date of incident: November 23, 1992
Place: Ar-Ram, north of Jerusalem, West Bank
Remarks: Jabbar was not armed.

Summary of Incident

Soldiers, traveling in an unmarked civilian car, intended to intercept high school students who had thrown stones at an Israeli bus in the vicinity minutes before Amjad's death. They encountered a group of

youths and ordered them to stop. When the youths fled, a soldier opened
fire, fatally wounding Jabbar in the back. The soldier has since been
convicted and sentenced to a prison term.

Description of Incident

On February 16, 1993, a Middle East Watch researcher traveled
to Ar-Ram and separately interviewed two civilian eyewitnesses to the
killing, thirteen-year-old Shadi Riyash Thalji Jabbar and thirteen-year-old
Ra'ed Muhammad Nimer Awad. The researcher then visited the site of
the killing.

Shadi Jabbar said that on November 23, 1992, he mounted a
public bus with his cousin, Amjad Jabbar, at about 6:45 a.m. The bus took
them from their home in el-Bireh to al-Umar Grade School in Ar-Ram,
a suburb of Jerusalem. On the bus they met their seventh-grade
classmate, Ra'ed Muhammad Nimer Awad, of Qalandia refugee camp.

According to both Shadi Jabbar and Ra'ed Awad, all three boys
got off the bus, which stopped on the main road directly across the street
from al-Umar High School, at approximately 7:30 a.m. When the bus
neared the stop, the boys said they saw students running from the main
road toward the high school.

The two boys said they then crossed the street, intending to walk
past the high school toward their grade school, located some 300 meters
up a street that intersects the main road. When they reached the other
side of the main road, they saw an Israeli bus to their left, driving slowly
northward, some seventy-five meters away. The two witnesses said they
assumed that the bus had been stoned by the youths they saw running
toward the high school.

The boys entered the side street that runs from the main road to
their grade school at the top of the hill. To their left was a large, open
field and beyond that, the high school soccer field. The three boys stayed
to the right of the road, keeping close to a line of shops and a car-wash
garage on their right. The shops were mostly still closed and there were
few people on the street.

After walking some fifty meters down the side road, they saw a
white Peugeot turn into the street and begin to drive toward them,
heading in the direction of the main road to their rear. Shadi said that
the car "seemed normal, like a regular car. It had blue [i.e., West Bank]

license plates. It had maybe three people inside, the driver and another two." Shadi and Ra'ed said they were walking together, slightly behind Amjad. The Peugeot pulled up and stopped in the middle of the road some six meters from the youths. At that moment, Ra'ed said, "people wearing Bedouin clothes and *keffiyehs* jumped out of the car and yelled 'Halt, army!'" (*"Waqqif! Ej-jeish!"*)

The men were holding firearms described by Shadi and Ra'ed as "longer than pistols, but shorter than big guns." Ra'ed said that at first, "I thought of staying there but they began to shoot, so we all began to run away."

Ra'ed and Shadi turned and fled toward the main road. Amjad, who stood several meters away from his two companions, ran in the opposite direction, away from the main road. While they were running, Ra'ed heard "a second bunch of shots. All the time while we were running to the main road there was shooting."

Shortly before reaching the main road the two boys looked back to see whether Amjad had managed to escape. From a distance of approximately fifty meters, both boys clearly saw Amjad lying face down in the dirt, some ten meters from the white Peugeot, and saw the plainclothesmen approaching Amjad's body. Then both boys rounded the corner and fled down the main road.

The Official Version

On November 24, 1992, a day after the killing, *Hadashot* quoted official military sources as saying Amjad Jabbar died when undercover soldiers of the Duvdevan unit launched an operation aimed at capturing stone-throwers. According to the military, the soldiers encountered a group of youths building barricades and throwing stones near ar-Ram junction and ordered them to halt. When the youths failed to obey the command, the army said, the soldiers opened fire, killing Jabbar.[20]

On November 25, *Haaretz* reported that Brig. Gen. Moshe Ya'alon, the commander of IDF troops in the West Bank, had conducted his own investigation into the killing and concluded that the killing was unjustified. Gen. Ya'alon said Amjad was killed by the commander of the

---

[20] See also IDF Radio, November 23, 1992, as reported in FBIS, November 23, 1992.

undercover unit, identified only as "Second Lt. Ofir," who shot Amjad with his pistol at a distance of fifteen to twenty meters. According to Gen. Ya'alon, the undercover force should have attempted to capture the youths without using their guns. He promised that the CID would investigate the case promptly.

Within three months, the second lieutenant was court-martialed and sentenced for causing death through negligence and violating the procedure for apprehending a suspect.

According to an account provided to Middle East Watch by a journalist who attended the lieutenant's sentencing on May 10, 1993, the defendant said he had been ordered not to carry out the procedure for apprehending suspects against persons under the age of sixteen. Even though he guessed that Jabbar was under sixteen, he thought he could execute the procedure because Jabbar had thrown stones. The lieutenant testified that he had first shouted a warning, fired into the air, and then at the ground near the victim, and only then did he aim at the victim's legs. No Palestinian witnesses gave testimony at the trial. (The two youths interviewed by Middle East Watch said they had never been questioned about the incident by investigators from the IDF.)

The military court sentenced "Second Lt. Ofir" to twelve months, of which six were suspended. Of the remaining six months, he is to spend three in prison and three doing army work. The court decided not to demote the officer because of his "dedication and sacrifice" and "excellent service," as well as "internal pressures" and "the overall context of the circumstances."

Analysis of the Official Version

The IDF's swift response in this case is laudable. The apparent misconduct was acknowledged promptly and led to a timely prosecution. Unfortunately, the leniency of the sentence for killing a twelve-year-old undermined the message that wrongdoing by soldiers is punished appropriately.

The soldier fired on a twelve-year-old in violation of the written rule prohibiting gunfire to apprehend a suspect who is under fourteen years of age. But this is only one of the abuses committed in this case.

Although Amjad disobeyed an order to halt, soldiers are prohibited from shooting fleeing persons unless they have good reason to suspect the suspect has committed a "dangerous" crime. If the crime is stone-throwing, the arrest procedure must be conducted immediately following commission of the offense, or else opening fire is not allowed. Even if Amjad had been involved in the stone-throwing — contrary to his companions' statements — the special forces confronted the youths away from the scene of the incident and minutes after it had occurred, when they were posing no danger to others.

In addition, soldiers are permitted to open fire on fleeing suspects only if there is no other means to apprehend them. Had the undercover soldiers who drove up to the youths in their car made an effort to do so, they probably could have caught a twelve-year-old running in a nearly empty street. Apparently, no such effort was made.

Finally, the soldier testified at his court-trial that he had aimed at Amjad's legs, as required by the open-fire regulations. The court did not reject his claim. The difficulty of refuting such an assertion, except when the suspect is shot in the upper body at point blank range or when exceptional forensic evidence is obtained, underscores our point that the order to shoot at the legs is virtually impossible to enforce.

Soldiers frequently kill fleeing suspects, including stone-throwers, outside of life-threatening situations and are rarely punished. The only remarkable feature of the Jabbar case was the age of the victim.

Case 12: Mahmoud 'Issa Shalaldeh

Age: 16
Date of incident: May 7, 1992
Place: Village of Sa'ir, Hebron district
Remarks: Shalaldeh was not armed.

Summary of Incident

A Volkswagen van with Israeli license plates, carrying Israeli undercover troops, was stoned as it drove past youths in a schoolyard. Its occupants opened fire and wounded one youth in the leg. Mahmoud Shalaldeh, who was in the schoolyard at the time, carried the wounded youth to the road, stopped a passing car, got in with the injured youth and asked the driver to drive to a clinic in the next village. As the car set off, the Volkswagen van began chasing it. The car stopped and Shalaldeh jumped out and began to flee up a hill beside two houses. Two men in civilian clothing jumped out of the van, and one shot Shalaldeh in the back. The two men then drove off in the van without collecting the body.

Description of Incident

On October 27, 1992, two Middle East Watch researchers traveled to Sa'ir and interviewed two witnesses to the killing of Shalaldeh. The description of the events that led up to the killing is based on information provided us by Sa'ir residents, as well as B'Tselem's report on the undercover units.[21]

Zahi Jaradat, al-Haq's fieldworker for the Hebron district and a resident of Sa'ir, told Middle East Watch he saw a Volkswagen van with yellow Israeli license plates[22] when it first entered Sa'ir at approximately 3 p.m. in the afternoon of May 7, 1992. He said he initially assumed the van belonged to Israeli settlers.

The van drove slowly through the village. When it passed near a group of youths playing soccer, one of the car's occupants reached out of the window and placed an Israeli flag on the van's roof, both B'Tselem and al-Haq reported. The youths threw stones at the van. The distance between the stone-throwers and the Israeli vehicle was approximately seventy-five meters.

One of the van's occupants opened fire from the vehicle's window, wounding sixteen-year-old Amin Jaradat in the leg. Mahmoud Shalaldeh lifted Jaradat and carried him to the main road. He flagged down a passing Peugeot, driven by a Sa'ir resident. Shalaldeh and Jaradat got into the back seat and then the car headed in the direction of the clinic in the neighboring village of Shuyoukh.

---

[21] B'Tselem, *Activity of the Undercover Units,* pp. 67-68.

[22] Vehicles registered in Israel use yellow license plates, while vehicles registered in the West Bank and Gaza Strip use blue or white plates. Israeli settlers living in the occupied territories use yellow license plates. Most undercover missions by the special forces involve the use of cars with blue or white plates; this incident is an exception.

The van circled round the school and approached the Peugeot as Shalaldeh was putting the wounded youth into the back seat. As the Peugeot drove off, the van gave chase. Zahi Jaradat, al-Haq's fieldworker, said he watched the two cars drive out of the village at high speed.

The two cars had gone over one kilometer from the school when they suddenly halted, for reasons that remain unclear. According to some villagers, there was an electricity pole lying across the road, blocking the way. The Peugeot slammed to a stop, and the van pulled up several seconds later, stopping a few meters behind it. Shalaldeh opened his door and began to run up a gentle slope on the left side of the road. The slope offers no natural cover; it has no trees or underbrush. The only buildings are both at least twenty meters to the left of where he was running.

Khadhra Muhammad Salem Warasneh, a forty-three-year-old mother of nine, was sitting on her verandah with her cousin, Omar Issam Warasneh, when she heard shots and the sound of a car speeding up the hill toward her home. Seconds later, she told Middle East Watch, the two vehicles slammed to a halt some fifty meters away from where she sat.

> The [first] car was a Peugeot....It stopped....The second vehicle was a "Flux" [Volkswagen] van with an Israeli flag. It was only a couple of meters behind the Peugeot. A youth ran out of the Peugeot. Then the driver of the Peugeot got out and raised his hands. A third man [presumably the wounded youth, Jaradat] stayed in the Peugeot.

Then, Warasneh said, two men climbed out of the Volkwagen van while a third remained with the vehicle. She said that all three men were wearing civilian clothes and yarmulkas, the skullcap worn by observant Jews. Warasneh said:

> one guy chased the youth up the hill, and the second ran up the road. The man who was chasing him shot him as he tried to climb up a stone terrace on the slope. There were no warning, no firings in the air.

Warasneh said the youth was shot from a distance of twenty meters away.

A second woman,[23] whose home overlooks the road from a different but equally close vantage point, said she watched from her bedroom window as the cars stopped and a boy began to run toward her home. She then moved to a second window in the room. She said:

> I saw the youth was lying face down on the ground. The men went up to him and lifted his hand. They were wearing street clothes and yarmulkas. They did not lift or drag the body anywhere.

Then, both women told us, the two men returned to their van and drove away. Men from the village arrived and took Shalaldeh's body to his family's home.

Some sixty minutes after the shooting, Warasneh said, the Volkswagen van returned, accompanied by several military jeeps. The soldiers dismounted, stood talking among themselves for several minutes, and then drove off. Warasneh, her cousin Omar Warasneh, and the second witness interviewed by Middle East Watch all said that no military investigators had questioned them about what they had seen.

Both Ms. Warasneh and the other woman interviewed by Middle East Watch said they had heard no warnings shouted before the plainclothes gunman shot Shalaldeh.

According to al-Haq, Shalaldeh's family said that Mahmoud had been shot with one bullet in the head. There was apparently no official autopsy in this case, since the family obtained custody of the body directly.

The Official Version

Although the gunmen looked as though they could have been Israeli settlers, the army said that its soldiers were responsible. The IDF issued two descriptions of the incident. As is the case in many killings, the initial statement differed substantially from the later official version of events.

On May 7, 1992, the day of the killing, the IDF spokesman stated:

---

[23] This witness would not give her name to Middle East Watch.

> During an operation initiated by the IDF this afternoon
> around 5:30 p.m. against rioters and disturbers of the
> peace, in the area of the village of Sa'ir in the Hebron
> District, soldiers of the force identified two young Arab
> men throwing stones at a car which was passing by. The
> soldiers from the force shot at them, and as a result both
> were wounded, one moderately and the other critically,
> and they were taken to the hospital for medical
> treatment.[24]

The next day, B'Tselem reported, the IDF issued a statement saying that
Mahmoud Shalaldeh died from his injuries in Ramallah hospital.

In response to questions posed by Middle East Watch, the IDF in
December 1992 provided a somewhat different account of the case:

> The investigation to date suggests that the shots were
> fired during an attempt to catch residents who were
> throwing stones at passing vehicles and endangering the
> lives of passengers. The soldiers moved to detain the
> stone thrower, who escaped in a car, in accordance with
> the procedure for detaining a suspect. At the end of the
> chase the deceased ran from his car as the soldiers fired
> toward his legs in order to stop him. The deceased was
> wounded and died. The circumstances of the incident are
> being investigated by the Military Advocate General. (See
> Appendix.)

In May 1993, the IDF informed us that the legal deposition in the case
had not yet been given and therefore it could provide no further details
of the investigation.

Analysis of the Official Version

This case is in some respects a familiar one: a fleeing suspect
posing no imminent threat is shot dead by an undercover soldier who
"fired toward the legs in order to stop him." A few points about the case

---

[24] B'Tselem, *Activity of the Undercover Units*, p. 67.

are worth noting, however. The victim in this case was neither "wanted" nor masked. He was a sixteen-year-old suspected of stoning a car, and the evidence suggests that the stone-throwing incident was not even a serious one: the car was not moving quickly, and the rocks were thrown from a considerable distance. It appears, moreover, that the undercover soldiers disguised themselves as Jewish settlers and drove around the village, which is off the main road, in an apparent effort to entrap stone-throwers.

The IDF initially provided an account of the incident that was highly misleading. As B'Tselem pointed out, it "did not in any way address the fact that Mahmoud Shalaldeh was shot over one kilometer from the place where the stones were thrown, and not at the time when the stone-throwing was taking place, but when he was running away and not endangering anyone."[25] The IDF did not address this point when responding to B'Tselem's report.[26]

The IDF's later, interim account of the event bears a closer relationship to the account provided by village residents. Shalaldeh ran from a car, well after the end of a stone-throwing incident, and was shot dead while attempting to flee. The IDF does not explain how this incident comports with restrictions in the rules of engagement on the use of gunfire to apprehend fleeing stone-throwers. As we understand the rules, fleeing stone-throwers may be shot only "if real [mortal] danger exists and the arrest is performed immediately during the incident." Interestingly, the initial IDF account of the event was worded so as to create the impression that the shooting directly followed the stone-throwing. The second version makes clear that a car trip intervened. Whether there are legal consequences for the soldiers remains to be seen; the investigation was not yet complete one year after the incident.

---

[25] *Ibid.*, p. 68.

[26] *Ibid.*, pp. 125-128. The IDF's response refers to seven out of thirteen cases documented by B'Tselem in its report, but not the Shalaldeh case.

Case 13: Muhammad Isma'il abd as-Salaam al-Ja'afreh

Age: 15
Date of incident: April 1, 1992
Place: Tarqumia, district of Hebron
Remarks: Al-Ja'afreh was not armed.

Summary of Incident

On April 1, 1992, an army jeep vehicle drove into the main square of the village of Tarqumia, and was pelted with stones and bottles. The jeep came to a halt at the edge of the square. Youths pelted the jeep steadily with stones and bottles for some time from nearby roofs and alleyways. The soldiers stayed inside the jeep. Then an unmarked Peugeot drove up the main approach to the village and drove into the square. About six men burst out of the Peugeot and began chasing and firing at the youths. Some of them chased al-Ja'afreh down an alley behind the square and fatally wounded him in the chest.

Description of Incident

On October 27, 1992, a Middle East Watch researcher traveled to Tarqumia, a relatively remote village built on hills northwest of Hebron. While the circumstances at the exact moment of the fatal shooting remain unclear, the events that led up to the killing raise disturbing questions about how undercover troops have been deployed against stone-throwing youths.

According to several witnesses, the incident began when a jeep drove into the main square and was pelted with stones. The owner of a café on the main road a few meters off the main square recalled:[27]

> A [security-forces] jeep stopped in the square, and the
> youths threw bottles and rocks at it from every direction.
> The jeep had three persons in it, I think. They stayed in
> the jeep. It sat there for about forty-five minutes without

---

[27] The café owner declined to give his name.

moving, and the youths just kept throwing stones and bottles at it.

Then, I saw a Peugeot 504 station wagon coming up the main road, driving quickly. There were six or seven persons in the car, one looked like an Arab woman, with a white head covering, the others were dressed in streetclothes. When they reached the square, the Peugeot stopped and all but one of them jumped out, and began running and shooting with pistols.

The café owner stated that the soldiers did not shout any warnings.

A fourteen-year-old youth who was with al-Ja'afreh when he was killed and who was himself wounded by a bullet, described what he saw. The two youths were positioned at the corner of the square where the main road continues into the village. They were not wearing masks. The youth, who asked that his name not be used, said:

We were all throwing rocks at the jeep that was parked in the square when this car drove up and stopped right near Muhammad and me. When the men jumped out of the car we turned around and ran. I started to run straight [away from the square] and Muhammad turned left and ran into an alley. Before I could get away I was hit by a bullet.

I managed to get up, and when I looked down the alley I saw a soldier catch up with Muhammad and shoot him in the chest. I tried to get away, but I fell after a few meters. I waved to a car that was passing, but when it got close I saw it was filled with [undercover] soldiers.

The soldiers stopped the car, got out, and put me inside. They drove to the mosque and put me on the ground outside. Muhammad was laying nearby, and they were trying to revive him. They loosened my pants, and gave me glucose. I didn't lose consciousness.

The witness was later transported to a hospital, where he says he spent eight days. He said the bullet entered his buttocks and exited near the navel, and showed scars that supported this claim. He said he was not arrested.

A fifty-five-year-old woman, whose house faces the alley where al-Ja'afreh was shot, saw five or six youths fleeing together. Behind them she saw al-Ja'afreh, limping for several meters before falling on the ground.

A forty-two-year-old Tarqumia man who had been praying in the mosque at the time of the shooting, said that he heard a lot of commotion outside the mosque. When he went outside he saw that soldiers had placed three wounded youths on the ground and were preventing villagers from approaching them. "There were fourteen men in civilian clothing, and about four soldiers in uniform," he said. "A uniformed soldier opened [al-Ja'afreh's] shirt. He was losing a lot of blood. He had already lost consciousness." The soldiers announced a curfew over a megaphone. Eventually, a military ambulance evacuated al-Ja'afreh, and a Palestinian ambulance transported the other wounded youths.

The father of al-Ja'afreh told Middle East Watch that the IDF returned the body of Muhammad late the same evening, without conducting an autopsy. He later obtained an IDF death certificate that corroborated the testimony of the fourteen-year-old witness that Muhammad had been shot at close range in the chest. The certificate also noted an exit wound in the upper back.

Al-Ja'afreh's father recounted a conversation he had after the killing with an officer at the local Civil Administration office in Idna. He recalled:

> I told him, You made a terrible mistake: my son did not throw stones. He answered, We made a mistake in another village. This time, we did not make a mistake. We saw him throwing stones. It's like when someone goes into Israel without [the required] permission. He gets away with it ten times, and then the next time he gets caught and pays a heavy fine. Your son threw stones and got caught, so he has paid a heavy price.

The Official Version

In May 1993, the IDF informed Middle East Watch that it decided that the soldier had acted justifiably in killing al-Ja'afreh because he reasonably felt threatened by a large rock that he believed al-Ja'afreh was about to throw at him from close range. The IDF added that the soldier would face disciplinary proceedings for negligence because he had wounded two youths under sixteen years of age in the legs.

Analysis of the Official Version

Middle East Watch did not find eyewitness testimony that was sufficient to challenge the IDF's conclusion that al-Ja'afreh was threatening the soldier with a large rock. Nevertheless, there are other disturbing facets to the case.

The operation was apparently set in motion when youths threw stones and bottles at an IDF jeep. Such vehicles are well-protected with grills over the windows, and the soldiers inside were in no apparent danger, even though the stone-throwing was by all accounts vigorous. The soldiers parked and waited. They did not drive away nor did they get out to disperse the stone-throwers or to open fire in self-defense. The IDF statement did not suggest that the jeep was disabled.

Instead, the soldiers apparently radioed to a command post and remained on the scene as bait for stone- and bottle-throwers until the undercover force arrived. When it came the plainclothesmen leaped out and, according to two eyewitnesses, opened fire without warning at suspected stone-throwers. The IDF's acknowledgment that two suspects were wounded in the legs is inaccurate: soldiers saw to the treatment of one of the wounded, and must have been aware that he was hit by a bullet in the buttocks that exited near his navel. While the difference between legs and buttocks is inches, the difference in consequences is potentially enormous, and underscores the unjustifiability of shooting at the legs as a means of apprehending suspects outside of life-threatening situations.

In both this incident and Case Twelve, undercover soldiers ignored the apparent prohibition in the rules of engagement on firing to apprehend stone-throwers unless their actions are posing a mortal danger. In these two cases, the operations seem to have been designed to bait stone-throwers and then use undercover units to mete out summary punishment, within the framework of firing at fleeing suspects, killing Mahmoud Shalaldeh (Case Twelve) and injuring the fourteen-year-old Tarqumia youth in his abdomen (Case Thirteen).

Middle East Watch believes that the same legal standards should apply to security-force encounters with "wanted" activists as to the encounters presented in the previous chapter. Lethal force should be used as a last resort and meet the tests of necessity and proportionality. Reliable information that a suspect carries and has used a firearm is, of course, relevant to a soldier's assessment of the level of danger in a situation. However, such information must never become a pre-approved basis for opening fire. The circumstances of each encounter must be judged on their own merits when determining if lethal force is justified.

In this chapter, we present four cases we investigated in which we believe that soldiers killed "wanted" persons unjustifiably. In two of the cases, the IDF did not claim that the Palestinians were armed when killed; the IDF stated only that they were fatally wounded while attempting to flee. We also discuss a third case that was researched by other human rights organizations in which undercover soldiers burst onto a soccer field and gunned down an unarmed "wanted" Palestinian. Although authorities claimed that he was shot while trying to flee the stadium, the circumstances of the killing illustrate, at the least, how the orders on apprehending fleeing suspects amount to shoot-to-kill policy.

The two other cases presented in this chapter involve Palestinians who were killed while holding firearms. In one, however, the testimony we gathered indicates that he was shot dead on sight, without warning. In the other, soldiers ambushed a meeting of suspected activists and then opened fire indiscriminately as they tried to escape, killed three men, including two who were neither "wanted" nor armed when killed.

Case 14: Muhammad Sadeq Kemayel Taktak

Age: 20
Date of Incident: October 3, 1992
Place: Qabatiya, Jenin district
Remarks: Taktak was not armed when killed.

Summary of Incident

Plainclothes soldiers burst into the courtyard of a house where six men had gathered, including Taktak. As soon as the men realized what was happening, they climbed out a window and mounted a ladder toward the roof, intending to escape on the other side of the house. The soldiers fired on them as they reached the roof, injuring one man in the leg and fatally wounding Taktak with a bullet in the upper body.

Description of Incident

On October 23, 1992, two Middle East Watch researchers visited the house in Qabatiya where the killing had occurred three weeks earlier, and interviewed witness Sana' Ahmed Nazzal, twenty-one years old, who was in the house at the time of the shooting. We have also drawn on interviews conducted by B'Tselem and al-Haq, which are on file at their offices.

On October 3, six men had gathered in a house in Qabatiya. The house is separated from the street by a continuous wall and a large courtyard. Abutting the outer wall, inside the courtyard, are a couple of small rooms. The main part of the house is on the other side of the courtyard. When standing in the courtyard and facing the house, the kitchen is on the right and a small sitting room is on the left. The men were in the sitting room.

One of the men in the room, Muhammad Ahmed Suleiman Saba'neh, is the nephew of the owner of the house, and lives in the house next door. He told al-Haq that at about 12:30 p.m., while still at his own house:

> I observed a woman who appeared to be poor. She came toward me wearing a *dishdash* [a long, loose-fitting dress] and a white kerchief, and carrying a purse. Her face was young and pale. She seemed to be in her twenties. She asked for some alms, and I gave her some coins and some rice. She left and headed next door to my uncle's house....I turned to this poor woman and said that I had just given her some alms and then I went in [to the uncle's house] and locked the door behind me.

Sana' Nazzal described what happened minutes after her neighbor came in:

> I heard a hard knocking at the [front] door. I left the kitchen and went [across the courtyard] to open the door. Before I got to the door, they had climbed over the wall and onto the roofs of the little rooms. Some of them were in women's clothing. They had guns. They yelled at me, "Go inside," and fired two bullets at the house, near the kitchen. I went back in.

A person who stands on the roof of the rooms near the street wall has a clear view of the house's roof near the top of the ladder. The special-force soldiers stood there and fired toward at least some of the men as they mounted the ladder or reached the roof. Confined to the house, Nazzal did not witness what happened next. But Saba'neh, who was with the men in the room, told al-Haq,

> I heard a loud knock on the door....Then I heard someone say "Halt!" Immediately, the guys and I fled to the roof over the room we had been in. We used the nearby ladder. I heard the sound of heavy gunfire. On the roof I felt blood pouring from my right knee. I began crawling from the roof [of the room] in an effort to reach the courtyard of my father's house. Then I lost consciousness for a few minutes. When I regained consciousness and started crawling again, I saw more than twenty soldiers closing in on the three youths who were cornered in a room in the courtyard of my father's house.

Saba'neh said that three of the six men were arrested. He was evacuated to a hospital and not arrested.

Nazzal's brother-in-law, Hani Tawfiq abd ar-Rahman Saba'neh, twenty-five years old, lives in the house and was among the men in the sitting room. He was the only one of the men to escape both injury and arrest. He told B'Tselem:

When I heard gunshots I told the "wanted" person
[Taktak] to leave immediately. Everyone who was sitting
with us in the room got up and went out of the room.
We climbed up a ladder, onto the roof, and each one of
us began to run in a different direction. Since they were
shooting at us on the roof of the house, I went down to
my neighbor's house and told the "wanted" person to
accompany me. He said he was wounded, and I saw
blood on his chest. I said it was a light wound, and he
should come with me so we could get out of the place.
We went about forty meters together, until the gate of
the neighbor's house. There was firing right above us. At
the gate, Muhammad fell and I kept running toward the
fields.

The bullet that killed Taktak reportedly hit him in the shoulder.
Saba'neh said that Taktak was known to carry a gun, although he did not
see him carrying one on the day of the incident. He had reportedly been
"wanted" since 1991.

Nazzal told Middle East Watch that after the shooting, the
soldiers ransacked her house and confiscated money.

The Official Version

In the Hebrew press the day after the incident, military sources
were quoted as saying that an IDF force fired at two suspects after they
refused an order to halt, killing one and wounding another. In December,
Deputy JAG Col. Yahav gave the following interim finding:

During the attempt to arrest him, the deceased did not
heed the warning given to him to stop. The soldiers fired
toward his legs. The deceased was wounded and died.
(See Appendix.)

In May 1993, the IDF reported that a legal opinion on the killing had still
not been rendered by the office of the JAG.

Analysis of the Official Version

The IDF accounts to date are consistent with the testimony of Palestinian eyewitnesses: Taktak was shot while trying to flee, after refusing an order to halt. He was known to carry a gun, but either did not have it on his person the day he was killed, or made no attempt to draw it.

This case resembles several other cases presented in this report in which Palestinians are shot dead by soldiers who are supposedly following the procedure to fire at the legs of fleeing suspects. The soldiers, firing from close range, managed to hit Saba'neh in the legs, while hitting Taktak, the main target of the mission, in the upper body. This does not prove intentionality, but it raises suspicion. The frequency of this sort of killing reinforces the impression that the shoot-at-the-legs order is often a fig leaf for a "wanted: dead or alive" policy.

Case 15: Abd al-Qader Yousef abd al-Qader Masarweh

Age: 21
Date of incident: April 9, 1992
Place: Nur Shams refugee camp, Tulkarm district, northern West Bank
Remarks: Masarweh was not armed when killed.

Summary of Incident

According to the only known civilian eyewitness to the incident, a group of uniformed IDF soldiers fired one bullet at close range at Masarweh, hitting him in the head. According to his father, Masarweh had been on the GSS's "wanted" list for two years prior to his death. He was not, according to the eyewitness, armed at the time of his death, nor has the IDF claimed the contrary.

According to the eyewitness, Masarweh had been attempting to escape from uniformed soldiers by scaling a stone fence surrounding the garden of the eyewitness' home. He abandoned his efforts to get over the fence and then walked back toward the soldiers. He was shot in the head by a soldier facing him at a distance of less than ten meters.

According to the eyewitness, there was a large contingent of soldiers in the immediate vicinity at the time of Masarweh's death.

Description of Incident

On August 27, 1992, a Middle East Watch researcher visited Nur Shams refugee camp and spoke with Masarweh's father, Yousef abd al-Qader Masarweh and Ms. Rasimia Hassan Mari', in whose yard Masarweh was killed.

Masarweh's father, a resident of Nur Shams camp, told Middle East Watch that soldiers came searching for his son every ten or fifteen days during the two years he was "wanted" by the authorities. He said:

> Twenty days before my son's death, I had another visit from the army and the *mukhabarat* [intelligence]. Several uniformed soldiers came, very young, and several men in plainclothes. The *mukhabarat* agent told me that if Abd al-Qader didn't immediately surrender to the Civil Administration, he would be killed. Then they searched the house. They overturned all of my possessions. They threw everything down onto the floor.
>
> This *mukhabarat* agent did not say who would kill Abd al-Qader if he didn't surrender. He simply told me, Abd al-Qader will come home dead if he doesn't turn himself in.

On April 9, 1992, Abd al-Qader Masarweh was surprised in Nur Shams by soldiers who were apparently searching for him. A large force of uniformed soldiers took up positions around the area. One group of soldiers entered the yard of the Mari' family home, apparently in an effort to block Masarweh's potential escape route.

Ms. Mari' was alerted by a neighbor to the presence of soldiers in her yard and hurried home. She pushed past several soldiers standing at her front gate and attempted to enter her front door. The door was locked from the inside and she had no key. Her husband was in his small grocery shop at the other end of their yard, some sixty meters away. Ms. Mari' sat down on the steps in front of her door. She recalled:

> There were soldiers near the gate where I had entered
> and there were soldiers down at the bottom of the yard,
> near the back entrance. Altogether there must have been
> about thirty soldiers. One soldier told me to get in the
> house. I said, "I can't get in, the door is locked." He said,
> "You must go in."

Suddenly, Ms. Mari' said, she saw a young man dressed in a green t-shirt jump over the wall to her right and sprint across her yard. He crossed the thirty-meter width of her backyard and then tried to climb over the wall. Soldiers at the top of the yard where she was standing and at the bottom of the yard, where her husband's shop was situated, shouted at the young man to stop and levelled their weapons in his direction.

According to Ms. Mari', the young man slipped off the wall and landed back in the yard. He turned to face the soldiers, hands raised, and then began to walk back toward the center of the yard. At that point another soldier appeared, leaning over the wall to the right of Ms. Mari'. This soldier pointed his rifle at the young man and shouted in Arabic, "*Waqqif!*" (Stop!). Then, Ms. Mari' said:

> The youth raised his hands, took several steps forward,
> right where that almond tree is, and then slipped and fell
> on a patch of ground that is steep and has lots of loose
> gravel and dirt. He then got up and began to walk slowly
> toward the soldier leaning over the wall.

> The soldier called out to him "*Waqqif!*" three times. The
> youth was still moving, very slowly and carefully, toward
> the wall where the soldier was standing. Each time the
> soldier yelled out to stop, the youth took another slow
> step forward. He was not attempting to escape; he was
> walking toward the soldier, walking slowly.

Ms. Mari' could not explain why Masarweh did not stop when ordered. But she said she did not believe he was threatening the soldiers or had any possibility of escaping.

After the third "*Waqqif!*" the soldier leaning over the wall shouted something — Ms. Mari' said it was "*Khudh!*" (Take this! in Arabic) — and fired one bullet at Masarweh. There were about fifteen meters between the two when he shot him.

> The youth fell. The soldier climbed over the wall and went up to him. One of the soldiers standing near me put his gun to my head and ordered me not to make a sound.

Soldiers then approached the body, pulled Masarweh's I.D. from his pocket, and called out his name to the surrounding troopers. At this point, Ms. Mari' said, the soldiers cheered and clapped. Soldiers then ordered Mr. Mari'[1] out of his small shop at the bottom of the yard. Mr. Mari', who said he was unable to see the killing from his shop, was told to identify the body lying in his back yard.

> I walked over and saw Abd al-Qader Masarweh lying on the ground. He had blood on his head. He was dead....There were about fifty soldiers in my back yard.

Masarweh's body was then taken from the yard by the soldiers. His father was summoned by the local Civil Administration office and informed of his son's death. Five days after the killing, the Civil Administration summoned him again to receive his son's body. The father said the body contained a bullet entry wound in the right temple and an exit wound in the left temple. The IDF provided no reply to Middle East Watch's request for information about the autopsy findings.

The Official Version

IDF sources cited in *Haaretz* the day after the incident stated that a military force engaged in an "initiated operation" in the refugee camp of Nur Shams encountered Abd al-Qader Masarweh, a "wanted" activist, and ordered him to stop. Masarweh ignored the command and attempted to escape. The soldiers opened fire, severely wounding Masarweh, who later died in the hospital. An article the same day in another daily, *Davar*, reported that Masarweh was killed by a special-force unit.

---

[1] Mr. Mari' declined to give his first name to Middle East Watch.

The IDF informed us in May 1993 that a legal opinion on the killing had still not been rendered by the office of the JAG. In December 1992, Deputy JAG Col. Yahav provided these interim findings:

> [D]uring the attempt to arrest him, the soldiers' presence was revealed and the deceased started to escape. He was warned then one of the soldiers tried to stop him by firing at his legs. Unfortunately it seems that due to conditions in the field, the soldier hit the deceased's upper body and killed him.

Analysis of the Official Version

Both the IDF and the sole known civilian eyewitness to the killing agree that Masarweh was not threatening the soldiers in any way when killed. But the witness disputes the official version that Masarweh was trying to escape when killed. Indeed, she suggests that he was shot while in the *de facto* custody of the large contingent of soldiers on the scene, after he had clearly abandoned his attempt to escape. Whether or not Masarweh's situation amounted to *de facto* custody, this killing represents at the very least another example of an unjustifiable killing within the framework of the orders to shoot fleeing suspects in the legs. The killing seems that much more deplorable in view of the large number of soldiers in the area, whose presence made it likely that Masarweh could have been captured alive had he attempted to flee.

Case 16: Ayman Muhammad Hussein Majadbeh

Age: 23
Date of incident: April 21, 1992
Place: Village of 'Allar, Tulkarm district, northern West Bank
Remarks: Armed at time of death.

Summary of Incident

Majadbeh had been on the GSS's "wanted" list for over a year, according to relatives, and was armed with a pistol when killed. He appears to have been shot by an IDF sharpshooter hidden in a vacant building some 150 meters from where he was walking. The soldiers, who were hiding and in no immediate danger, appear to have made no effort to arrest Majadbeh before shooting him dead.

Description of Incident

On August 27, 1992, a Middle East Watch researcher travelled to 'Allar and interviewed persons who witnessed the immediate aftermath of the killing.

According to residents of 'Allar, at approximately 11 a.m. on April 21, 1992, Majadbeh exited a friend's home and began to walk down the main street of the village. Villagers said Majadbeh had been "wanted" for over a year, and usually carried a pistol in his belt.

Neither Middle East Watch nor al-Haq, which investigated this killing separately, could find anyone who was watching Majadbeh shortly before and when the bullets struck him. There were, however, villagers who were on the scene moments after shots rang out.

Dr. H.,[2] a thirty-five-year-old physician, ran to the window of his clinic after hearing two shots. The window provides a view of the entire area, including the main street where Majadbeh had been walking. Dr. H. said he saw a body lying on the ground, near where the street levels out before it slopes uphill. The body was near an intersection. He said:

> Up the road from the intersection, I saw several soldiers
> coming out of a building that stands directly opposite my
> window. I don't know how many came out. They began
> to run down toward the intersection.

---

[2] Dr. H. requested that his name not be used in this report. His full name and identity card number are on file with Middle East Watch.

The building that Dr. H. mentions is clearly visible from his window, about 250 meters away as the crow flies. It is about 150 meters away from the intersection where the body lay.

After hearing the shots, Dr. H. said, a boy ran into his office and said that someone had been shot. Immediately, the doctor said:

> I rushed out of my clinic and ran toward the government clinic next door. It is on the way to the intersection where the body was lying. I called out to a nurse who works in the government clinic, and we ran together toward the body.

When Dr. H. reached the intersection he encountered soldiers dragging Majadbeh's body up the hill in the direction of the house from which they had emerged. "There were three soldiers dragging him," he said. "Two were in army clothes, while the other was wearing civilian clothes."

Dr. H. said he then approached the soldiers and explained in Hebrew that he was a physician and wanted to care for the wounded man. When they did not respond, Dr. H. recalled:

> I took out my doctor's identity card[3] and showed it to them. I was speaking in both Hebrew and English. They would not listen to me, then they shouted at me to go away. When I did not leave, they began to fire in the air to frighten me off. I left.

The doctor said he made one more attempt to assist Majadbeh. He returned to his office, got into his car and drove toward the soldiers, who had by then dragged Majadbeh up the street to the abandoned building:

> There were now about seven or eight soldiers standing around the body. The others had come out of the building. I again asked to be allowed to take care of the wounded person, whom I saw had blood all over his shirt.

---

[3] Palestinian doctors carry cards issued by their professional association.

The soldiers again denied Dr. H. permission to give Majadbeh first aid, fired in the air, and ordered him to leave the area. The doctor stepped back but kept in sight of the soldiers.

Ms. N.,[4] a thirty-six-year-old mother of ten, lives across from the abandoned building used by the soldiers. She said she too saw soldiers emerging from the building after the first shots were fired:

> I looked out of my window after I heard the shots. My window is directly across the street from the vacant building.[5] I saw two soldiers coming out of the door. One was wearing a white shirt and jeans. The other was wearing an army uniform.

> I watched them as they ran down the road. Several moments later they came back, dragging Ayman. I recognized Ayman, of course, he lived here in the village. They were dragging him by his arms, and his legs were flopping behind them on the ground.

Shortly after, Ms. N. said, a military jeep drove up to the front of the vacant building. Then the soldiers mounted the vehicle together with Majadbeh's body and exited the village.

Ziyad Majadbeh, Ayman's thirty-three-year-old brother, showed us a photograph[6] of his brother's body taken while being prepared for burial. There appeared to be two entry bullet wounds in the lower right-hand side of Majadbeh's back, just above his right hip. Ziyad Majadbeh said there were no exit wounds. The IDF did not respond to Middle East Watch's request for information about the autopsy findings.

Ziyad Majadbeh told Middle East Watch that during the four months prior to his brother's death, soldiers and GSS agents frequently searched the family's home for Ayman:

---

[4] Ms. N. refused to supply her name to the Middle East Watch researcher.

[5] The vacant building is owned by Faras Shadid, who said he was unaware that special forces had entered his property until the shooting started.

[6] A copy of this photograph is on file in the office of al-Haq in Ramallah.

In this last period they came often. They would break
things and yell at us. They threatened us, telling us that
we would be in trouble if we didn't make Ayman turn
himself in.

The Official Version

According to IDF sources cited in the Israeli daily *Davar* the day
after the shooting, soldiers confronted Majadbeh and called on him to
surrender. When he did not respond to the order, the reports said, the
soldiers shot and killed him.

Responding to Middle East Watch's questions eight months after
the killing took place, Deputy JAG Col. Yahav wrote:

The investigation to date suggests that the deceased was
suspected of carrying out dangerous crimes and
permanently carrying a firearm. During an attempt to
arrest him, the deceased was warned to stop and to give
himself up. The deceased did not respond to the warning
and began to flee. One of the soldiers fired a single shot
at his legs to stop him. Immediately after the shot, the
deceased appeared to draw a weapon. The soldier,
fearing for his life and the life of his comrades, fired an
additional shot. The deceased was wounded and died. A
search of the body revealed a pistol which was loaded and
cocked with a bullet in the breach.

In May 1993 the IDF informed us that a legal opinion on the killing had
still not been rendered by the office of the JAG.

Analysis of the Official Version

Deputy JAG Col. Yahav did not reply to Middle East Watch's
questions as to the location of the soldiers and their distance from
Majadbeh when they opened fire. If, as the testimony gathered by Middle
East Watch suggests, Majadbeh was killed by a sharpshooter from a
distance of some 150 meters, then the IDF's interim findings are

implausible. It is unlikely that the soldiers would have ordered Majadbeh
to halt, or aimed a bullet at his legs as he was walking: from a distance
of 150 meters, such measures would have given the long-sought suspect
too good a chance of escaping. (Moreover, at such a great distance, an
order to aim at the legs is meaningless.) Rather, it appears that the
soldiers made no effort to arrest Majadbeh, but rather, shot to kill on
sight.

**Case 17: Na'im abd as-Salaam al-Laham, Hajjaj Ibrahim Hajjaj, and
Imad Mahmoud Bisharat**

Ages: Al-Laham: 24, Hajjaj: 18, and Bisharat: 22
Date of incident: March 15, 1992
Place: Old 'Askar refugee camp, Nablus district, northern West Bank
Remarks: Al-Laham was armed when killed; the other two were not.

Summary of Incident

Special forces killed three youths, one or two of whom were
"wanted," after surprising them during a rooftop meeting of
approximately twelve youths. The youths attempted to flee, and were
met with automatic-weapon fire at close range. One of the youths was
armed with an assault rifle at the time, although the IDF has not claimed
that he attempted to open fire during the incident.

Description of Incident

On October 25, 1992, two Middle East Watch researchers
travelled to the Old 'Askar refugee camp, visited the scene of the killings
and interviewed residents who had witnessed the beginning and end of
the incident. However, the main witness to the killings declined to be
interviewed by Middle East Watch.

The testimony provided to Middle East Watch was consistent with
the findings of B'Tselem, presented in its report, *Activity of the Undercover
Units in the Occupied Territories*, and with the evidence collected by al-Haq.

According to witnesses' affidavits collected by al-Haq, the three youths were participating in a large gathering on the roof of a home. Mousa Khalil Erdaz, the fifty-one-year-old father of one of the youths who survived the clash, told Middle East Watch that there were about twelve youths on the roof, of whom five were "wanted" activists. (Among those who were killed, Bisharat and al-Laham were "wanted," B'Tselem reported. Others interviewed by al-Haq and Middle East Watch said they believed that only al-Laham was "wanted." By all accounts, al-Laham was armed with a rifle at the time of the incident.)

Witnesses told al-Haq that at approximately 1:25 p.m., camp residents noticed a number of persons dressed as Palestinians entering the camp, and identified them as special forces, alerting the participants at the meeting. But undercover soldiers had already taken up positions near the back of the house. Some of the persons on the roof descended via a staircase and managed to flee the area. Others tried to escape by jumping into the backyard from the five-meter-high roof. As they jumped, they were hit by automatic fire from special-force soldiers lying in wait below. Testimony gathered by B'Tselem indicates that the soldiers fired from a range of three meters.

The one known eyewitness to the fatal shootings is a woman who was inside the house at the time of the raid. When the shooting began she was beside a window underneath the spot from which the four youths had jumped. She gave the following account to al-Haq: looking out the window, she saw three special-force soldiers disguised as Palestinians concealed behind a fence in her yard. These "Palestinians" began shooting intensively in her general direction. She then saw four young men land on the ground in front of her bathroom window. She moved away from the window and heard many more bullets being fired. Hajjaj, one of the youths who had jumped, ran, wounded, into the house. As he entered, two more bullets were fired at him. Hajjaj collapsed into the arms of one of the residents of the house and died.

Both the woman and a youth who had remained on the roof told B'Tselem that they had heard no warning call shouted by the soldiers before the shooting began.

A photograph in B'Tselem's possession shows that the body of Hajjaj had at least five bullet wounds, two of which may be exit holes. The other two victims apparently died in the garden, according to testimony provided to al-Haq. Only one of the victims, al-Laham, was armed when killed. A photograph in B'Tselem's possession of al-Laham's body, shows at least six entry holes and two exit holes. B'Tselem also has a photograph of the third victim, Imad Bisharat, showing at least four bullet entry wounds. A fourth youth was injured but survived the incident.

The Official Version

B'Tselem followed the IDF's statements regarding the incident and detected serious contradictions between them (see pages 56-58 of *Activity of the Undercover Units*). The day of the incident, the Office of the Spokesman stated:

> The elite unit's force was operating in the Old 'Askar camp. The force identified a group comprising four terrorists....They called out to the terrorists to halt but the latter attempted to escape and opened fire at the soldiers. The soldiers returned automatic fire.[7]

On the day after the incident, the military commander of the Nablus region appeared on Israel Television and contradicted the assertion of the Spokesman's Office that the youths had fired at the special forces before being killed. "The terrorists did not have time to shoot," he said. "The force identified [a group of] four armed wanted persons. They jumped from the roof down to here, carrying their weapons, and when they jumped down, the force surprised them." The television program displayed weapons allegedly captured during the raid, which the announcer described as a Kalashnikov, a Samoval Russian machine gun, and a Carbine rifle. On March 17, "official military sources" quoted in the daily *Al Hamishmar* confirmed that the Palestinians had not fired at the soldiers, and that only one of the "terrorists" was holding a weapon in his hand when the soldiers opened fire.

In December 1992, the office of the IDF JAG stated that, according to the ongoing investigation, "The IDF force charged toward a terrorist squad, who according to earlier information was heavily armed and at the time of the incident one of the squad had an assault rifle which appeared to be a Kalashnikov (A.K. 47)." The account then concludes with allegations of past violent acts by al-Laham, but does not claim that the

---

[7] *Haaretz*, March 16, 1992.

killed activists were armed or threatening the lives of soldiers. In May 1993, the IDF reported that a legal opinion on the killing had still not been rendered by the office of the JAG.

Analysis of the Official Version

The testimony provided to al-Haq and B'Tselem suggests that undercover soldiers, acting on information that there were armed activists on the roof, shot to kill persons attempting to flee the roof without regard to whether they were armed or in a position to threaten the soldiers. It was likely, B'Tselem observed, that youths, even if armed, after jumping from a five-meter-high roof would not have been able to aim and shoot their weapons immediately. Thus, the soldiers were in an advantageous position and in no imminent mortal danger when they opened fire indiscriminately at the youths, killing three of them, only one of whom was carrying a firearm. In terms of the rules of engagement that Israel professes to uphold, two, if not all three, of the killings appear to have been unjustifiable.

Once the undercover soldiers were discovered and the youths began to flee, the operation apparently turned into a combat-style assault on the group. This impression is reinforced by the contradictions in IDF statements on the incident, which suggest an attitude that where "wanted" men and firearms are involved, the details of how the operation is then executed matter little.

***

In addition to the cases investigated by Middle East Watch, local human rights organizations have documented many cases in which "wanted" activists have been unjustifiably killed. One noteworthy case is that of Jamal Ghanem, twenty-three years old, who was shot dead in front of tens of witnesses by Border Police in a soccer stadium on March 22, 1992, in the town of Shweikeh, near Tulkarm, in the West Bank. Ghanem was unarmed when killed. According to B'Tselem:

> The [soccer] game was held in a stadium encircled by a concrete wall, on top of which there is a fence (approximately four meters high). The field is enclosed

by an additional fence two meters high, topped with
three barbed wires....There is one entrance to the
stadium.[8]

That entrance was used by plainclothes troopers to enter into the soccer
field, B'Tselem found. According to their report:

> Jamal Rashid Ghanem ... played on the Shweikeh team.
> During the second half of the game, when the Shweikeh
> team had a corner kick, and Jamal was exactly opposite
> the goalie, at a distance of approximately three meters,
> four persons in civilian dress entered the field.
> Immediately upon entering the field they drew large
> pistols and ran toward Ghanem.
>
> Ghanem tried to hide behind the referee, but the latter
> ran away and the four shot at Ghanem, according to the
> witnesses, without calling a warning and/or shooting at
> the legs. According to witnesses, Ghanem was shot when
> he was no less than fifty meters from the nearest exit
> from the field.

Members of Ghanem's family informed B'Tselem's researchers
that his body had two bullet wounds in his back and three in his chest. It
is possible that some of these were exit wounds, B'Tselem pointed out.

The Official Version

On May 1, 1992, Major General Danny Yatom, commander of
Israel's Central Command (which includes the West Bank), told the
"Yoman" program of Israel Television that soldiers had fired at Ghanem's
legs but that he had slipped and was hit in the upper body.[9] Gen. Yatom
also stated that Ghanem was running toward a hole in the fence when he
was shot.

---

[8] See B'Tselem, *Activity of the Undercover Units*, pp. 62-66.

[9] *Ibid.*, p. 66.

On August 12, 1992, *Haaretz* reported that police investigators had completed their investigation and recommended closing the file.[10] According to *Haaretz*, the investigators had concluded that the Border Police special forces had not deviated from the open-fire regulations governing the apprehension of fleeing suspects. They had followed each step of the procedure, first shouting a warning in Arabic, then firing in the air, and, only after he still appeared on his way to escaping through a hole in the fence, firing at his legs.

In a December 21, 1992 response to Middle East Watch's questions about the case, the Ministry of Justice described the investigation as follows:

[A]ccording to the Border Policemen's testimony, all the routine procedures for the arrest of a suspect were performed. The members of the...unit first shouted warnings to Ghanem and then fired shots into the air, at which point the suspect did not stop. Subsequently, two shots were fired toward the suspect's legs, but the suspect slipped in a puddle on the field and as a result was wounded in the back. The autopsy revealed that two bullets had entered into the lower back of the deceased. (See Appendix.)

The Justice Ministry repeated the assertion that Ghanem had fled toward a hole in the fence, but acknowledged that Palestinian eyewitnesses had argued otherwise. It stated that the Prosecutor for the Central District had ordered Israeli policemen to obtain statements from the witnesses who told B'Tselem there was no hole in the fence, "in order to clarify this issue and other questions regarding the circumstances of Ghanem's death."

In May 1993, the Justice Ministry informed Middle East Watch why it had decided to close the file. Its investigation, which it said included interviews with "several" Palestinian eyewitnesses, concluded that the Border Police had opened fire only after Ghanem had ignored orders to halt and warning shots, and continued to flee toward a portion of the

---

[10] Eitan Rabin, "Five Months after his Death the Police Has Stated: The Soccer Player Was Shot According to the Open-Fire Regulations," *Haaretz*, August 12, 1992.

wall that was low and without fencing on the top. The policeman had aimed at Ghanem's legs but Ghanem slipped in a puddle, causing the bullets to enter his upper torso rather than his legs. The Ministry wrote:

> In order for any officer to have been indicted in this case, the State Attorney's Office concluded that it would have had to have been proved that there was no possible escape route or that the officers did not follow the regulations for opening fire. Since no evidence was available to prove either, the file was closed due to lack of incriminating evidence.

Analysis of the Official Version

The official account conflicts with the testimony gathered by B'Tselem and al-Haq. The witnesses the organizations interviewed said Ghanem had no hope of escaping the field, and that he had not slipped or fallen shortly before he was shot. Not having investigated the case itself, Middle East Watch is not in a position to say which version is more persuasive. However, a few observations are in order:

The Justice Ministry did not mention how far Ghanem was from the possible egress when Border Police opened fire. B'Tselem's investigation concluded he was shot while still on the playing field and therefore not close to escaping. This raises doubts as to whether Border Police opened fire only as a last resort to prevent the escape, as the rules of engagement require.

The Justice Ministry states that Ghanem was hit by two bullets in the torso after he slipped. This raises the question whether the Border Police exercised the caution that the rules require before each use of a firearm. If Ghanem slipped and was then hit by a bullet in the upper body, why was a second bullet fired?

By all accounts, Ghanem was unarmed and posing no threat when he was gunned down. The questions that linger about the case underscore the impression that, at the very least, the rules for apprehending suspects are exceedingly difficult to police and effectively allow security forces to kill "wanted" persons rather than run the smallest risk that they will escape.

CHAPTER FOUR
OFFICIAL VERSUS UNOFFICIAL RULES

The IDF's Rules of Engagement in Judea, Samaria, and Gaza are in accordance with Israeli criminal law, with the rulings of the Supreme Court, and have been approved by the IDF Judge Advocate General and the Attorney General's Office....No one in the IDF has the authority to deviate from these regulations or to establish differing regulations for soldiers.
> -IDF Deputy JAG Col. David Yahav[1]

There was an unwritten set of practices that had no connection to the official procedures. The officers participated in it as well.
> -First Sgt. D.

Based on our case investigations, conversations with soldiers, and courtroom testimony, we believe that the following is a minimum statement of the parallel rules of engagement for troops engaged in the pursuit of targeted Palestinians:

1. **When encountering "wanted" activists,** undercover soldiers are permitted to shoot to kill the suspect with little or no warning, or if the suspect attempts to flee. Two concepts underpin this license to kill:

First, by classifying all "wanted" activists as extremely dangerous the IDF gives soldiers a pre-approved basis for shooting to kill them in "self-defense." Under these circumstances, soldiers can shoot and later claim without much difficulty that the suspect had made a "suspicious" move, even when it turns out the victim was unarmed and therefore had no rational motive for making suspicious moves. In at least four cases that Middle East Watch is aware of since December 1991, Palestinians who were neither "wanted" nor armed were killed after they were apparently mistaken for "wanted" Palestinians and, according to

---

[1] Letter from Col. Yahav to Middle East Watch, reprinted in Appendix.

authorities, appeared to threaten the soldiers (see the Khamayseh, Rahal, and Dihmes cases in Chapter Two and the Turkeman case, below). In a fifth case from October 1991, the IDF acknowledged killing a Palestinian in a case of mistaken identity.[2]

Second, the IDF places enormous emphasis on preventing the escape of "wanted" activists. Since the probability of escape is increased by obeying the official requirement that the soldier shout a warning, fire in the air, and then fire only at the legs, special-force soldiers are given a green light to aim at the torso or to abbreviate the warning procedure before opening fire, if that means removing even the slightest risk that the suspect will escape.

2. **When encountering masked activists,** undercover soldiers may shoot to kill when the suspect is among a group of masked persons that is sighted holding cold weapons and carrying out certain activities that are not life-threatening, such as manning roadblocks, participating in graffiti-writing, and ordering fellow Palestinians to observe political strikes. Such masked activists are sometimes killed before they are even given a chance to flee; more often they are shot dead while fleeing; in neither case are they shot while posing threats to the soldiers. In many of the cases discussed in Chapter Two, soldiers showed little effort to hit the suspects in the legs.

Three principal factors contribute to the kinds of unjustifiable killings described in Chapters Two and Three of this report:

(1) Written open-fire regulations that violate international standards by permitting soldiers to use lethal force against fleeing suspects even where there is no imminent threat to life.

(2) The great leeway special-force soldiers have to characterize encounters with "wanted" Palestinians as life-threatening and therefore warranting the use of lethal force under the open-fire regulations.

(3) Deviations from the written regulations that have become virtually institutionalized in the conduct of undercover units.

---

[2] The victim was 'Imad Nabil 'Atiq, from the West Bank village of Burqin. See B'Tselem, *Activity of the Undercover Units*, p. 20.

The first factor was analyzed in Chapter One. This chapter is devoted to the second and third factors. We present interviews with soldiers, press reports, court testimonies, and data from the case studies of Chapters Two and Three to show that the deviations have become so routine among soldiers pursuing "wanted" and masked activists that they form a kind of parallel set of rules of engagement. Undercover soldiers who violate the official rules but stay within the parallel rules when opening fire on "wanted" or masked activists are virtually assured of being cleared of wrongdoing.[3]

This and the following chapter trace the unofficial rules among special forces to:

• the training that special-force soldiers receive, which is more appropriate for combat than making arrests using minimum necessary force;

• oral orders given to soldiers by their superiors in pre-operational briefings that encourage them to use more force than is permitted in the official regulations;

• an aggressive hit-squad atmosphere within the units; and

• a lack of will among the IDF command to eliminate misconduct through strict orders, vigorous investigations, and appropriate punishments.

---

[3] In the two known cases of wrongful killings by undercover soldiers that led to courts-martial, the soldiers violated the unofficial rules or the practices surrounding them. In one case, the soldier violated both official and unofficial procedures by firing at a fleeing twelve-year-old boy. In the second case, the soldier followed unofficial rules by shooting at the torso of a fleeing suspect, but then violated the established routine of claiming to investigators that he had aimed at the legs. Instead, he admitted to aiming at the torso, saying this was a standing order in his unit. This claim led to the soldier's becoming a state witness in the court-martial of his commander. (See below.)

PREPARING FOR SPECIAL-FORCE MISSIONS

According to First Sgt. A., most special-force pinpointed missions against targeted Palestinians are initiated by the military commander of the area in which the operation is slated to take place, together with regional GSS operatives. The area commander typically summoned the commander of First Sgt. A.'s unit to inform him that the unit had been chosen for a certain operation. At this meeting, First Sgt. A. said, a GSS agent familiar with the area and with the "wanted" Palestinian was usually present. The GSS agent supplied the unit commander with the name, photograph, and description of the suspect and passed on other pertinent information. After the initial decision was reached to mount an operation, First Sgt. A. said, the regional commander and GSS agents usually left the operational details to the unit commander.

In the mission to assassinate a "wanted" Palestinian that was described by First Sgt. A. (see below), the unit commander described the target as a murderer with lots of blood on his hands, sketched the planned operation, and then assembled a team of soldiers to carry it out.

Several days before the operation, First Sgt. A. said, surveillance squads from the unit were sent out with GSS agents familiar with the area to survey the vicinity of the ambush. The surveillance squads took up positions in camouflaged observation posts, collected information on the movements of the "wanted" person, and chose the best spot for the ambush. During that time, participants in the ambush studied the photograph of the targeted suspect, prepared their equipment, and mastered the topography of the area.

First Sgt. B., who served in an administrative capacity in the Shimshon special unit in Gaza during late 1990 and early 1991, outlined a decision-making procedure similar to that described by First Sgt. A. First Sgt. B. said:

> The direct planning of these missions [all Shimshon missions] is done by the commander of the unit, the operations officer of the unit, and the commanders of the combat team involved. It is not planned by the regional commander of the brigade or of the division, although often these people are involved and make suggestions.

Other times, operations are requested by the "projector,"
the special Shimshon liaison with the regional division.
The "projector" sits in the Gaza Division headquarters
and will often come to the unit with requests [for
operations] from regional commanders.

First Sgt. A. said that in the ambushes in which he participated —
these, he stated, were not premeditated assassinations — soldiers lying in
wait were given the signal to challenge the suspect by GSS agents, who
were in contact with the commander of the ambushing force. According
to First Sgt. A.:

The GSS agents make a positive identification of the
person as he leaves the house and heads toward the path
where the ambush is waiting. They make sure it is the
right person and then tell the commander over the radio
that they have positive identification. In addition, our
own surveillance squads on the hill above the path
identify the "wanted" persons as they come toward the
ambush.

First Sgt. A. said that in ambushes he had participated in while in
southern Lebanon and the West Bank, night-vision equipment based on
thermal radiation was used to identify possible targets. The equipment
consists of a tripod-mounted scope which detects heat radiating from
living beings. Both thermal and starlight-based night vision equipment,
however, yield blurry images, even at close range. The ambushing force
sometimes uses searchlights or flashlights to make "final, positive
identification," First Sgt. A. said.

The way it usually works is that a GSS agent, who knows
the "wanted" person by sight, lies together with the
ambushing force. When they are in range, one of the
soldiers turns on a spotlight or a flashlight; the GSS
agent identifies the target and calls out "the one on the
right," or "the one on the left," etc.

According to First Sgt. A., there are some "wanted" activists whom
the GSS is eager to interrogate and is therefore eager to capture alive.

This instruction is passed along to the troops before the operation. In one such mission in a West Bank village, First Sgt. A. recalled:

> We were told prior to the operation that the GSS wanted the person alive. So when we went in, the soldiers did not fire a shot, even though the "wanted" person was armed with a pistol. They got him while he was lying in bed with the gun under his pillow.

EVIDENCE OF PREMEDITATED ASSASSINATIONS

It should be stressed that the IDF does not have, nor will it have a policy or a practice of killing "wanted" fugitives. IDF soldiers do not strike fugitives except in situations where they pose a threat to our forces, or during the procedure for apprehension of suspects — in which case the intention is to capture the suspect and not to kill him.

-IDF Spokesman[4]

Despite IDF denials, Middle East Watch believes that in at least a small number of cases, senior members of the security forces have targeted individual Palestinians for assassination. This belief is based upon evidence presented in this chapter, including our interview with First Sgt. A., quotations from other soldiers, as well as three cases presented in this report in which the circumstances strongly raise the possibility of premeditated killing (see below).

Although none of the evidence we offer is conclusive, we believe that cumulatively it is persuasive. Obviously, circumstantial evidence in killings may point to premeditation, but it is virtually impossible to rule out all plausible alternatives unless one obtains truthful testimony of premeditation from soldiers who participated in the preparation of the operation. In the three cases presented below, the possibility cannot be rejected that the decision to open fire was made on the basis of immediate circumstances, rather than in advance of the operation. We

---

[4] B'Tselem, *Activity of the Undercover Units*, p.116.

believe, however, that each case arouses strong suspicion that a decision
was made in advance to shoot to kill.

   The premeditation can be explicit or implicit. If, as this chapter
and Chapter One point out, soldiers are apparently permitted to shoot
without warning at anyone they identify as carrying a gun, and they are
told that a particular "wanted" individual carries a gun and is extremely
dangerous, then the distinction is slim indeed between such orders and
an order to shoot that individual on sight.

   First Sgt. A., who served in a combat capacity in an elite IDF
infantry unit, said it was common knowledge among his colleagues that
his unit as well as others carried out, on occasion, shoot-to-kill ambushes
of "wanted" Palestinians. He told us of one briefing in the winter of 1991-
1992 in which his unit commander informed fellow soldiers that their
unit had been ordered to carry out an assassination. According to First
Sgt. A.:

> Our unit commander called all the more experienced
> combat teams together and told us that the GSS had
> positively identified a "wanted" person, and that they
> wanted us to go for him. The guy was supposed to be a
> murderer. He had killed both Palestinian collaborators
> and Israeli soldiers. He was really dangerous, so we were
> not even going to try and arrest him. I guess also that
> the GSS was not really interested in interrogating him.

First Sgt. A. said that the assassination was to be carried out by
soldiers from his unit lying in ambush on a path near a village located in
the vicinity of the West Bank city of Nablus. According to First Sgt. A.:

> The unit commander said that we were going to lay an
> ambush and that the objective was to "stick" (לתקוע) the
> person. He said that we would send surveillance teams to
> the area for a day or two and that afterward, we would
> go in....

> To "stick" means to kill. There is no doubt about that.
> That is the term we use in Lebanon all the time. It
> means to shoot to kill. That is what everyone in the
> briefing room understood from the unit commander.

The unit commander, First Sgt. A. said, then told the assembled soldiers that anyone who did not wish to participate in the ambush would be excused. According to First Sgt. A., the unit commander was giving each soldier an opportunity to "follow his conscience." First Sgt. A. said:

> After the briefing, a few guys decided not to participate, including myself. I don't know how many decided not to go; I think maybe ten or fifteen. They only needed about fifteen soldiers anyway, so there were plenty to choose from.

After extensive preparations, some of which First Sgt. A. observed, the soldiers left the base to carry out the ambush. Upon the soldiers' return from the ambush, First Sgt. A. learned from his colleagues that they had killed the "wanted" activist.

The preparation, First Sgt. A. said, resembled preparations he had participated in for ambushes by his unit in southern Lebanon. He said they were more extensive than the preparations typically carried out before operations in the occupied territories whose aim was only to arrest "wanted" suspects. Each participant in the ambush knew in great detail his assigned position and role in the operation.

First Sgt. D., who served in the Gaza Strip, recalled a briefing by Maj. Gen. Matan Vilna'i, commander of the IDF's southern military region (which includes the occupied Gaza Strip), which supports First Sgt. A.'s contention that a small number of "wanted" suspects are targeted for death. First Sgt. D. told Middle East Watch that during his 1991 stint in one of the IDF's "territories companies" based in the Rafah refugee camp, Maj. Gen. Vilna'i addressed the company and spoke of a list of fifty "wanted" Palestinians in the Gaza Strip. The sergeant said Vilna'i "was talking about thirteen specific people, and said, I believe that if these thirteen people were to die the intifada would be over. At the least, we will have quiet for six months."

When we asked the IDF whether Maj. Gen. Vilna'i had made such statements, Deputy JAG Col. David Yahav said:

> [W]e completely deny that Major General Vilna'i ever made these remarks. An order has never been given to kill a man in place of arresting him. Any such order

directly contravenes the basic premises underlying the
State of Israel, legally and morally. (See Appendix.)

As stated above, there are two killings from 1992 that we
investigated and a third from December 1991, investigated by others, that
raise particular suspicion that they were premeditated, although we
cannot rule out other possibilities without learning the truth from the
soldiers involved:

Ra'ed abd ar-Rahman Dihmes (see Chapter Two): At dusk on
March 18, 1992, security forces ambushed a group of three Palestinian
men walking in a ravine toward their homes in the West Bank village of
Kufr Qadoum. The soldiers shot and killed Dihmes and wounded another
youth. None of the three men was armed or "wanted," and the two
survivors were not charged with any offense. It appears from IDF
statements that the soldiers were lying in wait for "wanted" men when the
confrontation occurred.
    It is of course conceivable that, as the IDF claims, the soldiers
fired only because in the fading daylight they mistook an object —
presumably a stick — one of the men was waving for a rifle. But this
explanation is suspect. The circumstances of this encounter favored the
soldiers more than nearly all of the other cases presented in this report.
They had set up their position well in advance, hiding behind large
boulders in a valley far from residential areas, where they could monitor
all approaches. They should have had time to observe whether a large
object that was being carried openly was a stick or a rifle. The fact that,
in spite of their advantageous position, the soldiers opened fire so quickly
at Palestinians some twelve meters away who turned out to be neither
"wanted" nor armed strongly suggests either that the killing was
premeditated or that the soldiers had in this case a license to kill.

Ayman Majadbeh (see Chapter Three): Majadbeh was "wanted"
by the authorities and was probably carrying a pistol at the time of his
death. Although we were unable to find any eyewitnesses to the actual
shooting, the testimony of persons who witnessed the aftermath made it
clear that he was probably shot without warning by an IDF sharpshooter
hiding at a distance of 150 meters.
    In answer to questions posed by Middle East Watch, Deputy JAG
Col. Yahav stated:

[Majadbeh] was warned to stop and to give himself up.
The deceased did not respond to the warning and began
to flee. One of the soldiers fired a single shot at his legs
to stop him. Immediately after the shot, the deceased
appeared to draw a weapon. The soldier, fearing for his
life and the life of his comrades, fired an additional shot.
The deceased was wounded and died. A search of the
body revealed a pistol which was loaded and cocked with
a bullet in the breach. (See Appendix.)

It is of course relevant in assessing the danger of the encounter
that Majadbeh was wanted for violent offenses and known to carry a
firearm, which may have been visible to the soldiers who spotted him.
But the strategy of deploying a sharpshooter from a great distance to
confront him raises questions about the intent of the mission. The main
witness interviewed by Middle East Watch, a Palestinian physician,
indicated that there were no other soldiers in the town except those who
were in hiding with the sharpshooter. (Middle East Watch asked the IDF
to specify the distance between the suspect and the soldiers who
confronted him but received no answer.) The physician also indicated to
us that he heard no warning shouted before shots were fired, and,
considering the great distance between the soldiers and the suspect,
shouting a warning would have entailed a perhaps unacceptable risk that
Majadbeh would have succeeded in running away if he had tried to do so.

Muhammad Muhannad Turkeman: The killing of Turkeman,
which was investigated by other human rights groups and by journalists,
also has the aura of a premeditated assassination. On December 10, 1991,
plainclothes security personnel shot and killed Turkeman as he sat in the
back seat of a taxi just north of the village of al-Zababdeh, near Jenin.
The personnel were members of the GSS, according to authorities.
Turkeman was neither armed nor on the "wanted" list at the time of his
death.

The Palestine Human Rights Information Center and *Haaretz*
reported that, according to the taxi driver, four plainclothesmen
approached the taxi when it had stopped, and then one of the four leaned

through the driver's window and shot three bullets at Turkeman, who was sitting in the back.[5]

The official versions of this killing were inconsistent on some details, but maintained that it was justified. Shortly after the incident, the authorities said that soldiers shot and killed Turkeman when he made a suspicious move after being ordered to stop. Sixteen days after the incident, however, the military stated that Turkeman was killed while sitting in a taxi, but said the car had attempted to flee when ordered to stop, and that Turkeman had put his hand in his pocket in a suspicious manner when it slowed down.[6]

The third statement, provided in December 1992 to Middle East Watch by the Ministry of Justice on the basis of the completed investigation, reported that Turkeman was killed while the taxi was stopped and being searched.

The Ministry of Justice stated that the file was closed on the grounds that the shooting was justified. (See Appendix.) The Ministry explained that roadblocks had been set up to capture an "armed terrorist" who had eluded capture during an IDF operation. "Information was received from reliable sources that the terrorist was a passenger in a local vehicle....A taxi with a number of passengers, among them Turkeman, stopped at one of the roadblocks and was searched by a member of the GSS who instructed those in the vehicle not to move." Turkeman, whom the GSS agent had incorrectly identified from a photograph as the "wanted" man, "suddenly inserted his hand into the inner pocket of his jacket. The GSS agent interpreted this act as an attempt to draw a weapon and, believing that he was in a life-threatening situation, he drew his gun and shot Turkeman, thereby killing him."

Although the Ministry acknowledged that the GSS agent had mistaken Turkeman's identity and that he was unarmed, it found that "in the unique circumstances of this case, the shooting was justified since the GSS man reasonably believed that he was in a life-threatening situation and as such had acted out of self-defense." This finding was based,

---

[5] PHRIC, "Targeting to Kill: Israel's Undercover Units," 1992, pp. 48-49; and Danny Rubinstein, "Sorry, We Shot the Wrong Person," *Haaretz*, January 25, 1992.

[6] Jon Immanuel, "Arab Was in Back Seat of Cab When Shot," *Jerusalem Post*, December 27, 1991.

according to the Ministry, on conclusive information that an "armed terrorist" was in the area and fleeing arrest; a remarkable physical resemblance between Turkeman and "the fugitive terrorist"; and Turkeman's sudden arm movement toward his pocket after having been warned not to move.

Although neither the driver nor any other witness whom Middle East Watch knows of was observing Turkeman during the seconds before he was shot, the official version seems improbable. It is difficult to understand why a father of four, who was neither armed nor "wanted," sitting in the rear of a taxi, would respond to the approach of four armed men by making a sudden arm movement that could be misconstrued as reaching for a gun.

Although the Justice Ministry did not name the activist for whom Turkeman was mistaken, it may have been a "wanted" man from the Jenin area whose name was also Muhammad Turkeman. The latter was arrested nearly one year later. On October 28, 1992, the IDF announced his capture and said he was one of two gunmen who had shot two Israeli settlers in the Jenin area earlier that week.[7]

THE PARALLEL PRACTICES: HOW SOLDIERS OPEN FIRE

As stated at the beginning of the chapter, the parallel rules of engagement are based on (1) excessive leeway in defining life-threatening situations and (2) taking liberties with the difficult-to-enforce rules for apprehending fleeing suspects.

Defining Life-Threatening Situations

Senior officers give soldiers pursuing targeted Palestinians broad discretion to define what constitutes a "life-threatening situation" in which they are permitted to open fire. Reserve First Lt. C., although not in a special-force unit, stressed the leeway that he felt he was granted when pursuing "wanted" activists:

---

[7] Jon Immanuel, "IDF Captures Suspect in Jenin Grocery Store Shooting," *Jerusalem Post*, October 29, 1992.

Theoretically, the orders we were given about shooting "wanted" people were on a relatively high moral plane. I myself received orders to arrest, rather than kill, a "wanted" person, unless I or my soldiers felt that the "wanted" person represented a threat to our lives. In practice, however, you do whatever you want and no one asks questions, especially if the person killed is "wanted."

First Sgt. A. said that the open-fire regulations with regard to "wanted" persons were never clearly spelled out to the soldiers in his unit:

The borders between making an arrest and killing someone are very thin. The issue of killing versus making an arrest is never seriously debated in the unit. No one pays the issue any attention....It is simply not something that people think about.

In general, regarding open fire orders, no one will come to you with complaints if you shot someone whom you thought was threatening you. No one will have you court-martialed. It is your judgment in the field....This is routine.

One senior officer in the West Bank told Israeli correspondents in a March 1992 off-the-record briefing that soldiers are ordered to open fire after they positively identify a "wanted" person. *Davar* correspondent Michal Sela, who was present at the briefing, noted that the case that the officer had been discussing involved a "wanted" person who was carrying a weapon but had not pointed it at soldiers. Sela continued:

Following several intermediate formulations, a reporter again asked, "If I see a "wanted" person, can I shoot? The senior officer replied, "Yes!"[8]

Sela related to us an incident described to her by an Israeli reservist who witnessed the incident in Bani Suheila, a village in the

---

[8] Michal Sela, "Yes and No," *Davar*, March 25, 1992.

southern Gaza Strip. The reservist, who requested that his name not be used, told Sela:

> The undercover forces were sitting in a local [i.e. Palestinian] car with a GSS agent. The GSS agent pointed out a "wanted" person in the street. The soldiers simply jumped out of the car and shot the guy dead, without warning him, without giving him a chance to surrender.[9]

The practice of shooting armed persons on sight without assessing the threat they pose was probably in place in some units long before the February 1992 change in the regulations. According to First Sgt. D., who served in Rafah refugee camp between 1989 and the autumn of 1991:

> The open-fire regulations, as I understood them, were that anyone who was armed, no matter whether it was with a knife, an axe, or a gun, was to die.

> Let me give you an example: Once, a masked person was holding a sword. He was standing about 100 meters away from me. I straight away shot at him, aiming to kill. I missed him, however, and he got away.

> Let me give you another example: In March of 1991, someone, I think it was a woman, tried to stab a soldier outside our base in Rafah. The soldier wore a protective vest, so the knife didn't penetrate. He hit her on the head with his rifle butt and then shot and killed her.

> My company commander often used this as an example of what we were supposed to do. He said that, "No matter what, anyone with a weapon has to die. Anyone with a knife, an axe, or a pistol, he should die. Automatically. I want to see you put a bullet through his mouth." Especially someone with a pistol. Even if he is

[9] Middle East Watch interview with Michal Sela in Jerusalem, July 16, 1992.

just carrying it in his belt. Are you kidding? An Arab with
a gun? He has to be killed immediately, on the spot.

Interpretations of the open-fire orders vary among units of the
security forces. According to First Sgt. A., soldiers in his unit knew that
they were required to wait until an armed person "made a move" before
shooting him dead. First Sgt. A. stated, however, that soldiers were
granted wide discretion in deciding what constituted a "threatening
move," and that no one would later second-guess their judgment.

Abuse of the Procedure for Apprehending a Suspect

The soldiers fired toward his legs in order to stop him.
The deceased was wounded and died.
                              -IDF Statement on killing of Mahmoud
                              Shalaldeh (Case Twelve)[10]

The case studies in this report indicate that, when pursuing
targeted activists, security forces frequently take liberties with the
procedure for apprehending fleeing suspects. The two warning stages are
often omitted or abbreviated, and bullets that are supposed to be aimed
at the legs all too often hit suspects in the back. These abuses are
particularly disturbing given the permissive nature of the official
regulations themselves, which permit soldiers to fire at fleeing suspects
who are posing no imminent danger to anyone. (See Chapter One.)

The virtual lack of accountability that surrounds the command to
fire only at the legs was illustrated by one of the few killing cases in
which the IDF said a plainclothes soldier had been disciplined for bad
aim. It was a case that attracted much attention, because it occurred in
broad daylight before dozens of witnesses in the relatively quiet and
affluent town of Ramallah, and because al-Haq published an extensive
report on it. On July 10, 1989, undercover soldiers chased "wanted"
suspect Yasir abu Ghosh, seventeen years old, through downtown
Ramallah. One of the soldiers fired at abu Ghosh as he ran down an
alley, hitting him with a bullet that, according to the autopsy, entered his

---

[10] Letter from Deputy JAG Col. Yahav to Middle East Watch, reprinted in
Appendix.

lower back and exited his chest. Witnesses claimed that the soldier had stopped and aimed his gun before shooting at close range. The soldier, according to the IDF, explained that he had aimed at the legs but the shaking caused by running had probably raised the gun, causing the bullet to land in the back.[11] The IDF's explanation of why only mild disciplinary action was appropriate illustrates the difficulty of holding soldiers to the requirement to aim at the legs:

> Due to the circumstances, and since opening fire was justified in the framework of the procedure for apprehending a suspect, and *since the only deviation was that the angle of the firing was apparently too high, and this is only a speculation, and since it is not possible to conclude exactly what happened,* and since the military advocate reviewed all the evidence and determined that there was no basis for charging the soldier with manslaughter or negligent homicide, he decided that it was sufficient to charge him with illegal use of arms [before an internal disciplinary court rather than in a court-martial].[12] (Emphasis added.)

There have been numerous incidents in which "wanted" or masked Palestinians have been fatally shot in what officials described as execution of the procedures for apprehending a fleeing suspect. This is hardly surprising, in view of the pressure felt by special forces to prevent the escape of targeted persons, the non-enforceability of the requirement to aim at the legs, and the relative ease of hitting the larger and slower-moving torso of the suspect.

Soldiers have in fact told Middle East Watch that the requirement to shoot at the legs of a fleeing suspect was treated as a legal fiction by their units. First Lt. C. said that in his experience, IDF soldiers routinely ignore the requirement to shoot at the legs:

---

[11] See Middle East Watch, *The Israeli Army and the Intifada*, pp. 205-207.

[12] Letter to B'Tselem, October 23, 1991. See B'Tselem, *Activity of the Undercover Units*, pp. 41-44.

Look, the whole thing is a joke. Even when you are using
a Galil rifle, which has a long barrel, the entire body of
the fleeing person fills the forward rifle sight when the
suspect is forty meters away. There is no way to aim at
the legs if the sight covers the body from the feet to the
head.

What everyone does is just fire to stop the person, and
then later, if necessary, say that they had fired at the legs
and missed. No one will give them any trouble for not
being a good shot.

First Sgt. B., who served in the Shimshon special force in an
administrative capacity, recounted one incident in which Shimshon
soldiers unjustifiably killed a Palestinian and then later claimed to CID
investigators that they had fired toward the legs:

It was in November or December [1990], right before the
Gulf war. It happened in the southeast section of the
[Gaza] Strip, near Bani Suheila.

A team [of Shimshon soldiers] was out in their car, and
were stopped at a roadblock by two masked persons.
When they jumped out of the car, one of the [masked
persons] ran away, and one of the soldiers, who is a very
good friend of mine, shot him with his pistol, and aimed
"at the center of the mass" [i.e., at the upper torso]. He
didn't hit him in the legs, he hit him in the back, and the
bullet went out through the stomach.

Afterward, in the debriefing, the team commander told
all of the team to lie and to say that the soldier had fired
at the legs, and that somehow he had hit him in the back.
I came into their room after the debriefing, and they
were talking about this. Some of them were pretty upset
at being told to lie. But when the CID investigators came
that night they lied.

In some units, the instruction to aim at the legs was abandoned completely. This emerged from the court-martial of Lt. Col. Ilan Rosenfeld, the former commander of the Gaza-based Shimshon special force. After one of the soldiers under his command killed a masked Gazan who was attempting to flee, manslaughter charges were filed against Lt. Col. Rosenfeld for having ordered his men to shoot fleeing masked persons in the upper body if they failed to hit their legs. In effect, Lt. Col. Rosenfeld was charged with having created a fourth, illegal stage in the procedure for apprehending fleeing suspects.

In the incident that led to the trial, Lt. Shahar Kanin killed twenty-four-year-old Maher Muhammad abu Qdama in al-Bureij refugee camp in the Gaza Strip in May 1989. Lt. Kanin became the prosecution's key witness against Lt. Col. Rosenfeld, testifying that Lt. Col. Rosenfeld had ordered all Shimshon officers and soldiers to shoot at the upper torso of fleeing masked suspects if shots fired at the legs failed to stop the escape. Other soldiers testified that it was common practice within the Shimshon special force to shoot to kill fleeing suspects.

The court-martial of Lt. Col. Rosenfeld ran from the autumn of 1991 into early 1992. During the October 22 session, first sergeants Eli Idud, Ya'akov Ben Nun, and Rafi Green all told the court that when they had heard the order to "fire at the center of the mass" of fleeing masked suspects they were not surprised because they were intuitively familiar with this procedure from the "anti-terror" course they had taken. They said the practice of shooting toward the "center of the mass" of fleeing suspects was widely used by Shimshon soldiers.

Soldiers who served in Shimshon when the illegal orders were in effect told the court they were frequently ordered simply to "shoot in an effort to stop" masked suspects who fled. The soldiers said they understood this order as an instruction to fire toward the "center of the mass."

Lt. Kanin killed abu Qdama with a Belgian-made Fabrique National (FN) 9mm pistol, which is standard issue for the undercover special forces. The effective, accurate range (i.e., the range at which the shooter can reasonably expect to hit the target) of the FN 9mm pistol is no more than twenty-five meters. Before shooting at the upper part of abu Qdama's torso, Lt. Kanin testified, he first fired several bullets toward abu Qdama's legs from a distance of fifty to seventy meters during a prolonged chase on foot.

In their summation, the military judges expressed surprise that IDF regulations did not specify a maximum distance from which soldiers were permitted to fire at the legs of fleeing suspects. The judges remarked:

> Hitting [the legs] at a range of fifty meters in the circumstances of the incident [Lt. Kanin's shooting of abu Qdama] required an extremely high level of marksmanship, if not a miracle.[13]

During the trial, presiding judge Col. Nili Peled asked:

> How do they expect that a soldier can accurately hit at a range of sixty meters, after an exhausting 300-meter-long dash while the soldier is aiming at the legs, when it is impossible to hit accurately at that range? So the commander of the forces said that he was simply following the procedure, and that's it. Why did no one draw attention to this?[14]

In their summation, the judges suggested that official regulations in effect granted soldiers a license to kill by permitting them to continue firing at the legs of fleeing suspects regardless of whether there was a realistic chance of hitting the legs:

> [I]t appears to us that this order [to shoot at the legs of fleeing suspects] must be limited in accordance with a realistic estimate by the person firing that he is able [accurately] to hit [the legs]...it appears to us that there was inadequate consideration of the significance of the order as it was understood, or liable to be understood, by the persons receiving the order — especially against the background of the soldierly approach that one shoots in

---

[13] Special Military Court file 2/91, ruling of the court, p. 6.

[14] "The Judge: How Does One Do Such An Idiotic Thing?...." *Haaretz*, January 8, 1992.

order to kill — that the order might be permission to kill.[15]

The judges said that Lt. Col. Rosenfeld's order to carry out a fourth stage of the procedure for apprehending suspects was influenced by the attitude of senior officers toward masked persons. In a key meeting between Brigade Commander Brig. Gen. Zvi Poleg and Lt. Col. Rosenfeld:

> The brigade commander insisted upon the crucial importance of catching masked persons, even to the point where...[senior officers preferred that soldiers] catch more masked persons by shooting them in the legs than catching a smaller number without causing injuries.[16]

The judges noted the difficulty of enforcing the IDF's shoot-at-the-legs policy:

> [A]s the range increases, it is more difficult to be accurate. No one asks and no one investigates after the fact where exactly the soldier who did the shooting was aiming. Even if he is asked, the soldier will reply that he did what the written orders say.[17]

Brig. Gen. Meir Dagan, an advisor to the IDF Chief of Staff on issues relating to the Palestinian uprising, testified to the court that the IDF had decided not to limit the range at which soldiers could open fire during the procedure for apprehending suspects:

> We did not set for ourselves a limit, we did not say that you are not permitted to fire at a range of sixty meters. If we were to set such a limit, we would create an

---

[15] Special Military Court file 2/91, ruling of the court, p. 8.

[16] Ibid.

[17] Ibid.

> operational problem for the IDF, since they, the Arabs, draw conclusions from our actions. If they know that we only fire at their legs and that at certain distances we don't even fire at all, an impossible reality would be created from our point of view.[18]

On July 2, 1992, the military court found Lt. Col. Rosenfeld guilty of negligence and five days later gave him a one-month suspended sentence. After the military prosecutor appealed the punishment as too light, the court on November 26, 1992 increased it by demoting Lt. Col. Rosenfeld one rank to major. (See Chapter Five.)

In February 1993, Lt. Col. Rosenfeld appealed his conviction to the Israeli High Court of Justice. According to press reports, he claimed in his appeal that the Military Prosecutor's office has collected files but not acted on many cases from 1988 to 1990 in which undercover soldiers shot at the upper bodies of fleeing suspects. He claims that these cases indicate that other undercover units also used an unofficial fourth stage in the procedure.[19]

The court-martial was a welcome recognition by Israel that officers should be held accountable when they give illegal commands to soldiers. It also provided a healthy exposure to public scrutiny of what happens to the official regulations under field conditions. Regrettably, the principle of accountability was undermined by the light sentence handed to Lt. Col. Rosenfeld, whose illegal orders were indirectly responsible for homicide.

In October 1992, Deputy JAG Col. Yahav told Middle East Watch that limits had been imposed on the range from which soldiers were permitted to shoot at fleeing suspects. He refused, however, to specify the range, saying that it was classified information.

Despite these supposed limits and the conviction in the Shimshon trial, fleeing suspects, including both "wanted" and masked activists,

---

[18] Eytan Rabin, "Brig. Gen. Dagan Testifies in the Trial of the 'Shimshon' Commander: 'We Did Not Limit the Range of Shooting,'" *Haaretz*, February 3, 1992.

[19] Hadas Manor and On Levin, "The Former Head of Shimshon: The IDF Prosecutor's Office Is Keeping Hidden Files Dealing with the Shooting of Wanted People," *Maariv*, February 7, 1993.

continued to be killed by bullets in the upper body in late 1992 and early 1993, as this report documents. Since the Shimshon trial, not one special-force soldier has been prosecuted for having aimed above the legs, although one who fatally wounded a twelve-year-old suspect was convicted for violating the rules against firing at fleeing suspects who are under fourteen. (The soldier's claim that he had aimed at the suspect's legs was not rejected by the court, even though he hit him in the back at close range. See the case of Amjad Jabbar, Chapter Two.)

Abbreviating the Procedure for Apprehending a Suspect

The IDF open-fire regulations permit soldiers in certain situations to bypass the three-step procedure to be used while attempting an arrest, and to open fire without warning. While the IDF confirmed to Middle East Watch the existence of an "abbreviated procedure," it has declined to divulge when it may be used and how it works. (See Chapter One.)

In practice, some form of abbreviated procedure appears commonplace. In very few of the cases investigated by Middle East Watch did witnesses report that the soldiers had fired at the victim only after shouting a warning and firing into the air. As long as the IDF does not disclose its rules on the abbreviated procedure, it is not possible to know in which of these incidents soldiers followed their rules. But the IDF's approval, whether explicit or tacit, of abridgements of the three-step procedure, when viewed in conjunction with the regulations on shooting at the legs, amounts to a shoot-on-sight policy that often results in death or serious injury.

Soldiers told Middle East Watch that with regard to "wanted" or masked activists, their units had been shortening the three-step procedure as early as 1989. First Lt. C. told Middle East Watch that the rationale for doing so was that the full procedure was too time-consuming:

By the time you shouted the warning in Arabic and fired in the air, the masked people are gone. If your aim is to stop them from escaping, it is absolutely counter-productive to go through the full, three-stage procedure for apprehending a suspect. It is simply too cumbersome.

What I and others would do is order one soldier to yell,
"Stop or I'll shoot!" I would order a second soldier to fire
in the air, if we even bothered with that. Then I would
take the best shot in the patrol and tell him to shoot
toward the suspect to stop him from escaping.

If we encountered a suspect — usually a masked person
— all three would do what they were supposed to do at
the same time. That way no one could say that he didn't
hear a warning shout or didn't see a shot fired into the
air.

After all, if you look at the official orders, they don't
specify how long you need to wait between each stage in
the procedure; as far as the official orders are concerned,
you can perform all three almost at the same time.

According to First Sgt. D., in late 1989 and 1990, soldiers in his
unit used a shortened procedure against masked activists:

There was a period when all masked people were to be
shot on sight. Yes, we were supposed to use the
procedure, but you can't hope to catch anyone if you
waste time yelling and shooting in the air. You simply
shot at them.

Later, they said that you needed a reasonable suspicion
that they had done something wrong. That usually meant
if they had a knife, an axe or a sword. If they had one of
these things you simply opened fire.

First Sgt. D. described an ambush in late 1989 or early 1990 in
which a masked Palestinian painting graffiti on a wall in Rafah refugee
camp was shot dead.

Right across from a school in the camp was a big white
wall which was usually painted on at night by masked
Arabs. So we were ordered to lay an ambush there and
catch them. One group of six [soldiers] would lie inside

the school, about fifty meters away from the wall.
Another group of three or four would be at the entrance
of the school, ready to run out and catch someone.

[Our orders were:] Everyone who walked along the wall
was to be fired on. They said to do the procedure for
stopping a suspect, but as I told you, we didn't really do
that. We were told, "The supreme goal is to stop the
person." ....We understood this to mean to shoot straight
away.

The way it worked in practice, however, was that the
group of six waited with a rifle fitted with a nightscope.
The minute the masked people appeared, the sniper was
supposed to shoot. I guess the sniper was told to shoot
directly at the legs, but you can't really aim at the legs
through a nightscope from a distance of fifty meters.

I lay in the ambush for several nights but they never
came. The night I didn't go out, I was in the
communications room. We heard over the radio that
there was shooting. Then the commander of the ambush
radioed in and said, "Receive we knocked one." (אחד
קבל רפקנו) We went out to collect the body. Later, they
told me that they had shot the masked person straight
off. They didn't tell that to the battalion commander,
however. They told him that they had "followed the
procedure." (For more details of the case, see Chapter
Five.)

**Israeli Witnesses Claim Soldiers Fired Without Warning on Graffiti
Writers**

On April 20, 1992, an Israeli couple witnessed by chance a
special-force unit opening fire on two graffiti-writers without warning.
The shooting of seventeen-year-old Mahmoud Fawzi Abd al-Latif and
nineteen-year-old Atef Mahmoud Kazaz was one of the very few during

the intifada that had eyewitnesses in addition to Palestinians and the
special-force soldiers themselves.

David Elimelech and his wife were visiting Mousa ar-Rajib, Mr.
Elimelech's partner in a small construction firm, at his home in the
southern West Bank village of Dura. Mr. Elimelech described the incident
to B'Tselem:

> At about 8:30 in the evening we sat on the veranda of
> [ar-Rajib's] house, around a table....Then one of the
> children sitting next to me said, "Look what's going on
> outside!"

> I turned my head and saw two masked persons. They
> were walking in the street below....They stopped near the
> wall across from where we were sitting and began to
> write slogans. They didn't have weapons....They were
> about ten meters away from us. The entire area was lit
> up with street lights, it was like daylight.

> Then I saw a Peugeot 305 with a blue license plate [i.e.
> West Bank Palestinian plates] draw up to their right,
> coming from the access road to the village. It stopped
> about six or seven meters from them.

> Immediately after it stopped, three men got out with
> guns. They were dressed as civilians and were masked.
> They ran until they were about two to three meters from
> the graffiti writers and opened fire, directly. It sounded
> like a burst [of automatic fire]. They shot straight away,
> without warning, without anything.

> They shot the masked people from behind, while their
> faces [of the masked persons] were facing toward the
> wall. They [the masked youths] did not turn around
> when the car came up, since other cars had passed by
> right beforehand.

> The two fell down on the ground. One of them cried out
> "*Ya ba!*" [Arabic cry of distress] Then one of the armed

men came and kicked him in the stomach. He stopped crying. I was as if paralyzed. I thought Arabs were shooting Arabs, and I thought they would shoot us as well.

Then my partner went down to the street....I heard him asking them, "Who are you?" They said, "Army."[20]

Several moments later, uniformed soldiers appeared on the scene. David Elimelech told B'Tselem that he confronted a uniformed army major, who ordered him to shut up, cursed him and his wife, and hit his Palestinian partner several times with the butt of his rifle.[21]

It is revealing to trace the shooting's aftermath for the soldiers, the masked youths and Mr. Elimelech. Regarding the soldiers, the IDF claimed to have opened an investigation. An inquiry had been requested by the Association for Civil Rights in Israel (ACRI) in a letter of April 29, 1992 to the IDF JAG. On May 22, the JAG replied that he had ordered an investigation. He wrote again on December 18, saying that the investigation had been completed and the file had been forwarded to the regional military prosecutor for consideration. He said that ACRI would be informed when a decision was taken. However, as of June 1, 1993 — more than one year after the shooting — ACRI staff attorney Eliahu Avram said that the organization had received no further information despite having sent letters to the IDF requesting updates.

Maariv journalist Avi Raz kept track of what happened to the victims of the shooting.[22] Although their alleged offense was presumably grave enough to justify their being shot, it took the army ten days to arrest Atef Kazaz and fourteen days to arrest Mahmoud al-Latif.

---

[20] Interview with B'Tselem, April 27, 1992. See also, "Israeli Couple Disputes Army Account of Shooting," *The New York Times*, April 22, 1992; and Susan Sachs, "Shooting First? Secret Israeli Occupation Units Target Arabs, Stir Outcry," *New York Newsday*, April 29, 1992.

[21] According to testimony taken by B'Tselem from Sahar Mousa ar-Rajib on April 26, soldiers returned the day after the incident, ordered her husband into the street, and then beat him, breaking his nose and causing other injuries.

[22] Avi Raz, "A Lesson In Truthfulness," *Maariv*, June 6, 1992.

Both were picked up after their release from hospitals, where neither had been under guard, *Maariv* reported.

On May 11, the two youths were brought to a military court in Hebron. The charge — "writing slogans and activity against public order" — and the prison sentence — eight days for one and eleven for the other, which matched the time they had already spent behind bars — suggest the court did not consider the youths to be serious offenders. Their treatment casts doubt on the army's initial claim that they had been shot only after threatening the soldiers with a metal chain after being ordered to surrender.

Raz concluded that "the press attention led to the persons' trial," suggesting that the only reason the youths were arrested or tried was to justify the shooting. Another journalist, Reuven Pedatzur of *Haaretz*, said he examined the IDF's file on the case and concluded that special-force soldiers routinely shot masked persons regardless of whether they had actually committed significant offenses. Pedatzur criticized what he termed this "new norm," asking:

> [S]ince when has writing slogans become a crime whose punishment is to be shot? It was clear to the officer [involved in the shooting incident] that the masked persons were not committing any crime other than writing slogans on the wall.[23]

David Elimelech was himself subjected to a criminal investigation. Police questioned him shortly after the incident, releasing him on a personal bond of 3,000 shekels (U.S. $1,100). On July 22, a newspaper reported that the police intended to bring charges against him for interfering with and insulting soldiers in the line of duty. Four months later, the State Attorney stated that Elimelech would not be prosecuted.

ATMOSPHERE WITHIN THE SPECIAL FORCES: TARGETED PERSONS WANTED DEAD OR ALIVE

Some U.S. experts on law enforcement have argued that the most effective safeguard against police excesses is swift and strict anti-abuse

---

[23] Reuven Pedatzur, "A Black Flag At Dura," *Haaretz*, May 4, 1992.

discipline imposed by officers on their subordinates. According to this school of thought, strict internal discipline is more effective than external oversight, anti-abuse legislation, or the criminal prosecution of abusive personnel.

Middle East Watch's 1990 report, *The Israeli Army and the Intifada*, charged that the IDF command, and by extension the Israeli government, lacked "the will to hold soldiers fully accountable for misconduct toward the population of the occupied territories" (p. 24). This failure, in effect, meant that authorities were condoning the abuses.

This conclusion even more aptly describes the official response to routine deviations from the official open-fire regulations that are committed by special-force soldiers when pursuing "wanted" or masked activists. Out of more than 120 killings by undercover forces to date, only two have led to courts-martial and one to a successful civil suit against the IDF. There are no indications that internal disciplinary measures within the special forces have significantly curtailed their abusive practices.

The atmosphere within the special forces is hardly conducive to the exercise of restraint. Rather, it is one of intense pressure to catch up with activists on the "wanted" list, and after all of the preparations and the lying in wait, not to let them get away. Little stress is placed on achieving this goal using the minimum degree of force necessary. According to some soldiers, the pressure translates into a not-so subtle and sometimes blatant dispensation to shoot to kill.

According to First Sgt. D., the tone was set by the commander of the IDF's southern military region (which includes the Gaza Strip), Maj. Gen. Matan Vilna'i. First Sgt. D. told Middle East Watch that he had attended a briefing in which Maj. Gen. Vilna'i named thirteen "wanted" persons and said the region would become quiet if these men were to die. (The IDF categorically denied the remarks attributed to Vilna'i. See Appendix.) First Sgt. D. stated that killing these thirteen persons became "an obsession":

> Their pictures were posted in the dining room, the briefing room, in the operations room....It was known that they were wanted dead or alive....At the nightly briefings, we were always told that these thirteen men had to die. The officers all said, "Keep your eyes open and kill them." My own company commander, L., said this to us many times.

First Sgt. D., not himself a member of a special-force unit, did not participate in the plans that were laid to find these thirteen "wanted" men. However, his platoon was assigned the auxiliary task of raiding the homes of "wanted" activists. Although the soldiers rarely found the activists at home, the raids were aimed at keeping them off-balance.

In one such raid in 1991, however, First Sgt. D, accompanied by two senior officers, did encounter a "wanted" activist. He recalled:

> I went with the commander in charge of Rafah camp and with my company commander to a "wanted" person's house. While the officers were standing near the house, someone jumped over the wall of a house into the main road. He was more than 100 meters away from us.
>
> A., who was standing next to me, immediately took aim and fired. He hit the guy in the back of the head, near the neck. A. had no idea who the person was and did not shout a warning or go through any of the official procedures for apprehending a suspect. He simply took aim and shot to kill.
>
> The commanders who were with us ran over to the body and turned it over. They saw that it was a dangerous "wanted" person. That evening, the battalion commander told A. he was lucky to have killed the right person, since he had not fired according to the regulations.

First Sgt. D. related that the regional commander sent his company a bottle of champagne to celebrate the killing, his custom whenever a "wanted" activist was killed or captured in the Rafah area. He said, "There was champagne in the office every time that a 'wanted' person was killed. We had five bottles during the time that I was a sergeant" [i.e., between January and October of 1991].

At the other end of the occupied territories, the city of Jenin and its environs are known to harbor many "wanted" activists. The area has also experienced a relatively high number of special-force killings, including Cases Three, Eight, and Nine in Chapter Two, and Case Fourteen in Chapter Three.

One of the special forces active in the Jenin area is the Border Police's Yamas. The atmosphere surrounding the Yamas force in Jenin was described by First Lt. C., who did a one-month tour of reserve duty in Jenin during April 1992. First Lt. C. said that the Jenin brigade's intelligence officer, who was responsible for coordinating the activities of special forces with those of the GSS, kept a large chart on the wall of his office on which he posted the names and photographs of "wanted" Palestinians slain or captured in the Jenin area since the beginning of 1992. First Lt. C. recalled:

> When a "wanted" person is arrested or killed, his page is torn out of the "wanted" persons booklet and pasted up on the chart. The ones who have been killed have big X's and something that looks like crossed swords over their picture.   The ones who were arrested have little handcuffs drawn under their pictures. Each kill has the name of the unit that did it and the date of the killing underneath. It was as though they were giving credit to the units that carried out the killing.

> I think that when I was there, there were twenty pictures up on the board, of both killed and arrested, which represents everyone taken out of the booklet since the beginning of the year [1992].

The cumulative effect of the manhunt atmosphere among officers within the Jenin regional headquarters, First Lt. C. said, was to create an atmosphere of "חיסול," a term meaning "elimination" or "liquidation."[24]

PRESSURE FOR QUICK RESULTS

Within the special forces, pressure is high to reduce the number of "wanted" and masked activists at large. This pressure originates with

---

[24] The Hebrew term חיסול (*hisul*) has violent connotations, such as when it is used idiomatically to refer to a gangster rub-out. However, it could also conceivably refer to "eliminating" a person in the sense of placing him in custody.

top IDF commanders and political leaders and has filtered down through the command structure to the special forces and the regional commands. This pressure was evoked during in the court-martial of Lt. Col. Rosenfeld. The presiding military judges remarked in their summation that IDF officers as senior as Brig. Gen. Zvi Poleg, military commander of the Gaza Strip[25] "stressed the importance of catching masked persons. They [the senior officers] even stated that it was preferable to catch more masked persons by wounding them in the legs than not catching them and leaving them unharmed."

The prevailing attitude of the commanders was characterized even more severely by "Yossi," a Shimshon enlisted trooper who testified at the trial. Speaking outside the courtroom to an Israeli journalist, "Yossi" alleged that Brig. Gen. Poleg had informed Shimshon soldiers "that he wanted to see more people wounded, and that out of each one of our operations [against masked persons] only one of them [masked activists] should remain [unwounded], so that this one could run and tell the rest of the guys [other activists] what had happened."[26]

In their summation, the judges also questioned the claim of senior officers that they had a "high regard" for the lives of masked activists. They expressed disquiet at "the reactions of the entire IDF high command, from the accused [i.e. the commander of the Shimshon unit] all the way up to the commander of the Southern Region....[E]ven though the operation ended in the taking of a human life, this did not prevent the commanders from treating the entire operation as a huge success."

Judge Peled noted that Lt. Kanin, the officer who unjustifiably shot dead the fleeing masked suspect,

> was considered a hero. No one ever asked him how he
> even dared to fire at such a distance....Why did no one

---

[25] Brig. Gen. Poleg commanded the Gaza Strip regional division at the time of the incident. The Gaza division includes all Gazan regional brigades, such as the Rafah brigade and the Gaza City brigade.

[26] Aviv Lavi, "Shimshonites Speak," *Kol Ha'ir*, March 13, 1992. "Yossi" spoke to the journalist on condition of anonymity.

say to him, "Why did you do such an idiotic thing?" After all, we are speaking about danger to human life.[27]

First Sgt. A. told Middle East Watch that in his elite infantry unit,

They are concerned only with professionalism. If you shoot well and run fast, you are respected....People do not have any notion of the value of human life. It is simply not something that anyone thinks about.

Investigative journalist Ariela Ringel-Hoffman of *Yediot Aharonot* interviewed a number of special-force soldiers and officers. She told Middle East Watch:

There is a sense of great pressure on these units to produce results. There is a desire to get as many of the "wanted" persons out of the field as possible. The army is entirely devoted to this now....Most of the attention is now focused on getting the individual "wanted" persons, what they term the "hard core" of the intifada. This category also includes some of the masked people.

The cumulative effect of this pressure, Ringel-Hoffman stated, "is a feeling that the 'wanted' person should be brought in at all costs; if a 'wanted' person escapes, the mission is a total failure. In a sense, it is better to kill the 'wanted' person than to let him escape."

In its report on the IDF's special forces, B'Tselem concluded, partly on the basis of interviews with unnamed IDF reservists, that the special forces operate in

an atmosphere which justifies fatal shooting by undercover units in general, and shooting at *wanted* persons in particular...In the zeal to capture *wanted*

---

[27] "The Judge: How Does One Do Such an Idiotic Thing?...." *Haaretz*, January 8, 1992.

persons, deviations from the official orders are understood as an unavoidable necessity.[28]

TRAINING

The actions of the special forces in the occupied territories are influenced by the instincts and ideology they absorb during their twelve- to fifteen-month training programs, according to soldiers and Israeli journalists who have investigated the special forces. There is, in our view, a fundamental incongruity between that training and the stated mission of the special forces. The stated mission is to apprehend suspects using the minimum force necessary; they adhere to rules of engagement that permit firing only in life-threatening situations or to apprehend a fleeing "dangerous" suspect (see Chapter One).

However, the training they are given is heavily combat-oriented and therefore at odds with their professed law-enforcement objectives. Little stress is laid on using the minimum force necessary to achieve their objectives, according to soldiers and Israeli journalists familiar with how the special forces are trained. Rather, as combat soldiers, they are instructed in using the maximum amount of force in the shortest possible time in order to eliminate any potential threat they encounter.[29]

The thrust of the preparation that special forces receive, like combat training worldwide, is to kill their enemies efficiently and quickly, while minimizing the real or perceived threats to their own lives. This training contrasts with that given in police academies in Western countries and in Israel itself. Although the practice is sometimes at variance with the training, police are taught that they are public servants who must respect the lives, property and rights of the members of the public.

Given Israeli officials' characterization of the ongoing offensive against "wanted" and masked Palestinians as a police, rather than a combat operation, it is reasonable to expect that special forces would be trained in law-enforcement techniques and philosophies. The need for

---

[28] B'Tselem, *Activity of the Undercover Units*, p. 79.

[29] The combat emphasis of their training is conveyed in a recent British Channel 4 documentary, *The Samson Unit*, released in April 1993.

police training is even more acute given that special forces in the occupied territories frequently disguise themselves to infiltrate crowded civilian areas.

To the best of our knowledge, however, the Israeli special forces receive little police-style training. According to First Sgt. B., who served in the Gaza-based Shimshon unit, Shimshon trainees never receive instruction from officers of the Israel Police. All of Shimshon's twelve- to fifteen-month training program is given by military instructors and is exclusively directed toward breeding aggressive, combat-oriented soldiers. The only non-military training the full-time special forces receive, First Sgt. B. said, is from civilian automobile instructors, who teach special-force drivers how to drive at high speeds; from psychological counselors, who help the special forces deal with stress; and from actors, who train them in techniques of disguise.

It is appropriate for special-force soldiers to undergo special training in the use of firearms. Many "wanted" activists carry arms and would clearly use them against the soldiers. As of June 15, 1993, Palestinian activists have killed at least six soldiers as they were engaged in the pursuit of "wanted" persons, according to our monitoring of press accounts (officials did not provide us with their count for this particular statistic).

However, it bears repeating that contrary to the image stressed by Israeli officials, a significant portion of the operations of the special forces have nothing to do with the pursuit of armed and dangerous "wanted" persons. They are frequently engaged in often-fatal ambushes of masked youths who are not carrying guns and whose identities are not known when confronted. If the training of special forces is excessively combat-oriented for the purported task of arresting fugitives who may be armed, it is wildly inappropriate for the task of arresting masked youths who are armed with at most a cold weapon.

According to First Sgt. B., the Shimshon unit's training includes the following:

A. Four and a half months of infantry basic training at the "Adam facility" training base just north of the Tel Aviv-Jerusalem highway. The "Adam facility" is used by all special forces as well as many of the part-time special-force units discussed in this report. The training given to recruits at this facility is similar to that supplied to most elite infantry units in the IDF.

B. Six weeks in the "anti-terror" training school at the "Adam facility."
One of the primary objectives of this course is to cultivate aggressiveness in the trainees. In addition, trainees are instructed in the use of small arms and combat in an urban setting.

Special-force instructors stress the need for trainees to "ensure killing" (לוודא הריגה) by firing a number of shots at close or even point blank range into wounded or dead enemies. The purpose of this order is to eliminate all potential threats from wounded persons in the midst of combat. In the course of the six-week training period, soldiers are drilled in "ensuring killing" as they pass by cardboard or poster targets representing the "enemy."

First Sgt. B. said that this reflex remains with graduates of the training course. At the Shimshon bases, the sergeant recalled:

> I used to see the soldiers fooling around in their room, playing as if they were shooting at a target. They would follow the procedure they were taught in the "anti-terror" school: run, slam to a halt, open fire, run, halt, open fire, and then run up to the body of the target and fire a bullet at close range to "ensure death." This was the procedure they were taught, time after time, in training. It's really important, this ingrained training, because when you are under pressure, and you are scared, it is the things that you have practiced until they are part of you that you do instinctively, without needing to think.

In at least one of the special-force killings that occurred in the Israeli-occupied West Bank and Gaza Strip during 1992, it appears that troopers did in fact "ensure killing" of a wounded suspect as he lay on the ground and threatened no one. Special-force soldiers fired several shots at eighteen-year-old Sa'd Khalil abd al-Karim Miqdad, according to four eyewitnesses, as he lay wounded on the ground. (See Chapter Two.) The same sort of training is reflected in some of the other cases, in which soldiers fired multiple rounds at the victims in situations that were not life-threatening; as, for example, in the al-Khatib and Dihmes cases in Chapter Two. Whatever the merits of opening fire in the first place, the multiple rounds may have made the difference between injury and death.

Repeated, rapid fire may be appropriate when confronting a suspect holding a gun in his hand. But the hazards of stressing this kind of aggressive posture is suggested by two cases where special-force soldiers inadvertently shot the wrong person.

First Sgt. B. recounted how Shimshon soldiers once "ensured the killing" of a Palestinian collaborator by mistake:

> I remember one operation, when two "wanted" people were trying to escape to Egypt by boat. A collaborator was with them in the boat. The operation was really complicated, involving the navy, helicopters, lots of soldiers. The navy was going to force the boat to shore, and our soldiers were going to be there to arrest them when they got to the beach. Anyway, something happened, and one of the three tried to run away. It was night, and one of our soldiers shot him, and then ran up and "ensured death" by shooting from up close. After, we discovered that the person who ran was the collaborator, the one on our side. We don't know why he ran. The one who shot him was really shook up, and later requested to be transferred from the unit.

In another case, an undercover soldier was killed by his comrades who evidently mistook him for a "wanted" Palestinian. On July 8, 1992, two soldiers from the West Bank-based Duvdevan special force shot dead Sgt. Eli Aisha, while raiding the town of Barta'a in search of "wanted" Palestinians. According to reports in the Israeli press, the IDF's official investigation into the killing concluded that the two soldiers mistook Sgt. Aisha for an armed Palestinian and fired several rounds into his body, including after he lay wounded on the ground. Summarizing the findings of the IDF investigation, *Maariv* reported:

> Second Lt. G. shot him in his back. Then Sgt. A. shot him in his chest. At the CID investigation, Lt. G. said that

Aisha was still alive after that, and therefore after he fell
he fired two shots to his head.[30]

In response to our questions concerning the incident, IDF Deputy
JAG Col. Yahav said that while "[T]he investigation into the death of Sgt.
Eli Eisha has not been completed...it is already clear that the soldiers fired
at him because they thought he was a terrorist who endangered them.
After he was wounded he continued to point his weapon at them. This is
why they fired on him again." (See Appendix.)

**C. One month of dramatic training in which Israeli actors from
professional theater companies train Shimshon soldiers how to disguise
themselves, use make-up and role-play.** This segment of the training
program prepares special-force soldiers to impersonate Palestinians.
Among other activities, First Sgt. B. said, Shimshon trainees impersonate
beggars in the Tel Aviv central bus station and Bedouin women in a
camel market in the Israeli desert town of Be'ersheva.

D. Three weeks of Arabic language training at the IDF Intelligence base
near the Gelilot junction just north of Tel Aviv on the highway leading
to Haifa.

COMBAT IN LEBANON: A PARADIGM MISAPPLIED

The combat-oriented training that special-force soldiers receive
is reinforced by the experience of IDF operations in southern Lebanon
against irregular Palestinian and Lebanese forces.[31] These operations

---

[30] Sima Kadmon, "The Duvdevan Affair: They Killed My Son Eli As They
Kill Old Horses," *Maariv*, February 26, 1993. See also, Eytan Rabin, "Tens of
Bullets Struck Eli Aisha, the Duvdevan Soldier Killed By Friendly Fire," *Haaretz*,
July 30, 1992. Other press reports indicate that a total of seven bullets hit Sgt.
Aisha, three in the chest, two in the back and two in the head. See also Ofer
Alfasi, "Hard Words in the Ears of the Army," *Hadashot*, August 21, 1992.

[31] Since 1985, Israel has occupied a self-declared "security zone" in southern
Lebanon after withdrawing most of its forces from the country, which it had
invaded in 1982. The "security zone" is currently patrolled by some 3,000 Israeli-

are understood by the IDF to be bona-fide combat operations against "terrorists." Soldiers are routinely authorized to shoot to kill suspected guerrillas on sight.[32] These operations include night-time shoot-to-kill ambushes, in which soldiers lie in wait and shoot at anyone who passes by. First Lt. C. stated, "All the civilians in southern Lebanon know that they are not allowed [out] at night, because they could get killed without warning."[33]

Most of the special forces that perform operations on a part-time basis in the occupied territories also carry out combat operations in southern Lebanon. Although the four full-time special forces do not usually operate in southern Lebanon, the attitudes and methods of operations developed in these combat situations have strongly influenced the thinking and methods of operation used by all special forces active in the occupied territories.

First Sgt. A. told Middle East Watch that in addition to operating against targeted Palestinians in the occupied West Bank, his unit often carried out night-time ambushes in southern Lebanon in which soldiers shot dead anyone walking through a pre-determined "killing zone" such as a specified ravine or path. Shortly after carrying out one such mission, he said, his unit was sent to the northern West Bank, where it carried out an operation against "wanted" Palestinians.

---

backed Lebanese militiamen of the Southern Lebanese Army (SLA) as well as some 1,000 Israeli troops.

[32] In a December 17, 1992 Supreme Court hearing on the deportation of 415 alleged Islamist activists to southern Lebanon, IDF Chief of Staff Ehud Barak told the court that the Israeli army "ambushes, shoots, bombs with aircraft, lays mines against, and shells" members of the Hizbollah guerrilla organization.

[33] This is not the place for Middle East Watch to evaluate the conduct and open-fire regulations of the Israeli army in southern Lebanon. Rather, the purpose of describing its conduct is to identify one source of the special forces' inappropriate combat-like tendencies when performing what the IDF characterizes as the policing task of capturing "wanted" and masked Palestinians in the occupied territories.

"ELIMINATING TERRORISTS":
OFFICERS' COMMENTS CONTRADICT STATED POLICY

The language used to refer to operations in Lebanon has been to some extent carried over to operations in the occupied territories. In Lebanon, suspected "terrorists" are to be shot dead without warning, or, as IDF personnel often put it, "מחוסל," meaning "eliminated" or "liquidated." In the occupied West Bank and Gaza Strip, "wanted" and some masked Palestinians are also commonly referred to by senior military officials and rank-and-file soldiers as "terrorists" (מחבלים). They have also sometimes used "elimination" to describe the aim of the hunt for these activists.

For example, on February 9, 1993, IDF Radio broadcast an interview with two company commanders of the Givati infantry brigade, "Captain Ron" and "Captain Yoram," who said:

> We conduct vehicular patrols, foot patrols, lookouts...around the clock, twenty-four hours a day, in order to catch these terrorists. I do not define them as "wanted" persons; they are terrorists in every sense of the word. My entire company is involved at this point in the hunt, in the pursuit after the terrorists walking around here. [My soldiers are not here] to deal with public disturbances and stuff like that, they move around like any force in Lebanon would now move. They are forces whose aim is to clash, to come into contact, to charge and to eliminate [לחסל] the terrorists, this is the only thing they [the company] are doing and this is the sole thing they are preoccupied with....

On August 27, 1992, shortly after a clash in Jenin between "wanted" activists and a Jenin-based Yamas contingent,[34] Commander Meshulam Amit[35] told Israel Television:

> [T]he unit dressed as Arabs (מסתערבים) operates routinely, almost every evening, in an attempt to increase and enrich our intelligence information, on the one hand, and to come into contact with and eliminate [לחסל] the Fatah[36] people and the armed terrorists who are in the area, on the other.

Shortly after a clash in Khan Younis refugee camp between members of the Gaza-based Shimshon special force and a "wanted" Palestinian suspect, the commander of security forces in the occupied Gaza Strip, Brig. Gen. Yom Tov Samiya, told a reporter that despite the death of one soldier in the course of the operation, "no one has characterized the operation in Khan Younis as a failed operation. The aim was to kill that terrorist, and we did kill him."[37]

In the interview, Brig. Gen. Samiya berated critics for calling Shimshon an "elimination squad": "Anyone who knows me well knows that I would not be willing, not even for one minute, to command a structure that includes a unit that could be termed, on one level or another, an 'elimination squad.'"

It is difficult to reconcile these officers' declarations that their objective is to kill "terrorists" with the IDF's official position that the special forces are engaged in a "police operation," attempting to capture suspects and resorting to force only when necessary.

---

[34] In the August 26, 1992 clash, special forces killed two armed and "wanted" activists and an unarmed twenty-year-old mother of two. The head of the Border Police unit was also killed in the gun battle.

[35] Commander Amit is responsible for the entire Border Police force, including the Yamas special unit.

[36] Fatah is one of the major PLO factions.

[37] "The Pride of Shimshon," *Hadashot* weekend edition, October 10, 1992.

CHAPTER FIVE
A LACK OF ACCOUNTABILITY:
INVESTIGATING AND PUNISHING ABUSES
BY SPECIAL-FORCE SOLDIERS

After I told the division commander that I had aimed toward the upper body with the intention of killing the guy, Erez Gershtein, my company commander, came up to me and asked me what I had reported to the Commander. I told him. He said that wasn't a good story, and that I should change it. He told me to say I fired at the legs.

I said, "Erez, that is not what happened." He said, "Negev, I'm telling you exactly what happened."

I ignored him and told the truth when the CID came. I was never charged. As far as Erez knew, however, I lied to the CID. He never asked me about it again.

-Lt. Negev Ahimiriam, former deputy commanding officer, "B" Company, Brigade 51, Golani infantry brigade.

A key indicator of official complicity in the conduct of individual soldiers is the response of the system to apparent deviations from the official regulations. Are possible deviations zealously investigated? Does improper behavior often result in criminal charges or appropriate disciplinary measures? Do the courts judge state agents in a fair manner and mete out appropriate punishments to those who are convicted? To the extent that the answer is no to any or all of these questions, state agents are likely to feel less accountable for their actions, and their superiors can be rightly accused of complicity in the abuses.

When it comes to the killing of Palestinians in the occupied territories, there is minimal accountability for actions that deviate from the official regulations. Although the IDF maintains a policy of investigating every Palestinian death in which its soldiers are implicated,

187

the investigations are lax, prosecutions are rare, and sentences that would
ordinarily be appropriate for the willful commission of a serious crime of
violence are rarer still. Middle East Watch believes that its conclusion in
the 1990 report, *The Israeli Army and the Intifada*, remains valid:

> [T]he few courts-martial to date represent only a small
> portion of fatal incidents in which there is prima facie
> evidence — credible eyewitness testimony in particular,
> but also medical evidence in some cases — that soldiers
> exceeded their open-fire orders....Part of the reason, we
> found, is that investigations into killings by IDF troops
> lack the vigor and resourcefulness needed to bring to
> justice those responsible for unjustified killings....
>
> The failure to establish ... an effective system of
> accountability ... must be taken to reflect a policy
> decision that the high number of Palestinians killed is an
> acceptable cost for asserting Israeli control in the
> occupied territories.[1]

Middle East Watch considers these conclusions to be particularly
germane to the killing of "wanted" and of masked persons by special-force
soldiers. In Chapters Two and Three, we presented seventeen such cases
in which we believed that there is prima facie evidence of wrongdoing by
the soldiers involved. To date, in only one of these cases were criminal
charges brought against a soldier (he was sentenced to twelve months, of
which six were suspended, for killing Amjad Jabbar). In fact, after more
than 120 killings by undercover soldiers, there is only one other case in
which charges were brought against an IDF or Border Police special-force
soldier, in connection with the killing of a Palestinian. (In a third case,
the survivors of a Palestinian killed by members of a special-force unit
successfully sued in civil court for damages, but criminal charges were
never brought.)
        Not all of the official investigations into the cases presented in
Chapters Two and Three have been closed, and it is possible that they
will lead to additional courts-martial or disciplinary measures against
soldiers. However, to deter abuse, the system must be overhauled. For

---

[1] Middle East Watch, *The Israeli Army and the Intifada*, pp. 5-7.

example, the long duration of most investigations, depicted by the IDF as an indication of their seriousness, in fact works against accountability; as we observed in *The Israeli Army and the Intifada*, "investigations into likely violations routinely drag on for months at a time, reducing the likelihood of a successful prosecution and reinforcing a lack of faith in the Israeli military justice system."[2]

Of course, some killings by soldiers have been justified by the imminent mortal danger they faced from the persons they were pursuing. Some Palestinian activists were killed only after they fired or attempted to fire at soldiers. Other killings were unjustifiable in Middle East Watch's view but consistent with Israeli open-fire regulations. Many such cases involved soldiers who followed the order to open fire toward the legs of fleeing suspects. Middle East Watch has urged and continues to urge Israeli authorities to bring the rules on apprehending suspects into compliance with the principles of necessity and proportionality. (See Chapter One.)

It is also not reasonable to expect a conviction in every case in which there is evidence of serious wrongdoing. The available evidence, even if diligently collected and presented, may be insufficient in quantity or quality to bring charges or, if charges are brought, to find guilt beyond a reasonable doubt. In at least some such cases, the soldiers should be subjected to internal disciplinary measures, which can be imposed without the high standard of proof that is required by a court of law. Since the IDF did not reply to a Middle East Watch request for information about such measures, we cannot say how often and which disciplinary measures have been taken against special-force personnel. From our conversations with soldiers, it is our impression that the more severe punishments that can be imposed by internal procedures, such as demotions and brief terms of detention, are rarely imposed on soldiers for causing death or injury during the pursuit of "wanted" or targeted Palestinians.

THE INVESTIGATIVE PROCESS

According to official policy, all killings by soldiers in the occupied territories are investigated. When an IDF soldier is suspected, the Military Police's Criminal Investigation Division (CID) investigates the killing.

---

[2] *Ibid.*, p. 6.

When a Border Policeman is suspected, the Israeli police conducts the investigation. According to First Sgt. B. of Shimshon, the post-operation investigative procedure typically includes an initial debriefing in which soldiers describe their actions during an operation to their commanding officer, who then summarizes their comments. Shortly thereafter, a CID investigator comes to the base to review the summary, interviewing the commander and the soldiers who participated in the operation.

Many of the soldiers we interviewed depicted the IDF investigations as perfunctory and unskeptical toward false accounts of events. First Sgt. B. said the commanders' summaries often contained legalistic clichés to describe killings. Common formulations included, "The soldiers carried out the procedure for apprehending suspects and the masked person died." In these summaries, First Sgt. B. said, the commander frequently failed to specify if and how the different stages of the procedure were carried out, what the distance was between the soldiers and the persons they fired upon, and other issues that would indicate whether the shooting was justified.

First Sgt. A. indicated that for the men in his unit, the CID was virtually invisible to the soldiers:

> I have never seen CID investigators talk to soldiers in
> our unit. I suppose that they must show up, but if they
> do, they only talk to the unit commander. They never
> talk to the soldiers who were involved in an operation.

With respect to the specific assassination operation he said his unit had carried out (see Chapter Four), First Sgt. A. said:

> The CID never came, at least not that I saw. For sure,
> they never interviewed individual soldiers who
> participated in the operation.

More often, the soldiers interviewed by Middle East Watch said CID investigators did come to investigate killings but were treated with disdain by special-force soldiers, who viewed them as desk-bound pencil-pushers with little or no sense of the hazards they faced in the field. First Sgt. B. said that while the CID investigators always came to the Shimshon base within twenty-four hours after a killing, "Everyone regards them as pests. The unit commander [commander of Shimshon] would hold them up at the gate of the base for a while."

First Sgt. D. recalled:

> The CID was always there, investigating, but no one treated them seriously. The guy they always used to send to question us was a skinny, scared kind of guy. He always ran away when we yelled at him. He would come, write what we told him, and then run off. If a CID officer ever came, that was different, but they didn't always come.
>
> Anyway, officer or not, you always made sure that you had a story for what had happened, so that nothing would happen to you. This was always done. The participants in whatever had gone on arranged things before the investigation, and made sure that everyone's story was the same. I have done this myself, not for killings, but for wounding, beatings, other things. We knew we were making up alibis.

First Lt. C. said that soldiers sometimes lied to CID investigators, who in turn did not probe their statements:

> It is possible, and I have heard of people doing this, to kill a person you think is in the "'wanted' persons booklet" and then later tell the CID that he had "made a threatening move" or that he had "tried to grab my gun." If a soldier chooses, he can kill the "wanted" person and no one will know or really care. All you have to do is to come up with a good story.

Lt. Negev Ahimiriam, former platoon commander and then deputy commander of company "B" in the Golani infantry's Brigade 51, related one incident in which a commanding officer ordered him to lie both to CID investigators and to senior officers conducting their own inquiry into a killing.

During a day of operations in the West Bank town of Nablus, a force commanded by Lt. Ahimiriam was repeatedly stoned while passing the same stretch of road. In an effort to capture the stone-throwers, Lt. Ahimiriam said, he ordered one group of soldiers to go past the same spot as "bait," while he and several other soldiers went around the back. While in the midst of this maneuver, Lt. Ahimiriam observed two youths preparing to throw a large stone from a mosque balcony onto the street below. Believing the soldiers serving as "bait" to be in danger, Lt. Ahimiriam shot at the youth holding the stone. He aimed at the upper body. Once the shot was fired, the two youths dropped to the balcony floor and disappeared from view. Lt. Ahimiriam later visited the balcony, saw no signs of blood, and concluded he had missed.

It was a day full of confrontations, Lt. Ahimiriam recalled, and he heard numerous shots fired by members of his battalion. At the end of the day, a senior officer informed Lt. Ahimiriam that a Palestinian had been killed, apparently by soldiers, and was asked whether one of his soldiers had fired his weapon. Lt. Ahimiriam confirmed he had and was then informed he was the only possible suspect in the killing, since no other officer in the battalion had reported using ammunition during the day.

In a debriefing by the commander responsible for all forces in the West Bank, Lt. Ahimiriam recounted that he had fired at the stone-thrower's upper body since he believed his soldiers' lives to be in danger. Two days later, his company commander, Erez Gershtein, learned what he had reported to the division commander and said he would arrange for a return interview with the division commander so that Lt. Ahimiriam could revise his story. Gershtein ordered Lt. Ahimiriam to tell the commander he had been confused during the first interview, and that he had in fact fired at the Palestinian's legs.

Lt. Ahimiriam said he objected, because he had no intention of lying and because in any event the balcony had a parapet that would have blocked any shot aimed below the youth's midsection. Lt. Ahimiriam said that Gershtein repeated his order to lie and then left. The return interview never took place, but a CID investigator did come to interview Lt. Ahimiriam. Lt. Ahimiriam said he stuck to his original account. After that, he heard nothing further about the case.

As mentioned in Chapter Four, First Sgt. B. of the Shimshon unit related how, in late 1991, a friend in his unit had aimed at "the center of the mass" of a masked Gazan, hitting him in the back. In the post-operation debriefing, the team commander told the team to lie and say that the soldier had fired at the legs. That is what they eventually told the CID investigators.

First Sgt. D. told Middle East Watch of incidents of unjustified killings by members of his unit that were never properly investigated and had no legal consequences. He said that following the incident described in Chapter Four in which his unit ambushed and killed a masked Gazan:

> The debriefing by the battalion commander was about to happen. I heard [the soldiers] right before the debriefing in the tent, getting their stories straight, together. They were making sure that everyone said the same thing. They were repeating it over and over. The sergeant in charge was S., a short little guy who used to be in [the] Golani [brigade]. There was one guy, D., who was a new immigrant. He couldn't get the story straight. So they told him to tell the battalion commander that he couldn't speak Hebrew well enough to talk.

The incident turned out "absolutely O.K.," First Sgt. D. said, meaning that, as far as he knew, the soldiers faced no tough questioning or disciplinary action.

Irregularities and bias in the investigations have been exposed when cases involving wrongful deaths have gone to trial. The CID was criticized by the judges in the "Givati trial" (concerning the beating death of forty-three-year-old Hani al-Shami in the Gaza Strip on August 22, 1988),[3] and, as discussed below, in the trial of the commander of the Shimshon undercover unit in the Gaza Strip and in the civil suit for wrongful death and injury committed by a West Bank undercover unit.

TRIALS

In the view of Middle East Watch, the courts-martial of soldiers for wrongful killings of Palestinians represent only a small fraction of cases in which there is at least prima facie evidence of wrongdoing that would warrant criminal charges against soldiers. Furthermore, the sentences that the courts have handed down against soldiers convicted in

---

[3] See Middle East Watch, *The Israeli Army and the Intifada*, pp. 153-154.

these cases have generally not been commensurate with the commission of a willful act of grave violence. These two factors contribute to the low level of accountability that exists for the conduct of soldiers.

However, some sense of accountability has been instilled in soldiers by the few courts-martial that have taken place. These cases have received a great deal of attention in the Israeli press and among the public, and have helped to place under intensive scrutiny some of the abusive practices of the IDF in the occupied territories.

Only two special-force soldiers, as far as we are aware, have been convicted for wrongfully killing a "wanted" or masked Palestinian. They are "Second Lt. Ofir," who killed Amjad Jabbar (see Chapter Two) and Lt. Col. Ilan Rosenfeld, the defendant in the "Shimshon" trial (see Chapter Four). In a third case, although no criminal charges were filed, Palestinians sued the State of Israel for civil damages after special-force soldiers killed one man and wounded another in 1988.

The court-martial of Lt. Col. Rosenfeld fit a pattern of Israeli justice that Middle East Watch has called "truth-telling without accountability."[4] When Israeli authorities show the will to pursue a high-profile instance of abuse, vigorous investigations and open trials shine a harsh light on misconduct by security-force members, their superiors, and the initial investigators. This healthy process, however, almost never culminates in appropriate punishments for those found responsible for wrongdoing.

Lt. Col. Rosenfeld was charged with manslaughter and negligence in connection with the shooting of Maher abu Qdama. The court accepted the testimony of the soldier who fired the fatal shot that Lt. Col. Rosenfeld had illegally instructed his soldiers to fire at the abdomens of fleeing suspects. The court wrote that this order deviated "from any sense of reason" and was "incompatible with the basic foundations of the State of Israel."[5]

Despite these stern conclusions in a homicide case, the court on July 7, 1992 gave Lt. Col. Rosenfeld a mere one-month suspended

---

[4] See Middle East Watch, *Israel's Truth-Telling without Accountability: Inquest Faults Police in Killings at Jerusalem Holy Site, But Judge Orders No Charges*, September 1991.

[5] "Special Squad Officer Guilty of Negligence in Palestinian's Death," *Associated Press*, July 2, 1992.

sentence on the negligence charge. The charge of manslaughter was dropped on the grounds that it was unclear whether Lt. Col. Rosenfeld had intended for his order to shoot at the "center of the mass" to result in the death of suspects. It was also unclear, the court said, whether abu Qdama was killed by the bullets aimed at his legs or by the ones aimed at his upper body.[6] The military prosecution appealed the lenient sentence, and a military court in November 1992 added the punishment of demoting Lt. Col. Rosenfeld by one rank to major.

The trial exposed misconduct on the part of the CID. When that agency probed the killing that led to the court-martial, the soldier who pulled the trigger, Lt. Kanin, told CID investigators that he first fired at abu Qdama's legs, and then, when this failed to stop his escape, went beyond the three-stage procedure by aiming at the fleeing suspect's upper body. The stage, he said, was routine in his unit and had been sanctioned by Lt. Col. Rosenfeld, the unit's commander.

In the course of the initial investigation, a CID investigator permitted Lt. Kanin to telephone Lt. Col. Rosenfeld in the investigator's presence and discuss the matter at length. Later, when asked in court what was said, the investigator claimed he could not recall the content of the discussion since he was busy writing.

In the CID's second interview with Lt. Kanin, the CID investigators, according to Lt. Kanin's testimony, coached him by suggesting he retract his initial testimony and testify instead that he had followed the official three-stage procedure and had only fired at abu Qdama's legs.

The judges also noted disapprovingly in their summation that the CID had failed throughout the investigation to question senior officers who had participated in the post-operation debriefing, including the commanders of the battalion and regional brigade. The investigators could have queried the senior officers on their immediate response to the killing: did they learn what the CID investigators were to learn later — that Lt. Kanin apparently believed he was carrying out an order to shoot to kill? If so, what actions did they take to end this illegal order?

Summarizing the CID's mishandling of the investigation, the judges observed, "All of these questions, in addition to Shahar's [i.e. Lt. Shahar Kanin] statement as to how the CID investigator helped him

---

[6] "Officer Given Suspended Sentence in Palestinian's Death," *Associated Press*, July 7, 1992.

retract his first statement, pose a large question mark as to the intentions of the investigation itself."

Col. Peled, the presiding judge, also commented on the general lack of interest in the IDF, before charges were filed, in discovering whether the shooting of abu Qdama was justified. The judge was quoted by *Haaretz* as saying:

> Until this charge sheet was submitted, this commander [Lt. Kanin] was considered a hero. No one asked him how he even dared to fire at such a distance....Why did no one say to him, "Why did you do such an idiotic thing?" After all, we are speaking about a threat to life. He fired according to the procedure, but a human being died.[7]

Had Lt. Kanin not openly acknowledged during his first CID interview the orders to shoot at the center of the mass, thereby compelling the CID investigator to record this testimony, it is very possible that the CID would have concluded the investigation without recommending prosecution.

***

A highly unusual civil suit for wrongful death and injury brought by Palestinians against the State of Israel also exposed the conduct of special forces and CID investigators to unflattering scrutiny.[8] The trial exposed a chain of perjury that included the GSS agents who initiated the

---

[7] "The Judge: How Does One Do Such An Idiotic Thing?..." *Haaretz*, January 8, 1992.

[8] Civil case #273/89 — *Jamal Qassem Beni Odeh v. the State of Israel*, and case #334/89 — *The Beneficiaries of Sa'oud Hassan Beni Odeh, Hassan Beni Odeh, Fatma Beni Odeh and Fatma Saleh Beni Odeh v. the State of Israel*. The case was tried in the Nazareth district court, inside Israel, and presided over by Judge Gideon Ginat. This incident is described at length in B'Tselem, *Activity of the Undercover Units*, pp. 37-40. See pp. 93-97 for excerpts from the testimony of the two soldiers who testified in the civil case.

fatal operation, the soldiers who carried it out, and the CID agents who investigated it.

The operation took place on August 18, 1988 in the West Bank village of Tamoun. According to trial testimony, the two Palestinian victims, twenty-seven-year-old Jamal Qassem Beni Odeh, and twenty-one-year-old Sa'oud Hassan Beni Odeh, were sitting with four other men in a metal workshop. A civilian car containing undercover and uniformed soldiers entered the village and approached the shop. The soldiers got out of the car and began approaching and surrounding the shop. The Palestinian men fled toward an open field. Within less than one minute, the soldiers opened fire, without first ascertaining whether the persons fleeing were indeed the suspects they had come to arrest. Jamal Beni Odeh was wounded in one knee and arrested, while Sa'oud Beni Odeh was mortally wounded by a bullet which entered his back and exited his stomach.

The soldiers later said they had been sent to arrest two suspects who were candidates for expulsion and, in addition, to arrest several other young men, including Sa'oud and Jamal Odeh. The state argued in the trial that Sa'oud and Jamal Odeh were dangerous suspects; consequently, the soldiers were authorized to shoot them if they disobeyed orders to halt. A GSS agent testified in closed court that Sa'oud and Jamal Odeh were well-known militants whose names were on a "wanted" list, and whose pictures had been distributed to the soldiers before the operation.

Although at least two soldiers testified that the GSS had provided them with pictures of targeted suspects before the operation, they could not recall whether the pictures they received included those of the men who were eventually shot. Notably, during the civil trial, neither the IDF nor the GSS presented these pictures or any written evidence, classified or otherwise, to back its claims about the victims. The plaintiffs' attorneys also alleged that the wounded man, Jamal Odeh, was detained for six months after his capture without being interrogated. This cast further doubt on the assertion that security forces believed him to be a dangerous "wanted" activist.

On November 11, 1992, over four years after the incident, the Nazareth court ruled that the plaintiffs were entitled to damages for the unjustifiable shooting. Jamal Odeh received 160,985 shekels (approximately U.S. $60,000) and Sa'oud Odeh's family received 50,000 shekels (U.S. $18,500). Judge Ginat said:

If the State is unable to present written documentation to the court, the only conclusion possible is that there is no such material to support the oral testimony against the plaintiffs.

In addition, Judge Ginat said, the soldiers had violated the open-fire regulations:

It appears to me that no other conclusion can be drawn other than that the procedure [for the apprehension of suspects] was not carried out by those who did the shooting....[I]t appears that the soldiers acted with abnormal haste. There is no doubt that in the few seconds that passed between their entrance into the metal shop and the shooting, they did not have an opportunity to identify which of the persons were "wanted." The soldiers acted, therefore, as if they assumed all persons in the metal shop to be suspects, an assumption that was without basis....No real attempt was made to chase after the persons who fled from the shop into an open field. The soldiers did not pause between the different stages of the procedure [for opening fire at fleeing suspects].

The judge's findings contrast sharply with the IDF's prior conclusions about the event. In April 1992, the IDF spokesman told B'Tselem that the file had been closed:

The opinion [of the military advocate] indicates that the soldiers acted in accordance with the procedure for apprehending a suspect, and that they tried to arrest the deceased, who was suspected of perpetrating grave attacks. Since he did not stop at the cry to halt and after the firing of warning shots into the air, the soldiers shot at his legs and wounded him. Shortly afterwards, he died from his wounds.[9]

---

[9] B'Tselem, *Activity of the Undercover Units*, p. 39.

In his ruling, Judge Ginat severely criticized the manner in which the CID had investigated the killing. For example, he said, the written statements taken by CID investigators from the soldiers shortly after the killing made no mention of the photographs of the Odehs that the soldiers later claimed to have been shown by the GSS. During the trial, however, a GSS agent and the soldiers testified that the agent had shown the soldiers photographs of the Odehs prior to the operation. The state explained this contradiction by stating that the existence of the photographs was noted in the original CID report, but this mention was later deleted for reasons of "state security."

If the CID had in fact been informed by the soldiers about the GSS-supplied photographs, the CID never requested to see them. Judge Ginat commented, "[A]ssuming that the pictures of the 'wanted' persons did in fact exist prior to the operation, I am unable to understand why they were not presented to the CID during its investigation." In fact, the judge noted, he had "never received an explanation from the State as to why the CID did not carry out such an inquiry at that time" or in the four years since the killing (i.e. an inquiry to check the GSS's claim that Sa'oud and Jamal Odeh were dangerous suspects, against whom soldiers would be permitted under the regulations to open fire to prevent their escape).

When asked whether the court's ruling in the civil case would lead to a reopening of the criminal investigation into the killing of Sa'oud Odeh, Shai Nitzan, deputy senior aide to the State Attorney, responded that the State was appealing Judge Ginat's decision. Nitzan said the State did not accept the conclusion that the soldiers failed to wait long enough between the stages of the procedure for apprehending the suspect. Moreover, he argued, the court ruling did not require the State to open a criminal case against the soldiers, since the level of proof required in a criminal case was much higher than that required in a civil suit. He added:

> Regarding a criminal case the State Attorney is of the
> opinion that it will not be possible today, over four years
> after the case. It would be impossible to obtain the type
> of trustworthy evidence able to meet the standards of
> proof required in a criminal trial, i.e., beyond reasonable
> doubt, which will prove negligence on the part of the

soldiers. There is therefore no choice but to close the file.[10]

Whether or not it is now appropriate to pursue a criminal trial against the soldiers, it is evident from the civil suit initiated by the Palestinian plaintiffs that the IDF closed its initial investigation into the killing on the basis of a false account of what had occurred.

Trial Exposes Abuses by Undercover Policemen in Jerusalem

A trial that ended in May 1993 traced some of the central themes of this report. In this case, however, the special-force members accused of opening fire without justification and then lying about the circumstances belonged to the "Gideon Unit" of the Israeli Police, which operates primarily in Israeli-annexed East Jerusalem, which for security matters is jurisdictionally under police rather than IDF authority.

The defendant in the trial, seventeen-year-old Yusuf abu Juma'a, was acquitted on May 5, 1993 of charges relating to a June 10, 1992 incident in which an undercover policeman shot him after he had allegedly threatened the policeman with an axe. Jerusalem District Court Judge Ruth Orr pointed out that the policeman's claim that Juma'a had been shot in the front of his body was called into question by the pathologist's finding that he had been shot in the back. According to the weekly *Kol Ha'ir*:

> From the judge's closing remarks it appears that the policemen concocted a story to "link" the axe that was found in the area to the young person they had shot. The policeman [said]...he felt his life was in danger, because an axe had been raised above his head. Orr did not accept this version of events: "Is it conceivable that after the axe was lifted above the policeman's head, he had time to take his gun out, cock it, cry "Halt, Police!" and

---

[10] Letter to B'Tselem, April 4, 1993. The letter was in response to an inquiry by B'Tselem to the Deputy JAG on November 11, 1992. B'Tselem's letter had been transferred from the IDF to the Ministry of Justice because the soldiers involved were no longer serving in the military.

then shoot the accused, and the accused had no time to bring the axe down on his head during this entire time?"

Orr also remarked that no attempt had been made to check the fingerprints on the axe ... and thus, the possibility had been prevented for making an objective investigation into the guilt or innocence of the accused.

Jawad Boulos, who represented the accused, said the police may have fabricated the story and brought the axe to the scene in order to justify an illegal shooting...."The absurd thing is that if Abu Juma'a had been killed, he would not have been brought to trial and the policemen's lies would not have been exposed. In such a case we would have heard the famous cliché on the radio that a masked person had attacked a police force and had been shot."[11]

---

[11] Hillel Cohen, "Police Undercover Soldiers Shot a Young Arab in the Back, and Then Lied about It To Convict Him," *Kol Ha'ir*, May 7, 1993.

APPENDIX
CORRESPONDENCE BETWEEN MIDDLE EAST WATCH AND THE IDF
AND
BETWEEN MIDDLE EAST WATCH AND THE JUSTICE MINISTRY

The following is the complete text of exchanges of correspondence between Middle East Watch and the IDF, and between Middle East Watch and the Justice Ministry, concerning killings by special-force units in the occupied territories.

To make the exchanges easier to follow, we have placed together, at the end of this appendix, all of the information from the correspondence related to specific cases. We have also repeated a few of the official statements when they were meant to apply to more than one case. For continuity, we altered the phrasing in slight ways that in no way affected meaning. We have also standardized the spelling of Arabic names throughout the correspondence.

The cases referred to in this exchange of letters do not correspond exactly to the cases presented in the report. This is because the report does not include every case that we investigated. However, all information provided by the government is reprinted below, including for cases that are not recounted in the report.

The chronology of the correspondence is as follows:

November 16, 1992: Middle East Watch wrote letters to IDF Deputy Judge Advocate General David Yahav and State Attorney Dorit Beinish. The cover letters to Col. Yahav and Adv. Beinish were similar to one another. Each was accompanied by: a list of the eighteen cases that Middle East Watch had investigated, with specific questions about each case; and a list of general questions for which Middle East Watch sought answers regarding each of the eighteen cases.

December 15, 1992: Middle East Watch received an undated response from Col. Yahav to its letter of November 16.

December 22, 1992: Middle East Watch received a response, dated December 21, from Adv. Tamar Gaulan, Director of the Human Rights and International Relations Department of the Ministry of Justice, to its November 16 letter to State Attorney Beinish.

April 27, 1993: Middle East Watch wrote follow-up letters to Col. Yahav and Adv. Gaulan seeking updates of the information they had provided in December.

Late May 1993: Middle East Watch received a reply from Adv. Gaulan, dated May 20, to its letter of April 27; and a reply from Captain Avital Margalit, Head of the Information Section of the IDF Spokesman's Office, dated May 21, to its letter of April 27 to Col. Yahav.

June 29, 1993: Middle East Watch releases the report in Jerusalem. Shortly before that date, the IDF issued a response to the report, dated June 25, apparently on the basis of a report summary delivered by Middle East Watch to the government in advance of the release date. It appears after the Appendix. The government did not reply to invitations to provide a more detailed reply to the report for inclusion in this edition. Invitations were made in person at the Israel Consulate in New York on June 23 and by facsimile to the Consulate, the IDF Spokesman's Office and the Justice Ministry's Human Rights and International Relations Division on July 2. We requested a reply by July 12 but as of July 14 had received none.

November 16, 1992   via fax and mail

Col. David Yahav
Deputy Judge Advocate General, Israel Defense Force
6 David Elazar Street, HaKirya, Tel Aviv, Israel

Dear Col. Yahav,

I wish to thank you for the time that you, Captain David Shabi of the
Chief Military Prosecutor's office and Lt. Col. Rami Kaydar of the
Spokesman's office took to meet with my colleagues and me on October
28 to discuss incidents in the occupied territories involving IDF
undercover units.

This letter is in response to your request that we submit to you all
remaining questions in writing. We will reprint in our forthcoming
report the full text of your answers to the following questions, provided
they reach us by December 14.

Many of our questions pertain to the sixteen cases about which we
requested information in our October 5 fax to the Judge Advocate
General. After further fieldwork, we have expanded the list to eighteen
cases (involving twenty deaths), all from the past twelve months. In each
case our investigation has yielded some evidence that security forces may
have employed excessive force.

Since you indicated that it would not be possible to grant our request to
interview the soldiers involved in the incidents, we are dependent on you
to furnish as much specific information as possible about how the army
views the sequence of events that led to each fatal shooting.

We are aware that some of the cases listed below involved IDF soldiers,
while others involved other security forces. We have therefore submitted
the questions and the entire list both to you and to State Attorney Dorit
Beinish at the Ministry of Justice. On the basis of the information we
have, the IDF forces were involved in cases 2, 3, 4, 6, 7, 9, 11, 12, 14, 17,
and 18, and other security forces (Border Police or the General Security

Service) were involved in cases 1, 5, 8, 10, 16. We do not know who is responsible in cases 13 and 15.

When we met on October 28, you discussed your findings in two cases from the list we had submitted on October 5. We have no further questions about the case of Majed 'Abed Khalil Jubour. However, in the case of Khalil Nader Khamayseh, we have followed your suggestion to submit remaining questions in writing (see below).

We also wish to ask four questions that are not related to the specific cases. When we asked the first two at our October 28 meeting, you asked us to submit them in writing.

(1) A soldier based in Gaza told us that in 1991 he attended a briefing by Gen. Matan Vilna'i, the commander of the Southern Command. According to the soldier, Gen. Vilna'i told the company, with regard to thirteen well-known wanted Palestinians, "I believe that if these thirteen people were to die the intifada would be over. At the least, we would have quiet for six months." Is this quote accurate? Does the IDF ever decide prior to an operation that a particular individual should be killed rather than arrested?

(2) How many members of undercover units have been court-martialed or subjected to disciplinary hearings during the intifada for actions that led to the death or wounding of Palestinians?   Please indicate the circumstances and the punishments, if any.

(3) In the recently decided civil court case stemming from a fatal undercover unit operation (*Jamal Qassem Beni Odeh, Hassan and Fatma Beni Odeh, and Fatma Salah Beni Odeh* v. *the State of Israel*, 273/89 and 334/89), we understand that Judge Gideon Ginat explicitly rejected the State's defense that because the death and injury occurred during what was essentially a combat operation, the soldiers were not obligated to weigh their actions and the damage they might cause the public good.

How can the State's defense in this case, i.e., that the legal framework is one of combat, be reconciled with your statement to us on October 28 that the IDF views its operations in the occupied territories, including those of undercover units, within the legal framework of law enforcement rather than combat? Please clarify the IDF's position on the legal framework applicable to undercover operations, including those against persons who are armed.

(4) On July 8, 1992, two soldiers from the Duvdevan special forces unit shot dead a third undercover soldier, Sgt. Eli Aisha, whom they apparently mistook for an armed Palestinian. According to an article in *Hadashot*, the soldier's father, Nissim Aisha, was later told by soldiers in the unit that after Eli lay wounded on the ground, soldiers fired several more bullets into his body. Is this true? If so, what are the reasons? In what situations are members of the security forces permitted to fire at a person who is already wounded and unable to flee?

Thank you for your attention to these matters. Do not hesitate to phone or write if you wish to discuss them.

Sincerely yours,

Eric Goldstein

cc: Lt. Col. Rami Kaydar, IDF Spokesman, Information Branch
       Mr. Shimon Stein, Political Officer, Embassy of Israel,
       Washington, D.C.
enc.:   List of General Questions, List of 18 Cases with Specific
       Questions (4 pp.)

November 16, 1992   via fax and mail

State Attorney Dorit Beinish
Ministry of Justice
29 Salah e-Din Street
Jerusalem 91010

Dear Ms. Beinish,

I wish to thank you for the time that you and your colleagues took to meet with the Middle East Watch delegation on October 29 to discuss incidents in the occupied territories involving undercover units.

This letter is in response to your request that we submit to you all remaining questions in writing. We will reprint in our forthcoming report the full text of your answers to the following questions, provided they reach us by December 14.

Many of our questions pertain to the sixteen cases about which we requested information in a October 5 fax to the IDF Judge Advocate General and an October 8 fax to the Minister of Justice. After further fieldwork, we have expanded the list to eighteen cases (involving twenty deaths), all from the past twelve months. In each case our investigation has yielded some evidence that security forces may have employed excessive force.

Since we have not interviewed the security force members involved in the incidents, we are dependent on you to provide us with as much specific information as possible from the official investigation into the sequence of events that led to the fatal shooting.

We are aware that some of the cases listed below involved IDF soldiers, while others involved other security forces. We have therefore submitted the questions and the entire list both to you and to IDF Deputy Judge Advocate General Col. David Yahav. On the basis of the information we have, the IDF forces were involved in cases 2, 3, 4, 6, 7, 9, 11, 12, 14, 17, and 18, and other security forces (Border Police or General Security Service) were involved in cases 1, 5, 8, 10, 16. We do not know who is responsible in cases 13 and 15.

We also wish to ask two questions that are not specifically related to the list of cases.

(1) How many members of Border Police undercover units have been charged or subjected to disciplinary hearings for actions that led to the death or wounding of Palestinians? Please indicate the circumstances and the punishments, if any.

(2) In the recently decided civil court case stemming from a fatal undercover unit operation (*Jamal Qassem Beni Odeh, Hassan and Fatma Beni Odeh, and Fatma Salah Beni Odeh* v. *the State of Israel*, 273/89 and 334/89), we understand that Judge Gideon Ginat explicitly rejected the State's defense that because the death and injury occurred during what was essentially a combat operation, the soldiers were not obligated to weigh their actions and the damage they might cause the public good.

How can the State's defense in this case, i.e., that the legal framework is one of combat, be reconciled with the IDF's statement to us on October 28 that the IDF views its operations in the occupied territories, including those of undercover units, within the legal framework of law enforcement rather than combat? Please clarify the State's position on the legal framework applicable to undercover operations, including those against persons who are armed.

Thank you for your attention to these matters. Do not hesitate to phone or write if you wish to discuss the questions in this letter.

Sincerely yours,

Eric Goldstein

cc: Tamar Gaulan, Human Rights Division, Ministry of Justice
     Shimon Stein, political counselor, Embassy of Israel, Washington, DC

enc: List of General Questions (2 pp.), List of 18 Cases with Specific
     Questions (4 pp.)

MIDDLE EAST WATCH'S
GENERAL QUESTIONS FOR ALL CASES
submitted November 16, 1992

Attached is a list of eighteen cases of Palestinians who were reportedly killed by undercover units of Israel's security forces. Please answer the following questions for each case:

1. WHOSE RESPONSIBILITY?

Agents of which security force were responsible for the killing (IDF, Border Police, General Security Service, other)?

Which unit was involved?

Were the forces in uniform or undercover?

2. WHO IS INVESTIGATING?

Which agency is conducting a criminal investigation into the killing, and what is the status of that investigation?

3. WAS THE KILLING JUSTIFIED?

If the investigation is completed, what conclusion was reached as to whether the killing was justified? And —

> — if the killing was *not* justified, what legal or disciplinary measures have been initiated against members of the security forces? (Please include charges, verdicts, and penalties.)

> — if justified, what circumstances justified the killing?

>> If the justification relates to a life-threatening situation, what are the specific facts that, together, created that situation?

If the justification relates to carrying out the procedures for apprehending a suspect, what are:

the specific facts that made the person a legitimate suspect as defined in the procedures?

the circumstances in which a fatal injury was inflicted when the orders oblige the soldier to aim only at the legs of the fleeing suspect?

the warning steps (shouting a warning, or firing in the air) or attempts to effect an arrest, if any, that were carried out before the person was fatally shot?

If the forces omitted any of the standard warning steps, or did not attempt to effect an arrest, what are the reasons?

4. AUTOPSY

Was an autopsy conducted?

If an autopsy was conducted, please provide us with a copy of the autopsy report (we will pay for photocopying and postage).

If it is not possible to provide the autopsy report, please indicate the number of bullet holes that the autopsy report found in the victim, their location and characteristics (entry or exit, and the distance from which the bullet was shot).

If an autopsy was *not* conducted, please explain why not.

5. WAS THE VICTIM "WANTED"?

Was the person who was killed previously "wanted" by the authorities? If so, what were the specific reasons he was "wanted"?

6. WAS THE VICTIM MASKED WHEN KILLED?

7. WAS THE VICTIM ARMED?

Was the person classified as someone thought to carry arms?

Was he carrying an arm at the time of the fatal encounter? If so, what kind of weapon was he carrying?

Did he use or attempt to use a weapon against the security forces involved in the fatal encounter?

Was a weapon recovered? Where is it now?

8. WHO WAS INTERVIEWED DURING THE INVESTIGATION?

In the course of the criminal investigation of the killing, was testimony collected from persons who are not members of the security forces? If so, please specify how many, and what kinds of individuals provided testimony.

Middle East Watch asked the State of Israel Ministry of Justice and the Israel Defence Force to provide information about the circumstances surrounding the deaths of the following individuals:

1. **Muhannad Muhammad Turkeman,** December 12, 1991 (Zababdeh, Jenin district, West Bank)

2. **Husam Yousef Muhammad abu Kheir,** January 4, 1992 (Khan Younis, Gaza Strip)

3. **Na'im abd as-Salaam al-Laham, Hajjaj Ibrahim Hajjaj, and Imad Mahmoud Bisharat,** March 15, 1992 (Old 'Askar refugee camp, Nablus district, West Bank)

4. **Ra'ed abd ar-Rahman Dihmes,** March 18, 1992 (Kufr Qadoum, Nablus district, West Bank)

5. **Jamal Rashid Ghanem,** March 22, 1992 (Shweikeh, Tulkarm district, West Bank)

6. **Muhammad Isma'il abd as-Salaam al-Ja'afreh,** April 1, 1992 (Tarqumia, Hebron district, West Bank)

7. **Abd al-Qader Yousef abd al-Qader Masarweh,** April 9, 1992 (Nur Shams refugee camp, Tulkarm district, West Bank)

8. **Zakariya Muhammad 'Issa Qabalan,** April 15, 1992 (Greater Abassan, southern Gaza Strip)

9. **Ayman Hussein Majadbeh,** April 21, 1992 ('Allar, Tulkarm district, West Bank)

10. **Jawad As'ad Rahal,** April 29, 1992 ('Arrabeh, Jenin district, West Bank)

11. **Khalil Nader Khamayseh,** April 29, 1992 (al-Yamoun, Jenin district, West Bank)

12.   **Mahmoud Shalaldeh**, May 7, 1992 (Sa'ir, Hebron district, West Bank)

13.   **Sa'd Khalil abd al-Karim Miqdad**, June 4, 1992 (Khan Younis, Gaza Strip)

14.   **Zakariya al-Mathloum**, July 17, 1992 (Gaza City, Gaza Strip)

15.   **Nuri Sharif abd al-Qader al-Aqqad**, July 27, 1992 (Khan Younis, Gaza Strip)

16.   **Abdullah Dibash Hamarshe**, September 9, 1992 (Ya'bad, Jenin district, West Bank)

17.   **Muhammad Sadeq Kemayel Taktak**, October 3, 1992 (Qabatiya, Jenin district, West Bank)

18.   **'Issam al-Khatib**, October 10, 1992 (Ar-Ram, West Bank)

The following section contains the letters that Middle East Watch received from the IDF and from the Israel Ministry of Justice.

Undated: Received at Middle East Watch on December 15, 1992.

**Military Advocate General
Office of the Deputy Advocate General
6 David Elazar Street
Hakirya
TEL AVIV
ISRAEL**

Mr. Eric Goldstein
Middle East Watch
485 Fifth Ave.
New York, NY 10017-6104
USA

re: REQUEST FOR DETAILS CONCERNING INCIDENTS
INVOLVING IDF SPECIAL ANTI-TERRORIST UNITS
IN JUDEA, SAMARIA AND THE GAZA DISTRICT

Dear Mr. Goldstein,

We read your letter of Nov. 16, 1992 with the greatest care. In our response, we will attempt to provide you with as many details as possible bearing in mind that we are limited in our ability to give you all the information at our disposal by two requirements. Firstly, we are constricted by our duty to protect the safety of the soldiers and secondly, by our responsibility to abide by *sub judice*, since some of the incidents to which you refer in your letter are still before the courts. We are certain that you will honor your assurance to present the facts in the manner in which they are put forth herein.

Before we answer the specific questions you raised, we would like to give you some background information regarding recent IDF activities in Judea, Samaria and Gaza.

The Background to IDF Activities Against Terror

The uprising in Judea, Samaria and Gaza has undergone a transformation. Until recently the situation was characterized by mass popular demonstrations. However, due to the changes that Palestinian society has undergone, the uprising is now largely characterized by the activity of terrorist groups. These groups (such as the PLO, the Popular Front for the Liberation of Palestine and the fanatical pro-Iranian HAMAS) attempt to keep the uprising going by increasing terrorist activity, with a heightened emphasis on the use of firearms.

The change in the nature of the uprising is expressed by, among other things, the reluctance of the local residents to join the mass demonstrations. Because of their desire to resume their routine, the uprising's leadership has had to enforce its authority by force. As time has passed, the need to use violent means has increased.

In accordance with the ideology that it is necessary for all segments of Palestinian society to "fall into line" in order to ensure the success of the uprising, the terrorist groups systematically act against those who refuse to abide by the instructions of the uprising's activists. Merchants who open their shops during strikes or who sell Israeli goods are beaten up and their goods burnt. Workers who want to work in Israel receive "night visits" from masked members of the "Shock Committees" who threaten them, take away their entry permits to Israel and beat them up.

The members of these terrorist organizations are also instructed by their leadership to attempt to destroy the Civil Administration and strike at its Arab employees. Policemen and other employees have been forced to resign. Those who have refused have been dragged from their homes and "interrogated" on suspicion of "collaboration" with the authorities. These "interrogations" involved the most heinous physical torture for those concerned including the severing of limbs. On many occasions, those "interrogated" have died following these sessions. In tandem with these activities, in an attempt to replace the local authority framework that have been damaged, and in an attempt to gain "legitimacy" with local residents, the "Shock Committees" have begun to operate against those suspected of drug offenses or other behavior deemed immoral.

From the second half of 1991, coinciding with the eve of the Madrid Conference, the wave of armed terrorist attacks directed against Israeli civilian and military targets carried out by armed individuals or groups whose identity is known to the security authorities has been strengthened.

The uprising has changed its form and has become much more murderous than in the past. In the words of the Palestinians themselves, it is now known as the "Red uprising." Criminals and murderers who once fled from their homes in fear of arrest and trial, are today organizing themselves in small armed bands. They are largely involved in attacking the IDF and Israeli civilians on the roads in Judea, Samaria and Gaza. Apart from that, they have instituted a reign of terror against the local population in order to maintain the impetus of the disturbances and in order to prevent the local population from resuming normal lives.

In the past, these activists shrank form the use of firearms. But today attacks on the IDF and Israeli civilians involving firearms have become a regular occurrence.

In the period between October 1991 (on the eve of the Madrid
Conference) - until October 31, 1992 there were 1886 attacks involving
the use of firearms in Judea, Samaria and Gaza. Fifteen Israeli civilians
were murdered by terrorists and 623 soldiers were injured during
operations duty. Up to date 808 Arabs have been murdered by other
Arabs. Two hundred and twenty-two of these murders alone occurred
during this year.

We don't know if you are aware of these facts, but if you wish to criticize
the IDF, you should be aware of the situation in which the security forces
are placed on a daily basis. Additionally, you would do well to turn your
attention to the suffering of the victims of Arab terror.

IDF Deployment

The disturbing increase in the murderous attacks on Israelis and Arabs
has obliged the IDF to deploy its forces accordingly.

We emphasize that the terrorists generally have the support and
protection of the local population—whether out of identification with their
actions, fear of retribution, or the belief that the withholding of support
is a betrayal of the cause. Consequently, it is almost impossible to stop
this terror by routine means. Every time an IDF force openly enters an
Arab village, the soldiers encounter opposition from local residents. This
opposition provides the terrorists with ample warning and as a result
enables them to evade arrest.

The solution to this problem has been found in the deployment of
undercover troops who can enter the villages without revealing their
identity and, as such, make contact with the terrorists and apprehend
them. These are the soldiers of the special units.

The disturbing increase in the activities of the terrorists has led to a
corresponding increase in the number of soldiers involved in this type of
activity. The only distinguishing feature of these units is that they do not
wear uniforms when on operations. The Rules of Engagement

(Regulations for Opening Fire) and all other military regulations apply to them in exactly the same manner they apply to all IDF soldiers.

To label these units "assassination squads," as the terrorist units have done in their propaganda, is to spread a malicious lie without any justification whatsoever. These units have no more authority to shoot to kill than any other IDF unit.

The Rules of Engagement

The IDF's Rules of Engagement in Judea, Samaria and Gaza are in accordance with Israeli criminal law, with the rulings of the Supreme Court, and have been approved by the IDF Advocate General and the Attorney General's Office. Briefly, IDF soldiers are permitted to open fire under two conditions:

A. If a soldier is in a life-threatening situation or in a situation where he is faced with serious physical harm.

B. If IDF soldiers are attempting to detain an individual suspected of crimes endangering another person, and there is no way to apprehend him without resorting to the use of firearms. In such circumstances, the soldier is permitted to open fire at the suspect's legs, after a warning has been given.

No one in the IDF has the authority to deviate from these regulations or to establish differing regulations for soldiers.

Response to General Questions

A. In your letter, you refer to an anonymous soldier who on an unspecified occasion reported things that were said by OC Southern Command Major General Matan Vilna'i. Despite the abstract nature of the claim, the matter was investigated. We completely deny that Major General Vilna'i ever made these remarks. An order has never been given to kill a man in place of arresting him. Any such order directly contravenes the basic premises underlying the State of Israel, legally and morally. As a citizen's army in a democracy, the IDF cannot allow itself to deviate from the laws laid down by the state. We are sure you are aware that Israel does not carry out capital punishment even against terrorists responsible for the murder of scores of Israeli civilians.

B. During the five years of the uprising, some 35 soldiers have been tried in military court for causing a death while deviating from the Rules of Engagement. Two of these soldiers were from the special units. These trials are still in progress, therefore we cannot comment on them. We would like to point out, however, that recently a lieutenant colonel who gave orders that deviated from the Rules of Engagement was tried for his offence. The said officer was demoted and sentenced to a month in prison which was suspended for two years. Without any reference to the offense, the said officer no longer holds the position he held at the time of the incident.

C. Judea, Samaria and Gaza are held by Israel as occupied military territory or hostile areas. According to International Law (Clause 43 in the Appendix to the Hague Convention-1907), the military is obligated to ensure peace and public security in areas under military control, not only when there is actual fighting going on, but also to put down hostile action. Keeping order and security thus falls upon the shoulders of the IDF, which employs military means to achieve these goals, changing them in accordance with events.

IDF soldiers keeping order in Judea, Samaria and the Gaza District therefore are carrying out a military operational role. In carrying out this role amidst a civilian population, IDF soldiers are required to behave in a certain manner. This includes specific Rules of Engagement because, of course, IDF soldiers in the territories are armed due to the nature of the mission.

The traditional international law, which is the legal basis of IDF activities in hostile regions, allows for considerable discretion regarding the use of fire by the army in fulfilling its obseverings (*sic*) to maintain security and public order. Orders for opening fire are derived from this law. *The fundamental concept underlying these instructions is based on the general principles of the Israeli criminal code.*

It was decided, as a principle of internal state policy, that the actual authority in the hands of the soldiers, and in general the orders concerning opening fire, will be based on the established principles of Israeli law. Concerning self-defense according to "necessary" defense, the justified defense stands with one fulfilling his role to disperse demonstrators in accordance with the law. These regulations are similar to the authority given to the police.

These regulations, we emphasize again, apply to all the IDF, including the special units.

The verdict of the Nazareth District Court exempting the state from damages

According to Israeli law, the state cannot be sued in civil court for damages inflicted as a result of IDF operational activity. The High Court of Justice, sitting as the Supreme Court, stated two principles on this point.

A. An action can be defined as "belligerent," even if it doesn't occur during wartime. The action itself has to be considered—and not the question if a war is in progress or not.

B. "Belligerent" activities are *usually* engaged in by the army during wartime. In accordance with these principles, the Supreme Court decided that guarding the borders in wartime is *not* a belligerent activity, as there are no belligerent characteristics.

In contrast, an operation in which a man was injured by Border Police fire during an ambush to apprehend terrorists in the Gaza District was labelled a "belligerent" operation.

You asked for an explanation why a resident of territories who was shot and injured when the IDF tried to arrest him cannot claim damages. We cannot take upon ourselves to explain the judgement of the Civil Department of the Attorney-General's Office. We think it proper that you approach them directly for an answer.

As mentioned above, any question about the obsevering [*sic*] of the state in question of damages in a war-time situation must be seen in the framework of the two conditions outlined above. Even if damage is caused by criminal negligence, the state is not liable under civil law because the action occurred under "belligerent conditions." When judging if an action is belligerent or not, the action must be examined in its entirety.

The question of where the action took place (within or without the "Green Line") is not decisive in judging if an action was belligerent or not.

According to Israeli law, when examining the liability of the state for damages in a belligerent action, the fact of any deviation from regulations is not relevant. Only the nature of the action itself can be taken into account, its aim and the extent and type of danger the soldier faced. In our opinion, judgements from international law cannot help us to define belligerent activities in an area under military control.

4. The investigation into the death of Sgt. Eli Aisha has not been completed, but it is already clear that the soldiers fired at him because they thought he was a terrorist who endangered them. After he was wounded he continued to point his weapon at them. This is why they fired on him again.

Answers to questions relating to incidents involving death

1. Only nine of the cases of death that appear in your list occurred as a result of IDF operational activity. The other cases were caused by other security elements and the IDF is not responsible for investigating them.

2. To the best of our understanding, your investigations are based on the one-sided reports given by individuals brought before you to give testimony by hostile groups who have an interest in marring the IDF's name. We hope you are aware of the fact that the "reports" of the local residents are not given directly after the incident in question. The reports you hear are "recycled" by people who have become "professional witnesses." In order to attack the IDF, they recount again and again the same propaganda lines used by the uprising's activists. We don't say that the reports you receive are an outright lie. But we ask you to take into account the fact that they were given by elements inherently hostile to the IDF and Israel.

3. It is interesting that in your wide-ranging investigation based largely on the tendentious reports of local residents you found that apparently only in nine cases is there any doubt about the legality of the shooting and force applied by the IDF.

The extent of the IDF's operational activities against terror is huge, encompassing *hundreds of special operations every year*. Therefore, the fact that you only found nine cases, once again based on one-sided reports, and that *maybe* there was unnecessary use of force, is in itself testimony to the high standards used by the IDF in its relationship with the residents of the territories.

Following are figures showing the results of IDF efforts in the war against terrorism during this past year, correct to October 1, 1992:

	Apprehended	Killed	Surrendered
Judea and Samaria	410	19	108
Gaza	81	7	27
Total	491	26	135

The statistics show that from the beginning of the year until October 1, 1992, in contrast to the approximately 500 terrorists who were detained, only 26 were killed. This shows that there is no foundation to claim that the IDF has a shoot to kill policy.

4. The IDF considers adherence to the law and regulations by IDF soldiers in Judea, Samaria and Gaza to be of primary importance. Every case of the death of a local resident is investigated by the Military Police. The material is transferred to the relevant military legal elements for a complete review. In the course of their activities to preserve law and security in the territories, hundreds of soldiers are forced to meet difficult and complex situations daily, as they face a hostile and violent population.

In a situation where so many soldiers are operating under such difficult conditions, some deviations are inevitable. The IDF is aware of this and tries to deal with the problem in various ways—education, preparation prior to operational duty in the territories, renewing familiarity with the regulations, briefings, etc. One of the important ways to deal with the problem is to take legal action against those who deviate from the standing orders. The policy of placing offenders on trial is a strict one. On more than one occasion soldiers have been tried for causing death through *negligence*. This is despite the fact that the IDF operates under conditions which are both difficult and complex, and where the possibilities for error are quite considerable.

5. The use of such methods has proved its effectiveness and it can be said with complete confidence that the number of deviations is minute in comparison with the entirety of the situation.

6. The soldiers in the special units are comprised of the best of our youth, the fruit of an open and democratic Israeli society. Since these activities demand forbearance and judgement under the most difficult of conditions, these units select soldiers of the highest quality. They are experts in their field and totally familiar with the Rules of Engagement. They have been involved in very few breaches of the regulations.

7. During our conversations and in your correspondence, you have described occurrences where Palestinian groups have often claimed that deaths were caused by illegal use of the Rules of Engagement. However, upon investigating the situation you found, based on the evidence of the local population alone, that the Rules were adhered to and that the force acted in accordance with the situation in which the soldiers found themselves. We are certain that you will also publish these facts.

Answers to General Questions

1. Our investigation has revealed that IDF soldiers were involved in only nine of the incidents mentioned in your letter; to be specific, with the incidents under the numbers 3,4,6,7,9,11,12,14 and 17. All the above cases have been or are being investigated by the Military Police's Criminal Investigation Department. It is worthwhile enunciating that an investigation is opened after every death in which the IDF is involved.

2. The investigation by the Military Police and the judicial review of the material has only been completed in one case. This the case of the death of Khalil Nader Khamayseh, resident of al-Yamoun. (No. 11 is in the attached list.) This is the only case we can relate. In the other cases,

because the issue is still under legal review, we cannot offer any details apart from a brief description of the incident.

[Note: Col. Yahav's letter provided details about the circumstances surrounding the deaths of the following Palestinians, all of which are reprinted below in the case section:

- *Khalil Nader Khamayseh*
- *Na'im abd as-Salaam al-Laham, Hajjaj Ibrahim Hajjaj, and Imad Mahmoud Bisharat*
- *Ra'ed abd ar-Rahman Dihmes*
- *Muhammad Isma'il abd as-Salaam al-Ja'afreh*
- *Abd al-Qader Yousef abd al-Qader Masarweh*
- *Ayman Muhammad Hussein Majadbeh*
- *Mahmoud Shalaldeh*
- *Zakariya al-Mathloum*
- *Muhammad Sadeq Kemayel Taktak.]*

Conclusion

The task of the special units is the locating and apprehending of armed and dangerous criminals and terrorists in order to bring them to justice. This is a daily operational activity. It is a dangerous one also, as it is aimed at armed squads who do not hesitate to murder anyone, including fellow Palestinians. These special units are comprised of men of the highest quality and standards who operate in a difficult, complex and dangerous environment. The IDF invests a great deal of resources in the choosing and training of these units.

These units operate in accordance with moral criteria which characterize the activities of the entire IDF, and are subject to all its rules and regulations, including those governing the opening of fire.

The regulations themselves are determined by Israel's democratic laws and the rulings of the Supreme Court, and they are not enacted without the prior approval of the appropriate legal authorities, including the Military Advocate General and the Justice Ministry.

The incidents involving the deaths of residents of the territories, which the IDF makes every effort to avoid, are investigated fully; action is taken when those involved are found to have deviated from regulations.

Any organization or body which wants to investigate the military system has first and foremost to investigate the entire picture and then present it, without trying to present the deviations as representative of the army or of some non-existent policy. Such a group also has to remember the difficult reality has been *imposed* upon the IDF and Israel with the outbreak of violence.

We do not purport to say that our soldiers have acted properly in each and every incident of the hundreds which have taken place in Judea, Samaria and the Gaza District and in which local resident are injured. We are convinced, however, that the number of these incidents in which IDF soldiers have not operated according to the regulations is quite limited; in such cases, justice is carried out to the fullest extent of the law.

In closing, may we ask you to compare the legality of the actions and the use of force employed by the terrorists acting in the names of the terrorist organizations in Judea, Samaria and the Gaza District. We are convinced that the results of such an investigation will open your eyes to the horrifying reality of the situation.

> Sincerely,
>
> David Yahav, Colonel
> Deputy IDF Advocate
> General

STATE OF ISRAEL
MINISTRY OF JUSTICE

Salah-a-Din Street, 29   TAMAR GAULAN, Adv.
P.O. Box 1087   Director, Human Rights and
91010 Jerusalem   International Relations Dept.

Telephone   (02) 708-569
Facsimile   (02) 869-473

December 21, 1992

Mr. Eric Goldstein
Research Director
Middle East Watch

Dear Mr. Goldstein,

With reference to your letters of 23 October and 16 November, 1992 addressed to the State Attorney, Mrs. Dorit Beinish, enclosed please find our response to your general and specific questions concerning cases in which local residents of the administered areas were killed.

We would appreciate it if this response appears together with your report which is due to be issued early in 1993.

Sincerely,

Tamar Gaulan

enclosure

Response of the Ministry of Justice Human Rights Department to Middle East Watch's Questions Concerning Cases in Which Local Residents of the Administered Areas Were Killed

We understand that the Deputy Military Advocate General has already sent you his response to the general and specific questions referred by you to him. Before we proceed to reply to the questions referred to the State Attorney in your letters of 23 October and 16 November 1992, we would like to make some general observations on the role of the Israel security forces and in particular on the conditions under which the undercover units operate and the rules governing such operations.

1. The role of the Israeli security forces in the administered areas is extremely complex, difficult and dangerous. Under Article 43 of the Hague Regulations of 1907, the relevant international law, Israel is obligated to maintain public order and safety in the administered areas. In fulfilling this duty, Israel's security forces must cope with ruthless terror organizations that do not hesitate to kidnap, torture and murder Israelis and even Palestinians. In fact, during five years of the intifada, more than 800 Palestinians have been murdered by intifada activists.

2. The goal of the undercover security forces is to locate terrorists, apprehend them and bring them to trial. The wanted terrorists are usually armed and determined to kill. They receive assistance and cover from the local population in the administered areas, often only out of fear. Were ordinary uniformed Israeli Defense Forces (IDF) forces used in such operations, the fugitives would likely be warned of their approach, thereby facilitating the escape of the wanted terrorists and/or increasing the likelihood of IDF casualties.

3. The members of the undercover units are subject to the same instructions as the rest of the security forces regarding the opening of fire. No license to kill has been given to the undercover units of the Israeli Police, the General Security Service (GSS), the Border Police, and the IDF, even as regards dangerous fugitives. The use of live ammunition is only permitted whether by undercover or regular security forces, in the following two situations:

a. **Danger to life**: Where there is a life-threatening situation or the danger of grave bodily harm to a member of the security forces or to another person in the immediate vicinity. In such circumstances one is allowed to shoot but using only the force necessary to neutralize the danger.

b. **The arrest of a suspect**: At the time of an attempted arrest when the man suspected of criminal offenses that endanger peoples' lives doesn't respond to warning measures (shouts and shots fired in the air), and continues to attempt to escape, the security forces are permitted to shoot single aimed shots at the suspect's legs.

As regards your two questions in your letter to the State Attorney of 16 November, 1992 we would like to note the following:

1. To date, no Border Policeman has been charged with illegally causing the death of a Palestinian during undercover activities. However, an investigation is opened in every case where a person's death is caused by a member of the security forces. Further, in all cases involving the death of any person not caused by an IDF soldier, the responsibility to determine whether to proceed with an indictment rests with the State Attorney. It should be noted that in the next few days a manslaughter indictment will be served on a Border Policeman stemming from an incident in which a rioter was killed in East Jerusalem.

2. Under Israeli law, the definition of "combat operation" is not dependent on the location in which the operation takes place, but rather upon the nature of the operation. The principles that guide the courts in determining whether a specific activity is "combat" thus relieving the government from responsibility for damages, have been developed by the Supreme Court of Israel. These principles state that a "combat operation" need not occur during a time of war. To ascertain if there has been a "combat operation", one must examine the activity itself to discover if the signs of battle existed. Therefore, a "combat operation" can occur inside or outside the borders of Israel or in the administered areas.

As regards your specific questions concerning five incidents of death caused by members of the GSS or Border Police, below are the details of these cases as provided to us by the authorities who conducted the investigations thereof.

[Note: Advocate Gaulan's letter provided information about the following cases:
- *Muhannad Muhammad Turkeman*
- *Jamal Rashid Ghanem*
- *Khaled Muhammad Saker Fahmawi*
- *Zakariya Muhammad Issa Qabalan*
- *Jawad As'ad Rahal*
- *Abdullah Dibash Hamarshe.*

Advocate Gaulan's comments are reprinted in full in the case section below.]

April 27, 1993

Col. David Yahav   via fax and mail
Deputy Judge Advocate General, Israel Defense Force
6 David Elazar Street, HaKirya, Tel Aviv

Dear Col. Yahav,

As you may have surmised, Middle East Watch has not yet issued the
findings of its research into the activities of special units of the Israeli
security forces in the West Bank and Gaza Strip. You will recall that my
colleagues and I met with you and your staff on this subject late last year,
and you were kind enough to send a written response in December to
many of our questions about this issue, including questions about specific
cases in which Palestinians were killed.

However, since the IDF investigations into nearly all of the cases that we
raised were at the time still incomplete, the information you furnished
about them was, as you stated, necessarily brief and tentative. This was
the situation with eight of the nine cases that you said involved the IDF.

Middle East Watch is now nearing completion of the report and wishes
to give you the opportunity to supplement the information you provided
to us about these cases. We will be able to incorporate into our report
any further information you furnish about the cases, so long as it reaches
us by Monday, May 17.

Please note that we remain interested in receiving copies of the official
autopsy reports. We have received none despite having expressed such a
request to you.

The eight cases for which you said the IDF investigation was incomplete
are:

1. Na'im abd as-Salaam Laham, Hajjaj Ibrahim Hajjaj, and Imad
Mahmoud Bisharat, March 15, 1992 (Old 'Askar refugee camp, Nablus
district)

2. Ra'ed abd ar-Rahman Dihmes, March 18, 1992 (Kufr Qadoum, Nablus
district)

3. Muhammad Isma'il abd as-Salaam Ja'afreh, April 1, 1992 (Tarqumia, Hebron district)

4. Abd al-Qader Yousef abd al-Qader Masarweh, April 9, 1992 (Nur Shams refugee camp, Tulkarm district)

5. Ayman Muhammad Hussein Majadbeh, April 21, 1992 ('Allar, Tulkarm district)

6. Mahmoud Shalaldeh, May 7, 1992 (Sa'ir, Hebron district)

7. Zakariya al-Mathloum, July 17, 1992 (Gaza City)

8. Muhammad Sadeq Kemayel Taktak, October 3, 1992 (Qabatiya, Jenin district)

I also wish to call to your attention the fact that neither the IDF nor the State Attorney claimed jurisdiction for investigating four of the 18 cases about which we wrote to you. These unclaimed cases are:

1. Husam Yousef Muhammad abu Kheir, January 4, 1992 (Khan Younis, Gaza Strip)

2. Sa'd Khalil abd al-Karim Miqdad, June 4, 1992 (Khan Younis, Gaza Strip)

3. Nuri Sharif abd al-Qader al-Aqqad, July 27, 1992 (Khan Younis, Gaza Strip)

4. 'Issam al-Khatib, October 10, 1992 (ar-Ram, West Bank)

Does the IDF maintain that IDF personnel were not involved in these deaths? If not, can you tell us which agency is responsible for conducting the investigations into these cases?

Again, in order for our report to reflect fully the depth and conclusions of the official investigation into many of the key cases that will be discussed, we need to receive your reply by May 17.

Thank you for your attention to these matters. Do not hesitate to phone or write if you wish to discuss them.

Sincerely yours,

Eric Goldstein

cc: Lt. Col. Rami Kaydar, IDF Spokesman, Information Branch

April 27, 1993

Tamar Gaulan, Adv.   via mail and fax
Director, Human Rights and International Relations Dept.
Ministry of Justice
P.O. Box 1087, 91010 Jerusalem, Israel

Dear Adv. Gaulan,

As you may have surmised, Middle East Watch has not yet issued the
findings of its research into the activities of special units of the Israeli
security forces in the West Bank and Gaza Strip. You will recall that my
colleagues met with you and State Attorney Beinish on this subject late
last year, and you were kind enough to provide a written response, dated
December 21, to many of our questions about this issue, including
questions about specific cases in which Palestinians were killed.

However, your reply noted that, of the five cases we raised that you said
the Ministry of Justice was handling, four were still under investigation.
Your comments on these cases were therefore brief and tentative, but you
indicated a willingness to "pass on relevant information when it becomes
available."

Middle East Watch is now nearing completion of its report and wishes to
give you the opportunity to supplement the information you provided to
us about these cases. We will be able to incorporate into our report any
further information you furnish about the cases, so long as it reaches us
by Monday, May 17.

Please note that we remain interested in receiving copies of the official
autopsy reports. We have received none despite having expressed such a
request to you and the IDF.

The four cases which you reported as still being under investigation are:

1. Jamal Rashid Ghanem, March 22, 1992 (Shweikeh, Tulkarm district)

2. Zakariya Muhammad 'Issa Qabalan, April 15, 1992 (Greater Abassan,
southern Gaza Strip)

3. Jawad As'ad Rahal, April 29, 1992 ('Arrabeh, Jenin district)

4. Abdullah Dibash Hamarshe, September 9, 1992 (Ya'bad, Jenin district, West Bank)

I also wish to call to your attention the fact that neither the IDF nor the Ministry of Justice claimed jurisdiction for investigating four of the 18 cases about which we wrote to you. These unclaimed cases are:

1. Husam Yousef Muhammad abu Kheir, January 4, 1992 (Khan Younis, Gaza Strip)

2. Sa'd Khalil abd al-Karim Miqdad, June 4, 1992 (Khan Younis, Gaza Strip)

3. Nuri Sharif abd al-Qader al-Aqqad, July 27, 1992 (Khan Younis, Gaza Strip)

4. 'Issam al-Khatib, October 10, 1992 (ar-Ram, West Bank)

Does the Ministry of Justice maintain that neither Border Police nor GSS personnel was involved in these deaths? If that is the case, can you tell us which agency is responsible for conducting the investigations into them?

Again, in order for our report to reflect fully the depth and conclusions of the official investigations into many of the key cases that will be discussed, we need to receive your reply by May 17.

Thank you for your attention to these matters. Do not hesitate to phone or write if you wish to discuss them.

Sincerely yours,

Eric Goldstein

cc: State Attorney Dorit Beinish

STATE OF ISRAEL
MINISTRY OF JUSTICE

Salah-a-Din Street   Tamar Gaulan, Adv.
P.O. Box 1087   Director, Human Rights and
91010 Jerusalem   International Relations Dept.

Telephone   (02) 708-569
Facsimile   (02) 869-473

                                            File 080.M
                                            May 20, 1993

By Fax: (212) 972-0905

Mr. Eric Goldstein
Research Director
Middle East Watch
485 Fifth Avenue
New York, NY 10017-6104
USA

Dear Mr. Goldstein:

      Further to the 18 May 1993 fax of Adv. Weiner in response to
your letters dated 27 April 1993, I am writing to furnish you with
additional information. Please find enclosed FACT SHEETS concerning
the deaths of Jamal Ghanem, Zakariya Qabalan, Jawad Rahal and
Abdullah Hamarshe.

      We have also made inquiries into the other four cases mentioned
on page two of your letters. According to the information that we have
received, the cases of Husam abu Kheir, Sa'd Miqdad, and Nuri al-Aqqad
were investigated by the Israel Police. We are waiting to receive the
results in these cases. As regards the death of Issam al-Khatib, this is
being investigated by the Military Police Investigations Branch and we
suggest that you contact Col. David Yahav, Deputy Military Advocate
General.

We trust that this information will be useful in the preparation of MEW's Report.

Sincerely,

Tamar Gaulan

enclosures
cc: State Attorney Dorit Beinish
cc: Colonel David Yahav, Deputy Military Advocate General

[Note: Advocate Gaulan's comments about the Ghanem, Qabalan, Rahal, and Hamarshe cases are reprinted in full in the case section below.]

IDF Spokesman
Information Branch

21 May 1993

Mr. Eric Goldstein
Middle East Watch
485 Fifth Avenue
New York, NY 10017-6104
USA

   re: **Request for Details Concerning Incidents Involving**
         IDF Units in Judea, Samaria, and the Gaza District

Dear Mr. Goldstein,

I am pleased to respond to your letter of 27 April 1993 as follows:

1.   A legal deposition has been handed down on only one of the
       cases you listed as those on which you have yet to receive the
       findings of the investigations. In the other cases, no legal
       depositions have yet been given; I therefore am unable to
       provide details beyond those already furnished in regard to those
       cases.

2.   A legal deposition was given in the investigation of the death of
       Muhammad Isma'il abd as-Salaam Ja'afreh, born in 1977.
       Ja'afreh died after being shot by an IDF soldier in a stone-
       throwing incident in April 1992. *[Note: the full text of Margalit's
       comments with respect to the case of Ja'afreh appears in full in the case
       section below.]*

3.   As for your request to receive copies of the official autopsy
       reports, we are unable to disclose them because of medical
       confidentiality. An autopsy report will be given only to a relative
       of the deceased if specifically requested.

4.   In regard to your query about the investigation of four cases which you refer to as "unclaimed", I am able to report that in fact three of the cases were investigated by the Israel Police, and not by the IDF. The fourth case is presently under investigation by the Military Police due to the fact that IDF soldiers were involved in the incident.

Sincerely,

Avital Margalit, Capt.
Head of Information Section

The following section lists the case-specific questions which Middle East Watch posed to the Ministry of Justice and the IDF. In addition, Middle East Watch requested responses for each case to the general questions (see above). The official responses follow the questions Middle East Watch asked about each case.

1.   MUHANNAD MUHAMMAD TURKEMAN, December 12, 1991
        (al-Zababdeh, Jenin district, West Bank)

MIDDLE EAST WATCH'S QUESTIONS: An official military source told *Hadashot* that Turkeman was shot after failing to comply with an order to stop and after making a suspicious move. Is this consistent with the finding of the official investigation? Please describe where Turkeman was situated when he was shot and any threatening moves he made that led to his being shot.

Was Turkeman wanted and/or armed when he was shot? Is there truth to allegations that he was the victim of a mistaken identity, i.e. that his pursuers mistook him for the Muhammad Turkeman who was arrested in late October 1992 in connection with the fatal attack that month on a Jewish settler in Jenin?

RESPONSES:
State of Israel Ministry of Justice (December 21, 1992): This case was investigated by the Jenin police. The findings of the investigation were transferred to the Northern District Attorney who decided to close the file after concluding that, under the circumstances, the shooting was justified.

On 12 December, 1991, an IDF unit surprised a Palestinian terrorist cell and succeeded in arresting its members, except one armed terrorist who managed to escape. Road blocks were set up in the entire region in order to apprehend the escaped terrorist. Information was received from reliable sources that the terrorist was a passenger in a local vehicle and was hiding among the other passengers. A taxi with a number of passengers, among them Turkeman, stopped at one of the road blocks and was searched by a member of the GSS who instructed those in the vehicle not to move.

From a photograph of the members of the terrorist cell the GSS man had seen earlier, he identified Turkeman to be the terrorist who had escaped.

While the vehicle was being searched, Turkeman suddenly inserted his hand into the inner pocket of his jacket. The GSS man interpreted this act as an attempt to draw a weapon and, believing that he was in a life-threatening situation, he drew his gun and shot Turkeman, thereby killing him.

The investigation revealed that the GSS man had mistaken Turkeman's identity and that Turkeman was not the fugitive in question. It was also ascertained that Turkeman had not been armed.

After reviewing the Police file, the Northern District Attorney determined that, in the unique circumstances of this case, the shooting was justified since the GSS man reasonably believed that he was in a life-threatening situation and as such had acted out of self-defense. The findings were based on the following:

1. conclusive information existed that an armed terrorist was in the area and fleeing arrest;
2. there was a remarkable physical resemblance between Turkeman and the fugitive terrorist; and
3. Turkeman made a sudden arm movement towards his pocket after having been warned not to move.

***

2. **HUSAM YOUSEF MUHAMMAD ABU KHEIR, January 4, 1992 (Khan Younis, Gaza Strip)**
    [*Note: In the end, Middle East Watch did not conduct extensive field work on this case.*]

MIDDLE EAST WATCH'S QUESTIONS: Was the victim masked when shot? Was he carrying a weapon when shot, and if so, had he made an attempt to use it? Describe any efforts that were made to arrest the victim before he was fatally shot. If none was made, please explain.

RESPONSE:
Ministry of Justice (May 20, 1993): The case was investigated by the Israel Police. We are awaiting to receive the results in this case.

***

3.   NA'IM ABD AS-SALAAM AL-LAHAM, HAJJAJ IBRAHIM
        HAJJAJ, and IMAD MAHMOUD BISHARAT, March 15, 1992
        (Old 'Askar refugee camp, Nablus district, West Bank)

MIDDLE EAST WATCH'S QUESTIONS: Which, if any, of the victims were
armed at the time that they were shot?

MEW's investigation indicates there are over 40 bullet holes in the side
of the house where the incident took place. If this number is correct, why
were so many bullets fired?

How far away were the soldiers from each of their victims when they first
opened fire? Did the soldiers execute the three-stage procedure for
apprehending suspects? If not, why?

According to our investigation, Hajjaj was killed not in the first burst of
fire, but later, inside the house, after having fled from the soldiers in the
garden. Please explain how and when he was shot. Did the soldiers fire
more than one volley? If so, why? Which of the victims died in the later
volleys?

RESPONSE:
IDF Deputy JAG (undated, received December 15, 1992): Because the
issue is still under legal review, we cannot offer any details apart from a
brief description of the incident. Material from the investigation to date
suggests that an IDF force charged towards a terrorist squad, who
according to earlier information was heavily armed and at the time of the
incident one of the squad had an assault rifle which appeared to be a
Kalashnikov (A.K. 47). It should be noted that the terrorist squad
consisted of murderers. Na'im Laham was a former prisoner who was
imprisoned on no less than four occasions for different crimes. According
to reliable information and the evidence of his partners in the act who
were captured, he was party to a number of terrorist attacks involving
firearms directed against Israeli citizens and the security forces.
Moreover, he tortured a number of local Arab residents and shot and
wounded others whom he suspected of "collaboration."

IDF Spokesman (May 21, 1993): No legal deposition has yet been given;
I am therefore unable to provide details beyond those already furnished
in regard to this case.

***

4.   RA'ED ABD AR-RAHMAN DIHMES, March 18, 1992 (Kufr
        Qadoum, Nablus district, West Bank)

MIDDLE EAST WATCH'S QUESTIONS: Shortly after the killing, military
sources quoted in the press stated that Dihmes was killed when soldiers
opened fire at a group of three masked men, one of whom brandished a
knife and a large stick at the soldiers.

Did the official investigation conclude (1) that the youths were masked?
(2) that they had made threatening moves? If so, please describe the
threatening moves, who made it/them, and please specify the distance
separating the soldiers and the youths at that moment. Also, please
describe the location where the soldiers were located, and whether they
were in a position to take cover if necessary.

RESPONSES:
IDF Deputy JAG (undated, received December 15, 1992): Because the
issue is still under legal review, we cannot offer any details apart from a
brief description of the incident.

The investigation to date suggests that the soldiers, whose aim was to
arrest murderous and armed terrorists, fired at the legs of the deceased
and his friends. During the operation, the soldiers saw the deceased
waving an object which seemed to be a rifle. The soldiers, who feared for
their lives, shot and killed him.

IDF Spokesman (May 21, 1993): No legal deposition has yet been given;
I am therefore unable to provide details beyond those already furnished
in regard to this case.

                                   ***

5.   JAMAL RASHID GHANEM, March 22, 1992 (Shweikeh,
        Tulkarm district, West Bank)

*[Note: Middle East Watch submitted questions about this case on the basis of
extensive reporting on it by journalists and human rights organizations. We did not
conduct our own fieldwork.]*

MIDDLE EAST WATCH'S QUESTIONS: What was the distance between the security forces and Ghanem when they first opened fire? Was Ghanem running away from them or was he standing facing them when they opened fire?

Major General Daniel Yatom, military commander for the Central Region, told Israel Television on May 1 that Ghanem was running towards a hole in the fence when he was shot. Did the official investigation verify the existence of this hole? If there was a hole, why did the security forces fail to guard it to prevent its use as an escape route?

RESPONSES:
State of Israel Ministry of Justice (December 21, 1992): Jamal Ghanem was killed during a routine arrest. Thus far a decision has not been made whether to issue an indictment.

Ghanem was wanted by the security forces following his participation in terrorist activities. On 22 March, 1992, reliable information was received that he was located at a soccer field. A Border Police unit that was coincidentally in the vicinity was sent to the field in order to arrest him. According to the Border Policemen's testimony, all the routine procedures for the arrest of a suspect were performed. The members of the Border Police unit first shouted warnings to Ghanem and then fired shots into the air, at which point the suspect did not stop. Subsequently, two shots were fired towards the suspect's legs, but the suspect slipped in a puddle on the field and as a result was wounded in the back. The autopsy revealed that two bullets had entered into the lower back of the deceased.

The Border Policemen's testimony also stated that one of their reasons for shooting was that the suspect was fleeing in the direction of a hole in the fence and they feared that if they did not shoot towards his legs he would succeed in escaping. The human rights organization, B'Tselem, brought to the attention of the Central District Attorney two local witnesses who claimed that there was no such hole in the fence. The District Attorney instructed the Israel Police to obtain a statement from those witnesses in order to clarify this issue and other questions regarding the circumstances of Ghanem's death.

State of Israel Ministry of Justice (May 20, 1993): Immediately following the death of Jamal Ghanem, the Office of the Israel State Attorney requested that an investigation of the matter be commenced by the police. The Police conducted the investigation and then recommended that no charges be brought because of insufficient evidence in the case. The case was then reviewed as well by the office of the State Attorney and the Central District Attorney, both of whom accepted the recommendation of the Police to close the file due to insufficient evidence.

The following facts, detailed in the investigation, led to the closing of the file:

1) On March 22, 1993, undercover police were sent to a Tulkarm football field in order to arrest Jamal Ghanem. Ghanem was wanted for violent acts against both the security forces and local Arab residents of Tulkarm.

2) According to the police, when they arrived at the field, they yelled to Ghanem in Arabic "Stop, Army!" Despite this order, Ghanem began to flee and the policemen fired warning shots into the air. Ghanem tried to hide behind the game's referee, but the referee fled. Then Ghanem began to run towards the northwest corner of the field where the wall was low and without fencing on top. Only when Ghanem continued to flee towards this gap in the fence were two shots fired at his legs.

3) On the day of the incident, police reports indicate that rainy weather had caused the entire field to be filled with puddles. Each of the policemen at the scene of the shooting was questioned individually, and each testified that Ghanem had slipped in one of the puddles as two shots were fired by one of the policemen at his legs. This caused the bullets to enter his upper torso rather than his legs. Immediately after the shooting, one of the policemen, who was trained as a medic, began to administer medical attention to Ghanem, but when an ambulance arrived at the scene Ghanem was pronounced dead by the ambulance doctor.

4) The police explanation for the shooting was that Ghanem was attempting to escape and that an escape route was available to him. Each of the policemen who were present stated that their colleague who opened fire had followed all regulations by announcing his presence and ordering the suspect to stop, by firing in the air, and by firing at the suspect's legs.

5) In addition to the testimony given by the policemen, testimony was taken from several local Arab eyewitnesses. This testimony was conflicting, i.e. some denied there was an opening in the fence and another confirmed that there was; some heard shots fired into the air, others did not. One eyewitness was asked about testimony he had allegedly given to a newspaper. The newspaper had reported that this eyewitness had seen the deceased running with his hands in the air. The eyewitness denied the story and denied ever having said this to a reporter. He said that, in fact, he did not know whether Ghanem fell because of a gun shot wound or because he slipped in a puddle. He is quoted as saying, "There were many puddles on the field."

On the basis of all the evidence which was compiled in this case, the following conclusions were reached.

a) Despite the allegation by several local Arab eyewitnesses that no escape route was available to Ghanem, all of the police officers and one of the other Arab eyewitnesses agreed that there was a break in the fence in the northwest corner of the field.

b) All of the police and two local Arab eyewitnesses agreed that the officers had fired first into the air. This is in accordance with the regulations for opening fire.

c) The policemen's account of Ghanem slipping in a puddle was corroborated by the pathologist who examined Ghanem's wounds. The pathologist concluded that Ghanem's wounds were consistent with the description of the manner in which the policemen said he fell as the shots were fired.

d) In order for any officer to have been indicted in this case, the State Attorney's Office concluded that it would have had to have been proved that there was no possible escape route or that the officers did not follow the regulations for opening fire.

Since no evidence was available to prove either, the file was closed due to lack of incriminating evidence.

***

6.   MUHAMMAD ISMA'IL ABD AS-SALAAM AL-JA'AFREH, April 1, 1992 (Tarqumia, Hebron district, West Bank)

MIDDLE EAST WATCH'S QUESTIONS: Was al-Ja'afreh armed or masked when he was shot? What are the specific circumstances that justify his being shot? His death certificate, signed by an Israeli doctor, notes an upward entry wound in the chest and an exit wound in the back, and says the shot was fired from a "face-to-face" (*panim al panim*) position. According to the official findings, how far was the soldier when he shot at al-Ja'afreh? Was al-Ja'afreh shot from the front or from behind?

RESPONSES:
IDF Deputy JAG (undated, received December 15, 1992): Because the issue is still under legal review, we cannot offer any details apart from a brief description of the incident.

The investigation to date suggests that during the operation to capture people throwing stones at passing cars one of the soldiers managed to catch a stone-thrower. Meanwhile the second soldier spotted an Arab resident holding a large stone in his hand which he was about to throw at him. The soldier, who feared for his life, fired one bullet at the attacker, and he appeared to drop the stone and escaped. It is likely that the deceased was the same person who was about to injure the soldier. The proceedings of the investigation are incomplete.

IDF Spokesman, Information Branch (May 21, 1993): A legal deposition was given in the investigation of the death of Muhammad Isma'il Abd as-Salaam al-Ja'afreh, born in 1977. Al-Ja'afreh died after being shot by an IDF soldier in a stone-throwing incident in April 1992.

a.   After careful study of the findings of the investigation, the Military Advocate issued instructions that no statutory or disciplinary action be taken against the soldier involved. The Advocate determined that the soldier had acted in self-defense in a life-threatening situation.

b.   The shot was fired during an action aimed at apprehending and arresting residents who were hurling heavy stones at close range at an IDF vehicle carrying soldiers.

Two soldiers disguised as residents—one of whom fired
the shot in question—succeeded in reaching one of the
groups of stone-throwers. One soldier jumped on a
stone-thrower, in order to subdue and arrest him.
Meanwhile, the second soldier called out a warning in
Arabic ("Halt, Army") and fired a warning shot into the
air. At this point, a youth standing one meter's distance
from him turned to face him, and then advanced towards
him waving a stone in his hand in a threatening manner.
This youth would later be identified as the deceased al-
Ja'afreh. The soldier believed that al-Ja'afreh was about
to hurl the stone at him at point blank range, and felt
himself to be in immediate danger. He fired a single
bullet at the deceased in an act of self-defense.

The deceased dropped the stone and fled. He was later
found wounded close by. Medical treatment immediately
rendered to him by the soldiers, an army medic, and an
army doctor who arrived at the scene was of no avail,
and al-Ja'afreh died of his wounds.

c.   The soldier's testimony was corroborated by the second
       soldier who was with him. Testimony from local residents
       present at the scene was not provided. It must be kept in
       mind that those residents present at the scene
       participated in the stoning of the military vehicle.

d.   According to the report filed by the doctor who treated
       the deceased and according to his testimony, al-Ja'afreh
       was wounded by a single bullet. The bullet entered
       through the chest and exited from the upper back; this
       shows that the shot was fired from the front. The body of
       the deceased was turned over to his family who did not
       request that an autopsy be performed.

e.   The deceased was not wearing a mask.

f.   After firing at the deceased who had endangered his life,
       the soldier fired at the legs of stone-throwers fleeing the
       scene. According to the soldier, these shots were fired at
       the legs of adult residents who had participated in

stoning the military vehicle. Later it was found that two youths under the age of 16 received leg injuries as a result of these shots. In the light of these findings, the Military Advocate determined that apparently there was prima facie evidence that the soldier had acted negligently. He therefore ordered that the soldier be tried in disciplinary proceedings before a high-ranking IDF officer. A judgment has yet to be handed down.

***

7.   **ABD AL-QADER YOUSEF ABD AL-QADER MASARWEH, April 9, 1992 (Nur Shams refugee camp, Tulkarm district, West Bank)**

MIDDLE EAST WATCH'S QUESTIONS: What is the official investigation's conclusions regarding why a soldier fatally shot Masarweh? If the soldier believed that his life was in danger, what was the basis for this belief?

What warning steps or arrest attempts, if any, were carried out before the soldier fatally shot Masarweh? What was the distance between the soldier and Masarweh when he fired? Does the autopsy report show entry wounds in the front or the back of Masarweh's body?

If Masarweh was shot according to the rules for apprehending a suspect, was opening fire necessary to stop him, or was he already effectively trapped in an enclosed area surrounded by a large number of soldiers?

RESPONSES:
IDF Deputy JAG (undated, received December 15, 1992): Because the issue is still under legal review, we cannot offer any details apart from a brief description of the incident.

The investigation to date suggests that the above was suspected of carrying out dangerous crimes and, as such, an operation was launched to capture him. During the attempt to arrest him, the soldiers' presence was revealed and the deceased started to escape. He was warned then one of the soldiers tried to stop him by firing at his legs. Unfortunately it seems that due to the conditions in the field, the soldier hit the deceased's upper body and killed him. It should be noted that the use of firearms for the purposes of arrest always includes the danger of a fatal outcome or harm, to the other person, even if used carefully. And that is due to the possibility of unpredictable accidents which can always occur.

IDF Spokesman (May 21, 1993): No legal deposition has yet been given; I am therefore unable to provide details beyond those already furnished in regard to this case.

***

8.   ZAKARIYA MUHAMMAD 'ISSA QABALAN, April 15, 1992
         (Greater Abassan, southern Gaza Strip)

[Note: after initial fieldwork, Middle East Watch decided to omit this case from the report.]

MIDDLE EAST WATCH'S QUESTIONS: After Qabalan was first wounded, did security forces shoot him again while he lay wounded on the ground? If so, what are the reasons?

The IDF initially identified the victim as Salaameh Muhammad Salaameh Barka. What was the cause of this error? Was the operation conceived to apprehend Barka?

RESPONSES:
State of Israel Ministry of Justice (December 21, 1992): The events surrounding the 15 April, 1992 death of 'Issa Qabalan are still under police investigation and the file has yet to be transferred to the State Attorney. It would therefore be inappropriate for us to comment on this matter at this time.

State of Israel Ministry of Justice (May 20, 1993): Zakariya Qabalan was shot by a Border Policeman on 14 April 1992 in the area of Abassan Ha'katana in the Gaza District. His death was investigated by the Gaza Police. The findings of the investigation were forwarded to the Office of the Southern District Attorney. It was determined that Qabalan was armed when he was spotted by the Border Police. They attempted to stop him but he initiated fire in their direction. They returned fire, killing

Qabalan. Thus, the Southern District Attorney decided to close the file since the shooting by the Border Policeman was justified under the circumstances.

***

9.   AYMAN MUHAMMAD HUSSEIN MAJADBEH, April 21, 1992
        ('Allar, Tulkarm district, West Bank)

MIDDLE EAST WATCH'S QUESTIONS: What is the official investigation's conclusions regarding why a soldier fatally shot Majadbeh? If the soldier believed that his life was in danger, what was the basis for this belief?

What warning steps or arrest attempts, if any, were carried out before Majadbeh was fatally shot? Please indicate at what distance from Majadbeh, and in what location, was the soldier who shot him.

Was Majadbeh "wanted," and if so, for what offenses? Was he armed at the time of his death? If so, what kind of weapon was he carrying? Was it recovered?

Did Majadbeh die at the scene of the shooting, or later?

RESPONSES:
IDF Deputy Judge Advocate General (undated, received December 15, 1992): Because the issue is still under legal review, we cannot offer any details apart from a brief description of the incident.

The investigation to date suggests that the deceased was suspected of carrying out dangerous crimes and permanently carrying a firearm. During an attempt to arrest him, the deceased was warned to stop and to give himself up. The deceased did not respond to the warning and began to flee. One of the soldiers fired a single shot at his legs to stop him. Immediately after the shot, the deceased appeared to draw a weapon. The soldier, fearing for his life and the life of his comrades, fired an additional shot. The deceased was wounded and died. A search of the body revealed a pistol which was loaded and cocked with a bullet in the breach.

IDF Spokesman (May 21, 1993): No legal deposition has yet been given; I am therefore unable to provide details beyond those already furnished in regard to this case.

***

10.   JAWAD AS'AD RAHAL, April 29, 1992 ('Arrabeh, Jenin district, West Bank)

MIDDLE EAST WATCH'S QUESTIONS: How many soldiers participated in the operation that led to Rahal's death? If only two, as MEW has been told, why were so few sent to carry out the operation?

What warning steps or arrest attempts, if any, were carried out before the soldier fatally shot Rahal? If none, what are the reasons?

Was Rahal in possession of a weapon? Was he himself carrying it when he was shot? If so, what kind of weapon, was it a real or toy weapon, and is it currently in the IDF's possession? What threatening move did he make, if any, that led to his being shot?

Was Rahal shot a second time as he lay wounded on the ground? If so, what are the reasons?

RESPONSES:
State of Israel Ministry of Justice (December 21, 1992): An investigation into Jawad Rahal's death was carried out by the Jenin police and was completed just recently. The findings of this investigation are in the process of being forwarded to the Central District Attorney. At present, we are not able to provide you with information concerning this case. However, we will pass on the relevant information when it becomes available to us.

State of Israel Ministry of Justice (May 20, 1993): On 29 April 1992 Jawad Rahal was shot in Jenin, by a Border Policeman who was attempting to arrest him since he was suspected of committing serious terrorist crimes. He died of his wound. According to intelligence information Rahal was believed to have a pistol in his possession at the time he was shot. However, after the shooting, a search of his body did not reveal any firearms.

A police investigation was carried out into the circumstances of Rahal's death. The findings of this investigation were transferred to the Office of the Northern District Attorney. During the time when the file was under review in that Office, additional information regarding the circumstances of Rahal's death came to the attention of the Police investigators. The file was therefore returned to the Police for completion of the inquiry. The inquiry is currently underway. Once it is finished, the file will be returned to the Office of the Northern District Attorney for a determination of what measures should be taken.

***

11.   **KHALIL NADER KHAMAYSEH, April 29, 1992 (al-Yamoun, Jenin district, West Bank)**

MIDDLE EAST WATCH'S QUESTIONS: Were the soldiers able to approach Khamayseh without his noticing their presence? How far from him were they when one of them opened fire? Was Khamayseh in possession of a weapon? Was he himself carrying it when he was shot? If so, what kind of weapon, was it a real or toy weapon, and is it currently in the IDF's possession? What threatening move did he make, if any, that led to his being shot?

RESPONSES:
IDF Deputy JAG (undated, received December 15, 1992):

1. + 2. The shots from which the deceased was injured and died were fired by soldiers who were *not* members of the elite units. The reasons for his death were investigated by the Criminal Investigation Department of the Military Police and the findings were presented to the Military Advocate General for his legal opinion.

3. After checking of the investigative material, the Military Advocate General decided to close the inquiry file without taking any steps against any of the soldiers. It was found that the soldiers fired since they were convinced that their lives were in danger. According to their testimony,

the soldiers discovered the deceased standing on the roof of a house armed with a weapon and binoculars, which he was using to scan the area. The soldiers, convinced that he was an illegally armed terrorist, started running towards him. The soldiers shouted a warning in Arabic and the deceased turned towards the soldiers holding the pistol in his hand. One of the soldiers, an officer, who saw that the deceased was aiming the pistol at him, fired at him and killed him. Later it was found that the pistol the deceased [was holding] was not real. The inquiry file was closed after it became apparent that the reasons for the incident was a mistake on the part of the officer, who was concerned with the danger to his life. This was a completely honest mistake and the conduct of the officer who was convinced that his life and the life of his soldiers were in danger, was reasonable.

4. During the investigation another resident, Nayif Kamanji, who was with the deceased during the incident, was questioned. It was noted that the same resident, although he stood close to the deceased, was not injured in any way since he did not endanger the soldiers. According to Kamanji's testimony he and the deceased were drinking tea at the time of the incident. Before that, the deceased, who was aged 17 at his death, came to him wearing an army shirt and cap and was carrying a plastic pistol, binoculars and a knife.

5. It was noted that, according to the testimony, the soldiers charged at the house where the deceased was from a distance of 15 meters and that they fired from range of ten meters. The soldiers were unable to reach the deceased without drawing his attention and risking their lives (remember that, at the time of the incident, the soldiers were convinced that the deceased was holding a real pistol). It should be noted that the attempt to arrest the deceased was not based on earlier information which linked him to terrorist activity, but occurred since the deceased was carrying a pistol and was behaving suspiciously.

6. Three entry wounds and one exit wound were found on the body of the deceased.

***

12.   MAHMOUD SHALALDEH, May 7, 1992 (Sa'ir, Hebron district, West Bank)

MIDDLE EAST WATCH'S QUESTIONS: MEW has collected evidence indicating that men dressed in the attire of observant Jews fired fatally at Shalaldeh, following a car chase, as he fled from a car approximately one kilometer from the location where the men's vehicle had been stoned.

Is this account true? If true, what circumstances justified the fatal shooting at such a great distance from the incident, and what made Shalaldeh a legitimate target for gunfire?

If this account is not true, please describe the circumstances in which the fatal shooting occurred, including the procedures to warn or to attempt arrest that were followed prior to the fatal shot. Also, please respond to the allegation that shots were fired at the Palestinian vehicle during the car chase.

RESPONSE:
IDF Deputy JAG (undated, received December 15, 1992): The investigation to date suggests that the shots were fired during the attempt to catch residents who were throwing stones at passing vehicles and endangering the lives of the passengers. The soldiers moved to detain the stone-thrower, who escaped in a car, in accordance with the procedure for detaining a suspect. At the end of the chase the deceased ran from his car as the soldiers fired towards his legs in order to stop him. The deceased was wounded and died. The circumstances of the incident are being investigated by the Military Advocate General.

IDF Spokesman (May 21, 1993): No legal deposition has yet been given; I am therefore unable to provide details beyond those already furnished in regard to this case.

***

13.   SA'D KHALIL 'ABD AL-KARIM MIQDAD, June 4, 1992 (Khan Younis, Gaza Strip)

MIDDLE EAST WATCH'S QUESTIONS: Was Miqdad first wounded in the legs and then shot again while he lay on the ground? Please explain the circumstances for each volley of gunfire, if there was more than one, and specify the distance between Miqdad and the soldier who fired each time. How many bullets were fired in the incident?

RESPONSE:
Ministry of Justice (May 20, 1993): The case was investigated by the Israel Police. We are awaiting to receive the results in this case.

***

14.   ZAKARIYA AL-MATHLOUM, July 17, 1992 (Gaza City, Gaza Strip)

MIDDLE EAST WATCH'S QUESTIONS: MEW has collected evidence indicating that undercover forces infiltrated a demonstration, and that the masked youths whom they confronted mistook them for members of a rival Palestinian political group and may have resisted. Did the soldiers clearly identify themselves before confronting the masked youths? What was the distance between al-Mathloum and the soldiers when they opened fire, and what were the reasons they opened fire?

RESPONSES:
IDF Deputy JAG (undated, received December 15, 1992): The investigation to date suggests that the deceased was shot when he attacked an IDF soldier with a club. According to the investigation, an IDF force entered into a fight with a group of masked men armed with clubs and axes. During the clash the deceased was shot. Two soldiers were injured and needed medical attention.

IDF Spokesman (May 21, 1993): No legal deposition has yet been given; I am therefore unable to provide details beyond those already furnished in regard to this case.

***

**15.   NURI SHARIF ABD AL-QADER AL-AQQAD, July 27, 1992
(Khan Younis, Gaza Strip)**

MIDDLE EAST WATCH'S QUESTIONS: Where was al-Aqqad situated
when he was fatally shot? From what distance was he shot, and for what
reason? Was he in an enclosed room when he was shot? If so, did the
soldier first attempt to remain outside the room and call on al-Aqqad to
surrender? If not, why not?

RESPONSE:
Ministry of Justice (May 20, 1993): The case was investigated by the
Israel Police. We are awaiting to receive the results in this case.

***

**16.   'ABDULLAH DIBASH HAMARSHE, September 9, 1992
(Ya'bad, Jenin district, West Bank)**

MIDDLE EAST WATCH'S QUESTIONS: Was Hamarshe armed or masked
when he was shot? What specific actions did he take that justify his being
shot? What steps were made to warn or attempt to arrest him before he
was shot? How far away was the soldier who shot him?

RESPONSES:
State of Israel Ministry of Justice (December 21, 1992): The Israel Police
are still investigating the circumstances of Abdullah Hamarshe's death
which took place on 9 September, 1992, are therefore we are unable to
comment on this case.

State of Israel Ministry of Justice (May 20, 1993): Abdullah Hamarshe
was shot by a Border Policeman on 9 September 1992 in the village of
Ya'bad in the area of Shchem (Nablus). A Police investigation was opened
to look into his death. It was determined that Hamarshe was one of a
group of young, masked men carrying various weapons (such as knives,
axes, metal bars, chains and swords) who confronted a Border Police unit.
When the Border Policemen called for them to stop they attempted to
escape. After calling them again to stop, and shooting in the air to warn
them to surrender, Hamarshe continued to escape. According to

testimony that was taken, a Border Policeman then fired at Hamarshe's
legs. Hamarshe, however, was fatally wounded by the bullet. The findings
of the police investigation were transferred to the office of the Northern
District Attorney. The decision of whether the shooting was justified, or
whether the Border Policeman involved should be prosecuted will be
made by the Northern District Attorney.

***

17.   MUHAMMAD SADEQ KEMAYEL TAKTAK, October 3, 1992 (Qabatiya, Jenin district, West Bank)

MIDDLE EAST WATCH'S QUESTIONS: Where was the victim situated
when he was fatally shot? What specific actions did he take that justify his
being shot? If he was shot while attempting to flee, was an effort made
to apprehend him without resorting to lethal force? How many soldiers
were in the immediate vicinity when he tried to flee, and were they
positioned in such a way as to make his escape almost impossible?

RESPONSES:
IDF Deputy JAG (undated, received December 15, 1992):   The
investigation to date suggests that the above was shot during an attempt
to arrest him. According to intelligence information and versions from
the investigation of those involved, the deceased was suspected of carrying
out a number of murders of local residents and shooting at IDF patrols.
Furthermore, there was information that the deceased always carried a
firearm with him.

During the attempt to arrest him, the deceased did not heed the warning
given to him to stop. The soldiers fired towards his legs. The deceased
was wounded and died. The proceedings of the investigation are
incomplete.

IDF Spokesman (May 21, 1993): No legal deposition has yet been given;
I am therefore unable to provide details beyond those already furnished
in regard to this case.

18.   'ISSAM AL-KHATIB, October 10, 1992 (Ar-Ram, West Bank)

MIDDLE EAST WATCH'S QUESTIONS: Was al-Khatib armed or masked when he was shot? What specific actions did he take that justify his being shot? What steps were made to warn or attempt to arrest him before he was shot fatally? From how far away was he fatally shot?

RESPONSES:
Ministry of Justice (May 20, 1992): This case is being investigated by the Military Police Investigations Branch and we suggest you contact Col. David Yahav, Deputy Judge Advocate General.

IDF Spokesman (May 21, 1992): The fourth case [presumably, a reference to this case] is presently under investigation by the Military police due to the fact that IDF soldiers were involved in the incident.

***

On October 23, 1992, Middle East Watch asked the Ministry of Justice for information on the killing of Khaled Muhammad Saker Fahmawi. In the end, Middle East Watch did not do extensive fieldwork on this case. However, in her letter of December 21, 1992, Adv. Tamar Gaulan of the Ministry of Justice responded to our request for information as follows:

> This case was investigated by the Jenin Police and the file was transferred to the Northern District Attorney, who decided to close the file after concluding that, under the circumstances described below, the commander of the Border Police unit involved in this incident acted in self-defense and was therefore justified in killing Khaled Fahmawi.
>
> Fahmawi was wanted by the security forces as a result of his involvement in terrorist activities. On 12 March, 1992 information was received that Fahmawi was located in a certain house and a Border Police unit was sent to arrest him. Upon the unit's arrival, Fahmawi jumped from a window of the house and began to escape. The Border Police pursued him and the commander of the unit shouted at him to stop and then fired warning shots into the air. When Fahmawi continued to flee, the commander fired shots towards his legs. Fahmawi then turned and drew a pistol, at which point the commander

fired another shot, directing his aim at the central part of
Fahmawi's body, thereby killing him.

IDF SPOKESMAN'S RESPONSE TO THIS REPORT
JUNE 25, 1993

The IDF utterly rejects the claims of the Middle East Watch regarding alleged violations of human rights in the territories by IDF soldiers. Moreover, the IDF categorically repudiates the MEW accusation that IDF soldiers purportedly shoot indiscriminately at innocent local residents.

The following is a detailed response by the IDF spokesman to the allegations of the Middle East Watch:

Terrorism in the territories - Background

In recent months, there has been an intensification of terrorist activity in the territories. Consequently, the security forces have had to take firm steps to prevent this violence. The hard core 'wanted' terrorists are responsible for much of this terrorism. Today there are about 200 armed terrorists "at large" operating in the territories, assisted by local Palestinians.

Their acts of terrorism have caused the death and the injury of Israeli citizens and IDF soldiers. In addition, these terrorists have murdered hundreds of fellow Palestinians, suspected by them of cooperating with Israeli authorities. Since January 1, 1993, 11 Israeli citizens, 8 IDF soldiers and 70 Palestinians have been killed in the territories by these Arab terrorists.

The Special Units Operating in the Territories:

The primary role of the special IDF units operating in the territories is to apprehend those who carry out acts of violence. A fundamental part of their task is to clearly differentiate between those engaged in terrorists activity and the local population who do not.

These units are exposed to daily threats to their lives. They are engaged in a constant confrontation with hard-core terrorists, who are not restrained by any law and who are armed with various lethal weapons, including firearms. The task of these units is complex and is carried out in a hostile environment, amid constant friction with the civilian population. However, it is stressed that all of these units must comply fully with the rules of engagement ("open-fire" regulations) which apply to all IDF forces operating in the field.

The Legal Basis of the Rules of Engagement:

The very title of MEW report — "A License to Kill" — is maliciously misleading, and totally untrue. The MEW alleges that IDF rules defining the circumstances in which a soldier may open fire have been adjusted in order to allow the special units to operate without restriction. This allegation is based on a total ignorance of the facts or a willful intention to distort the situation on the ground.

It should be emphasized, first and foremost, that the rules of engagement have undergone no basic change, and remain as follows:

IDF soldiers are permitted to use live fire in two situations only:

1. When a soldier finds himself in a life-threatening situation, in which case [the soldier] may direct fire toward the threat (the recent intensification of terrorism in the territories has demonstrated that one type of life-threatening situation encountered is that of a soldier engaging an individual carrying a firearm).

2. While carrying out the standard procedure for apprehending a suspect, in which case the fire is directed to halt the suspect and not to kill him. During violent rioting, soldiers may be permitted to use plastic and rubber bullets to disperse the rioters.

These regulations apply to all IDF soldiers, including those serving in special units.

Following the rise in violence in the territories and the new circumstances in which IDF soldiers find themselves, the regulations were updated and modified, without reference to the special units, in order to meet the immediate threat posed by those suspects identified as carrying weapons.

This update constitutes part of an ongoing process of adjustment and modification to situations in the field, without changing the basic legal basis of the regulations as detailed above. Furthermore, every such adjustment or modification is reviewed by the military advocate.

Dealing With Deviations From Orders:

As an army which operates within the law and subject to the above-mentioned restrictions, the IDF makes every effort to enforce its regulations. The IDF absolutely rejects the allegation by the Middle East Watch that its senior officers tolerate the killing of palestinians.

The IDF has routine and strict procedures regarding the investigation of cases in which Palestinians are killed. In cases in which deviations from IDF regulations and instructions have occurred, those responsible are brought to justice. In all cases of death, a military police investigation is immediately opened, and the findings are brought before the military prosecutor. In cases when those involved are found to have deviated from regulations, they are court-martialed.

The norm, whereby IDF soldiers or officers, including senior officers, are court-martialed and punished for these offenses, is proof of the resoluteness of the IDF penal system to prosecute these cases. This penal standard applies to the special units as well. For example, a senior special unit commander with the rank of lieutenant colonel was involved in an incident in which a local Palestinian resident was killed. He was found to have deviated from the rules of engagement, was brought up on criminal charges, and was punished. Moreover, the prosecutor submitted an appeal to the military court of appeals, and the sentence was increased.

Currently, there are two indictments pending against two officers from the special units suspected of involvement in cases in which local palestinian residents were killed as a result of the failure to abide by the rules of engagement.

It should however be emphasized that these cases are clearly the exception. In thousands of operations and life-threatening situations, the rules of engagement have been strictly followed — this under difficult conditions, when the soldiers' lives were in danger and when split-second decisions must be taken.

The Achievements of the Special Units in the War Against Terrorism:

While operating in accordance with the high ethical norms of the IDF, since their establishment, the special units have recorded many successes in the war against terrorism.

The greatest achievements have been against the hard-core terrorist groups and in the apprehension of fugitives.

Since January 1, 1993, 18 wanted terrorists have been killed, 7 have surrendered, 59 have been apprehended, and 42 have fled across the border.

Openness to Inspection:

As an army in a democratic state, the IDF operates in accordance with military law and the laws of the state as passed by its elected leaders. The IDF is subject to constant inspection and investigation by both military and civilian bodies.

Contrary to allegations by the Middle East Watch that the IDF conceals information, the IDF permits regular visits in the territories by human rights organizations from Israel and abroad, and allows unprecedented open and free press coverage in the territories. The Middle East Watch itself has in the past enjoyed the cooperation of the IDF and received replies to its hundreds of inquiries on questions of human rights in the territories.